THE POLITICS OF TEACHER UNIONISM

The Politics of
TEACHER UNIONISM

International Perspectives

Edited by Martin Lawn

CROOM HELM
London • Sydney • Dover, New Hampshire

British Library Cataloguing in Publication Data
The politics of teacher unionism: international
  perspectives.
  1. Teachers' unions
  I. Lawn, Martin
  331.88'1137   LB2844.58
  ISBN 0-7099-1696-5

Croom Helm, 51 Washington Street, Dover,
New Hampshire 03820, USA

Library of Congress Cataloging in Publication Data
applied for.

Printed and bound in Great Britain by
Biddles Ltd, Guildford and King's Lynn

CONTENTS

Contents

INTRODUCTION

Martin Lawn

This book consists of a series of case studies based in different national settings and concerned with the development of teacher unionism. They collectively deal with the politics of teacher unionism which, in this context, can mean the alliances teachers make, the educational policies they represent and the changing nature of employment in a public service. The study of teachers has moved some way forward in recent years, reflecting the complexities of teachers' working lives and eroding the functionalist monopoly of interpretation which, from a right or left perspective, saw teachers as determinedly apolitical and conservative; professionals within a benevolent State service. All those descriptions were loaded, selectively applied within a post-war period of growth of the Welfare State and the development of an extended professional service in different fields. The impetus for a re-working of the politics of teaching may have begun with tentative and ambiguous statements from American neo-Marxists, trying to end the separation of education from other kinds of production and finding this problematic. Fresh impetus has followed from the decisions of western governments to reduce the flow of resources into education while changing its direction. In England and Wales, State policy emanating from the Departments of Employment and Education seems to be guided by a radical but limited view of schooling as a process of commodity production, and this has had considerable implications for teachers as employees, not the least of which is the casting aside of the accumulated consultative committees, participative advisory boards and other apparatus of the partnership culture. Not even the old appeals to professional responsibility as defined by government, cut much ice when teachers are treated as disposable labour, paid according to supply and demand, and seen only in terms of their productive capacity. This is why the politics of teacher unionism, grounded in the development and struggles of unionisation in different educational settings, may be used to develop insights into the politics of the labour process in education. It is vital now in the development of studies of professional work ideologies in education, of the politics of struggle and the changing nature of work, and to enrich the study of teaching and more importantly, to act as a cultural resource to help teachers survive and organise.

CASE STUDIES OF WORK AND UNIONISATION

These case studies were specially commissioned from researchers having an interest in teacher unionism in their own or their adopted education systems. They were asked to explore sympathetically the development of a teachers' union or a contemporary problem in educational work. This request was made because the editor believed that work on teacher unionism seemed rarely to reflect the complexities of teacher work and ideologies. The case studies are ways of bringing other cultures and contexts in teacher unionism near to each other in order to generate insights and hypotheses about the way that our own union histories may have developed which, in turn, may generate new historical and sociological study. The studies may accumulate points of congruency on dilemmas in unionism, the changing nature of work and the contemporary situation in the education service. In some areas, the fact that there is little to refer to should point to the urgent requirement for more research; an important example of this is the neglect of women in teaching as a subject in its own right. Women appear in a number of different guises in these studies but the problems faced by women in their exploitation as a cheap source of labour, in national emergencies or as part-time workers needs serious study, as does the effectiveness of efforts to give the lie to the gibe that 'women teach and men manage', by campaigns in the National Union of Teachers for new union policies on child care facilities and equal promotion opportunities.

Case studies are not theoretically innocent. They are selections and interpretations, however much they lay claim to representing actuality. In the first instance, the authors were asked to be 'sympathetic' and although they interpreted this in different ways, in the main, the studies try to understand the insider's dilemmas, that is, the points of view of the organised teachers. Different theoretical or personal perspectives also colour these studies and generally, drafts of each study were commented upon by the editor. In other words, these case studies reflect a sympathetic investigation of issues in teacher unionism, a selection and interpretation of those issues and a concern for illuminating contextually-based problems in this area in a way which would generate new directions of research and action.

In England and Wales, and it is from this context that the introduction is written, there has been a productive period of work in the sociology of education in recent years which has produced a number of classroom ethnographies illuminating the environment and practices of teacher work. So far, these ethnographies lack an explicit reference to wider contexts of work such as union meetings and political and educational campaigns and to the changing nature of work as documented in historical studies. The production process in schools is shorn of its political and cultural aspects; classrooms are represented as 'natural' worlds of work, yet organised responses to it by groups of teachers are excluded. Every mode of production develops its own varied cultural identities and accumulation of experience, yet discussion of the labour process in teaching seems to be monopolized by one aspect of it, namely classroom interaction. This leaves the labour process of teaching vulnerable to the growing influence of management of education perspectives which interpret teachers' work as needing detailed supervision and control and the raising of standards of quality. The politics of the production process need to be drawn out and reassembled, connections made between the personal and the political/educational, the classroom and staffroom, the union branch and the union headquarters, the historical development of women and men as educational workers. One way to do

this would be through the life histories of
teachers; another is represented in this book in
the exploration of different political and
religious systems of education and their histories
and contemporary problems. What are the political
decisions, the disunities, the work policies and
the ideologies with which teachers have tried to
alter their world of work, the classroom and the
school?

The choice of the countries covered in the
studies is pragmatic, based upon academic networks
and contacts, and the countries which appear are
not claimed to be more important or more
'representative' than other countries. The book
falls into two main sections: 'Unions and
Political Strategies' and 'Problems in the Labour
Process'. In the first section, there are essays
on unionisation in Victoria, Australia (Spaull and
Mann), Portugal (Stoer), France (Duclaud-
Williams), Japan (Ota), Sweden (Boucher) and Malta
(Darmanin). These case studies may be read as
illustrating the ethnocentric paths unionisation
has taken, but there are also themes which occur
in more than one case; for instance, illegal
unions, conservative unions with radical
governments and vice versa, political alliances
and strategies. Each case is different yet there
are vicarious experiences which illuminate the
general problem of unionising teachers. The
second section of the book develops the study of
contemporary problems in educational work. There
are essays on merit pay (Urban), computerization
(White), teaching contracts (Ozga), stress
(Freedman) and organizing teachers (Jones). The
issues are grounded in particular settings (the
U.S.A., Australia, Scotland, U.S.A. and England
and Wales, respectively) but they reflect general
problems which are increasingly associated with
teaching and they may serve as bases for policy-
making by teachers in other countries.

Though each case of union development may be
different there are some broad similarities.
There is always the history of petty restrictions,
administered locally and centrally, and there is
the perennial issue of low pay. Sometimes the
restrictions are merely irksome, sometimes
fundamental as in the case of the marriage bar.
In each history there is the necessary attempt by
teachers to free themselves from the economic,
political and cultural control exercised over
their lives and the growth of strategies to

achieve their own educational aims, often produced in contradiction to management and sometimes involving wide educational alliances. These strategies do not add up to the consistent search for an upwardly mobile well-rewarded career, as they are sometimes described, but reflect the need to resist managerial domination and to search for policies and allies. Teachers move within specific material and cultural circumstances; even though they may not share them with other teachers, they are part of wider movements involving employees in the public sector, white and blue collar workers and radical and conservative social projects. It is mistaken to divorce the growth of teacher unions in England and Wales from their links with, or opposition to, the labour movement and its politics, from the progressive educational movements, from gender conflicts and from analogies with white collar or civil servant work. Neither a notion that unions are just pay-bargaining agents nor that they consist of classroom workers gives a feeling for their unique place in the warp and weft of the social fabric, a feeling which is essential for understanding the cultural and social identities of teachers. It is that past and its legacies, of disunity of sector, gender and ideology, all of which are in part creations of government policy, which will be the base-line for teachers' responses to the major onslaught in education and the restructuring of the teaching force today.

PROFESSIONALISM, POLITICS AND PRODUCTIVITY

It is suggested in much of the literature that the emergence of a national education system meant the fostering of professional groups acting as mediators for State policies, and in England and Wales there is some evidence for this. In periods of major State regulation and intervention, the two world wars and their immediate aftermath, the shortage of teachers and the need for a reconstructed education system meant benefits for teachers in terms of national pay awards, wage-bargaining agreements and investment in schools. It has also meant a revival and extension of a professional ideology, the creation of a certain kind of teacher identity, involving appeals to an expertise, increased responsibility and a recognised autonomy. Research in recent years has shown that this ideology was contested by some teachers, and in one period it was widely contested. However, the counter-hegemonic argument was often expressed in terms of professionalism, only this time it meant a sort of syndicalism, a guild of teachers running education on behalf of the community. The same key concepts of responsibility, service, expertise and autonomy were turned around, subverting the idea of a licensed professionalism and building a model for workers' control. Professionalism has contradictory meanings which is useful for teachers in combatting run-down of the service[1]. Several of the case studies reveal the problems teachers have had in being 'partners' in the running of the education system or alternatively, rejecting (after being excluded from 'partnership') dominant views of professionalism for a conscious proletarian ideology, in one case, to a combative professionalism in opposition to State authority, in another. The discourse of professionalism appears then to have a number of possible elements, most of which are capable of expressing employee protection arguments and being effective in uniting groups of teachers in opposition to local and national education policies. This discourse may become inappropriate when faced with a government unwilling to recognise any form of 'partnership' or when there is strong corporate decision-making in the education system.

There are sectoral variations in the ideology of teacher professionalism which reflect primary or secondary school training, the different generations and Church or State schooling. Further work is needed on competing definitions of professionalism that may exist between men and women in teaching, which may reflect ideologies of competition or collaboration, of career versus classroom commitment. More importantly, there must be a view of work coming from the economically oppressed majority in teaching which is not yet represented in union policies. Professionalism is a contested concept and may even be rejected altogether as an effective means of protection in some circumstances.

The discarding or re-working of particular forms of professionalism may be taking place in the present re-structuring of education; the use by the State of appeals to loyalty and a tradition of participation may lose their impact when the emerging criterion appears to be productivity.

Introduction

The efficiency of the service is now taking
precedence over the loyalty of the service. By
the same token, a direct defence of job tenure and
standard of living may have to produce a new
professional emphasis on teachers' definition of
quality in the service. The move in western
countries from public funding in education to
private capital (at all levels), from training a
well-qualified elite to a market economy of a
cheap supply and 'survival of the fittest', and
from autonomy to productivity, echoes earlier
periods in these countries' histories and current
policies in under-developed nations. The
extension and intensification of the workload[2] of
teachers is now to be institutionalised in
productivity agreements. Fixed-term contracts for
head teachers, their retraining in industrial
management skills and the tightening-up of
educational hierarchies are one contemporary
feature of education, another is the rise of
teacher assessment in the form of competency-
testing, delayed certification, school evaluation
and managerial consultancies. The case studies
discuss rating systems for teachers, teaching
contracts and the linking of tested productivity
to pay awards. The customs and practices of
educational work are to be radically altered.
Recent research projects have been funded on the
definition of teaching duties, conditions of work,
teacher surpluses and pupil-teacher ratios.
Productivity in education is no longer to be
associated with implied links between investment
and the creation of value but with job definition,
supervisory posts and staff management. It may be
associated with new technologies in schooling.
There is a revival of interest in proletarianisation theories. Are teachers losing not only
control over the ends and uses of their work
(ideological proletarianisation) but over their
craft knowledge and technical skills (technical
proletarianisation)[3]?
    In defence both of their skills in, and the
purposes of, education, teachers have not only
moved to union organisation but to local community
and parent alliances, essential for successful
strike action, and so to a redefinition of their
work in the light of parents' rights. This may
still be uncommon but it has roots in past
practice and case study evidence of revival.
Centralized systems of education appear, in
practice, to positively encourage the formation of

strong teacher alliances with opposition parties. The conflict between employers and teachers may create a bond with the opposition which, in turn, will involve teachers in some contexts as party candidates, cadres or advisors. The negative and reactive elements of the employer-teacher conflict are balanced by involvement in creating new education (and wider) policies with opposition parties. Divisions between unions may be accentuated by, or be a reflection of, different political allegiances. It is not clear exactly how a non-sectional, limited political, social and educational culture among teachers could be formed or sustained except as the product of total alienation from educational management and the State. Increasing stress and demoralisation among teachers may be alleviated by union involvement in breaking down isolation and by positive discrimination policies to ensure full membership participation. It is also an open question whether the phenomenal rise of peace studies is a response to institutional stress and part of the production of teacher-generated curriculum policies, something which has been the intention of some unions, if rarely the practice.

This introduction has concentrated on the labour process in teaching, but there is an interesting by-product of this emphasis and that is the changing nature of State policies and responses to public sector work and the role of the education service. These essays are full of insights into developments in State power and control and into contrasting definitions of the State.

This brief introduction has not attempted to draw together or theorize about many of the points raised in the case studies. In any case, this would contradict their usefulness as sources of vicarious experience, as sources of useful questions or as enabling new insights. Jointly, they are to be seen as a first instalment in a comparative study of the politics of production in education, suggesting links between work, politics and action, or, by omission or lack of emphasis, suggesting new studies of the hidden practices of teaching. Knowledge of these histories, shared by teachers and sympathetic researchers, and of their relation to managerial strategies and State policies could help to defend teaching, its separate and common traditions and its need to socially construct the craft skill of teaching in

Introduction

the face of imminent changes to the ideology, control and social relations of the mode of production in education in future years.

NOTES

1. The ideas in this section are derived from other work:
   Ozga, J.T. and Lawn, M.A. (1981) Teachers, Professionalism and Class, Falmer Press; and Lawn, M.A. and Ozga, J.T. 'The Educational Worker? A Reassessment of Teachers' in Barton, L. and Walker, S. (Eds.) (1981) Schools, Teachers and Teaching, Falmer Press.

2. Address by Yvon Charbonneau, President of the C.E.Q. (Centrale de l'Enseignement du Québec) to the 10th Convention of the Confederation of Canadian Unions, Vancouver, October 2nd, 1983.

3. Derber, R. Towards a new theory of professionals as Workers: Mental Labour in Advanced Capitalism G.K. Hall, Mass.

PART I

UNIONS AND POLITICAL STRATEGIES

Chapter One

TEACHER UNIONISM IN AUSTRALIA:
THE CASE OF VICTORIA

Andrew Spaull and Susan Mann

OVERVIEW

Australia's teachers' unions, with a combined membership of over 160,000 teachers, are amongst the strongest teachers' unions in the world, if measured by organizational unity and membership support. The pattern of a single organization representing all government school teachers, regardless of sex, function or location, in each state and the A.C.T., (except for Victoria), is one admired, but not easily attained, elsewhere. This has ensured that Austrialia's teachers' unions are the most visible of state white collar unions (Bessant and Spaull, 1972). Furthermore the single organization of teachers has meant that the teachers' union is generally an integral part of state educational policy-making. However in recent years this form of incorporation has become an ineffective means of teacher resistance to policies that have undermined state education and teachers' work. As a consequence the state teachers' unions have again become militant - with industrial disputation being replaced by political confrontation - including direct intervention in the electoral process.

There is also a national teachers' organization - the Australian Teachers' Federation (established in 1922), which is a loose federation of the state unions. Its major deficiency has been its inability to impose decisions on its state affiliates. It has also suffered from a relatively low level of capitation funding and apathy from rank and file members in the states. As a consequence, the ATF has never been a major political or industrial force in Australian education. This was evident between 1975-1980 by

13

its lack of momentum in resisting federal government financial cutbacks to education. This has led to a series of reforms within ATF which include:

. The transfer of the national offices from Sydney to Canberra with an increase in staff resources.

. An extension of its constitutional objectives to include the 'industrial, professional and social needs of teachers'.

. The possibility of developing ATF as a real federation of state teachers' unions as a result of it seeking registration as a trade union within the ambit of the Commonwealth Conciliation and Arbitration Commission in 1984.

Between 1855 and 1885 attempts to establish permanent organizations for teachers, modelled on English or Scottish associations, were unsuccessful because of official opposition (including in some cases, victimization of their leaders), the tyranny of distance, teacher apathy and sectional or geographical rivalry. The revival in teacher unionism between 1885 and 1895 was expressed in the formation of organizations in each colony that provide the direct, continuous link with today's unions. The first, the Victorian State School Teachers' Union formed in 1886, was the forerunner of the Victorian Teachers' Union (established 1926). The oldest surviving union is the Queensland Teachers' Union (established 1889). The impetus for union formation came from several sources: head teachers' response to the emergent state educational bureaucracy, reform of public service commissions, and the favourable climate for 'new unionism', which included the foundation of white collar unionism, especially in the government sector (Spaull, 1984a). The second stage of union development occurred between 1910 and 1925, when teachers' unions in most states came under the protective influence of compulsory (or Australian) industrial arbitration. In return for access to arbitration machinery, teachers' unions - at this stage often fragmented or internally divided on sectional lines - were required to establish and maintain a single teachers' union. In this and subsequent periods, state Labor governments and/or industrial arbitration courts encouraged the growth of teacher unionism by legislative mandate, industrial agreements and union preference clauses.

As such, the distinctive organizational character of teachers' unions owes much to Australia's unique arbitration system(s) and to the dominance of sympathetic Labor governments in most states (Spaull, 1983b). The contrast is apparent in Victoria, where the relative absence of both has produced a long, and at times sordid, history of teacher union fragmentation.

And yet despite, and in some cases, as a result of, separate teachers' unions, Victoria's teacher unionism has played a pioneering role in the articulation and realization of new conditions of industrial regulation and employment of state school teachers (e.g. it was the first state to abolish assessment of teachers by inspection), while being at the forefront in the uses of industrial disputation and political intervention in the electoral process. These recent developments will be the major focus of this chapter and also serve as an example of the new dimensions to teacher unionism emerging in Australia in the 1980s.

VICTORIA'S PATTERN OF TEACHER UNIONISM

Sectionalism, disunity, and fragmentation have been, and remain, the organizational condition of teaching derived from hierarchical, gender and structural relations in the modern school system and as well tensions between city and country teachers resulting from the geographical size of Australia's centralized education departments. As seen earlier, the State has encouraged and protected a unified, centralized teachers' union in the other Australian states. In Victoria the State through its distinctive industrial relations procedures, and at times through governmental practice, has recognized and fostered teacher union fragmentation.

Victoria's industrial relations system is not one based on <u>Australian</u> compulsory arbitration. Instead the Wages Board system is empowered to recognize employers and employees organizations as well as groups of industrial employers and employees and more than six individuals. This principle carried over into the legislation which established the Teachers' Tribunal in 1946. Thus organizations of teachers, even small and competitive groups, gain recognition, e.g. Victorian Association of Teachers (VAT) gained Tribunal approval with 4 per cent membership of all teachers. Union fragmentation has continued to

15

occur in two ways: first, the formation of breakaway unions from the parent union, in this case the
Victorian Teachers' Union (VTU). The forerunner of
the Victorian Secondary Teachers' Association
(VSTA) established 1948, and the Technical
Teachers' Union of Victoria (TTUV) established
1967, are classic cases of sectional breakaways,
which believed as specialized groups of teachers
that their policies and interests could not be
accommodated in the VTU because of its political
domination by the primary school teachers. The
second type of fragmentation is found in the formation of the VAT in 1976. It is not strictly a
breakaway group, in that it seeks to offer an
alternative organization to school teachers. It
was formed by teachers who were disenchanted with
militant, 'undemocratic' and 'party political'
unions. VAT now has the ideological support of the
political right wing, including the anti-communist
organization, the National Civic Council, which now
aims to counter 'radical' influences in all
Australian teachers' unions.

The overall effects of Victoria's fragmentation is that union density for Victorian teachers
remains low relative to other states. Sixty years
ago there were at least eight teachers' unions who
claimed a total support of about 40 per cent of
teachers; in 1983 there were eight unions who
claimed the total support of about 80 per cent of
teachers. The lower union density situation
continues because it is so easy for Victorian
teachers to avoid becoming union members, and
because of inadequate union organizing facilities.
Low union density, plus the separate organizations,
and government exploitation of this disunity, has
at last brought a sense of unity amongst the three
major unions who have been developing common
policies and joint negotiations and political and
industrial action (Spaull, 1984b). There are also
groupings of teachers in some regions, e.g.
(Melbourne) Western Suburbs Teachers' Federation.
In July 1984 the three unions formed the Teachers'
Federation of Victoria - based on equal
representation of the three unions to work in the
new industrial relations system (see later).

THE UNIONS' ORGANIZATIONAL CHARACTERISTICS

The government of Victoria's three major
teachers' unions varies in some detail, but all
adhere to a common polyarchical pattern. It

consists of active and passive rank and file
members belonging to the organization at the school
level (group of schools in the VTU) and delegating
responsibility for decision-making to an annual
conference and its administration and implementation to a monthly council meeting of about 40
teachers and an executive of about 10, the senior
executives being full time. The VSTA and TTUV, as
dissidents of the old centralized structures of the
VTU, constructed the school as the basic unit, the
branch or association, to give its members more
autonomous powers of local activity, providing that
they are consistent with the union's policies, and
the branch notifies the executive of any proposed
industrial or political action. The VTU has undergone significant changes in its basic structures in
the mid-1970s. It has abolished the sectional
branches for men and women in the Melbourne metropolitan area; it has yielded its right to recruit
post-primary teachers, although it has added other
sections to its membership, such as school inter-
preters. All three unions have established regions
of branches in order to make their organizations
more responsive to local issues and as a means of
electing members to council. These recent moves,
which have made the unions more accessible to the
membership, are a reflection of this changing
political style of teacher unions. There are
several reasons for the changes. First, the union
leaders have become concerned about membership
involvement because of the increasing reliance on
mass action in the form of political rallies,
teacher stoppages, and changes in the approach to
industrial negotiations such as in logs of claims.
Second, the teachers' unions were in danger of
becoming rigid bureaucracies, thereby further alie-
nating the classroom teacher from the political
processes in education, at a time when there were
increased opportunities for their involvement in
the school system. Finally many young teachers
brought to the unions in the early 1970s a more
clearly defined set of political attitudes and
expectations (Bessant and Spaull, 1976).

Although there have been attempts to directly
involve the membership in union decision making,
the unions are still faced with membership apathy.
Studies of the VSTA a decade ago, however, suggested that because of its 'crises period' and its
school-based branch activities, membership interest
was significantly higher than elsewhere in Australia. A 1982 survey found that, unlike 1971-72,

young teachers (under 26 years old) and others over 40 years, tended to be passive members, or did not belong to the VSTA (Spaull, 1984b). In all three unions policy-committees and sub-committees are not always filled by teachers, while annual conferences are not fully patronized. There are also organizational problems which reinforce the level of apathy. Open communications systems are required in large organizations and teachers' unions must keep close contact with rank and file dispersed throughout the state. In recent years the teachers' unions have recognized this with changes in the format of their publications. In 1980 the VSTA introduced a weekly tabloid. In 1981 the TTUV and the VSTA ran joint issues of their journals and this led to the Victorian Teacher. An off-shoot, the Australian Teacher, represents the beginnings of an attempt to produce a national teachers' union journal.

Among the active membership of the teachers' unions, there is still the internal factionalism endemic to organizations whose members hold divergent political views. The history of Australian Teacher unionism is marked by periods of intense factional discord.[1] This is not the case in Victoria today; instead there are more subtle factional manoeuverings, not only at the level of governing bodies and conferences but in the schools. The TTUV remains the most radical of the three unions, an umbrella of left-wing radical and Labor elements, while the VTU has moved to a more visible moderate ALP position. Within each of the teachers' unions there are factional coalitions, such as the left's 'Teacher Solidarity' group or a radical 'grass-roots' group in the TTUV, or feminist collectives to monitor women's policies. These factions initiate discussion on new policies and tactics.

THE WORK SITUATION OF TEACHERS

The role of the Victorian classroom teacher has become increasingly complex over the last decade as the modern labour process has moved into the non-manual sectors of production. This trend has occurred with noticeable contradictions: up-skilling in some tasks and deskilling in others where specialized personnel are assuming responsibility for certain roles, e.g. pupil welfare. The teacher's work has also broadened from strictly imparting knowledge and skills to now include pastoral and counselling functions, especially at secondary schools. Teachers have also been given considerable autonomy for the development and continuous evaluation of school-based curriculum. There has been a movement away from the centralized control of state schooling to a greater involvement in school governance and internal management by teachers, as well as in their developing and participating in school-community relations. This concentration/intensification of functions in the teachers' role has had the net result of increasing the overall workload of teachers.[2] This in turn has caused underlying conflict in schooling as regards identity, values, and purpose, as well as conflict externally imposed from such problems as youth alienation, chronic unemployment and ethnic tensions. Most teachers are ill-equipped by their initial training and by diminished in-service opportunities to deal with the increasing complexity of tasks.

Furthermore, in recent years teachers have been increasingly subjected to criticisms of incompetency in their inflated and diversified roles. This criticism has come from professionals more 'specifically trained', and the 'education right' who claim a decline in the basic functions of schooling, a corresponding decline in academic and student (and teacher) behavioural standards, and the inadequate preparation of secondary students for work or further education (Spaull,1983a).

Teachers are also operating within the context of competing and contradictory demands from students and parents, the local community, school council, employers, education pressure groups and the popular media. Criticism and polemical rhetoric of teachers have produced a 'siege mentality' amongst many teachers, especially those committed to their work. Not surprisingly teachers are eager to relinquish some of their tasks to specialized personnel. The trend towards specialization has burgeoned recently in 'career guidance' teachers, transition to work education officers - reflecting public concern for the schools' function in time of economic crises - subject and general curriculum consultants, pupil welfare coordinators, teacher librarians, and education personnel in multi-cultural education, non-sexist education and aboriginal education who are in the para-teaching positions which have flourished over the last decade in Victorian schools and the education department. Their growth has resulted in a narrowing of certain aspects of the teachers' task and an overall deskilling.

The teachers' work situation has been

exacerbated by eight years of federal and state monetarist and wages policies aimed at reducing public expenditures. As a result there was a relative decline in Australian teachers' salaries, to other occupations (until 1983), more so in Victoria because of the Teachers' Tribunal refusal to negotiate a major salaries award (see later). And like all other states, Victorian state education has had to bear serious curtailments in support services and physical resources to schools as well as witness decreases in employment opportunities (even job security for new teachers) and geographical and career mobility of teachers.

As a result, job dissatisfaction with teaching appears to have increased and is rising at all levels of schooling, but particularly among junior technical and high school teachers. Women teachers in primary schools, who by the mid-1970s came to expect better promotion opportunities, are increasingly dissatisfied with their lack of advancement (Stroud, 1982). Furthermore there has been a significant increase in the reported incidence of teacher stress related directly to the work situation; and as a response teacher welfare officers dealing with occupational stress are now employed on a restricted basis by the education department and the teachers' unions. The sum effect of these changes in the work situation of teachers can be seen in both the recent policies and behaviour of Victoria's teachers' unions.

Since the mid-1970s the teachers' unions have tended to act as dependent organizations as reflected in their tendency to react to events rather than shape them. "Unions are for the most time engaged in essentially defensive or protective operations stimulated by changing circumstances outside their control" (Martin,1975:134). Teachers' unions normally behave in this way when fulfilling their basic objectives of protecting membership interests; whether it be in resolving individual or group grievances with the Education Department, or complaining about variations in existing provisions such as teacher housing, allowances, or superannuation units. It is at the other level where teachers' unions were positive sources of change in teachers' and school conditions - the hallmarks of Victorian unionism in the 1960s and early 1970s - that the unions have been forced on to the defensive. They have had to yield ground because of the economic and political backlash against public education and teachers. As a result there has been confusion about strategies and tactics: whether teachers should accept the changed circumstances and hedge against further attacks; or whether they should make the offensive the basis of their defence, in particular confront the government with industrial and political campaigns.

In many areas, e.g. family leave policy, the unions have attempted to consolidate benefits gained in the earlier period, rather than initiate or extend policies to obtain new levels of benefits and concessions (Spaull, 1984b). However on certain issues which are considered fundamental to their members' interests, the teachers' unions have resisted government and departmental policies by taking the initiative through industrial and electoral action. Two of these 'fundamental' issues are considered here: the unions' recent reaction to the long-term unsatisfactory system of industrial relations in state education, and a more immediate problem, that of the employment conditions of new teachers.

The Industrial Relations System

The Teachers' Tribunal was rendered within the broad principles of the Victorian Wages Board system. There were, however, important exceptions to the typical Wages Board. These included firstly that no appeal mechanism existed from decisions of the Tribunal to the Industrial Appeals Court. The teachers' representative on the typical three-person Tribunal (government representative, and independent chairman were the other two representatives) was to be elected by the permanent members of the teaching service. The powers of the Tribunal were far more wide-ranging and complex in character than found in other wages boards' powers, and also exceeded the powers of any other industrial tribunal for teachers in Australia. There was also the increased scale of operation and administration of the Tribunal; its responsibility for some 8,000 teachers (and teachers in training) in 1945 being extended to some 60,000 teachers in 1980. The Tribunal did not have powers to handle grievances, or general industrial disputes, it being assumed in 1946 that teachers, like other public servants, would not engage in strike activity.

The establishment of separate divisional Tribunals marks the beginning of the first period of teacher union agitation for reform of the Tribunal. The proposed reforms were directed towards redefining and improving the arbitral roles of the government representative so that the

government's views would be known, and its instructions followed by its representative. As it became
obvious that it was almost impossible to bring the
education department into the ways of genuine
negotiations while a Tribunal existed, and with the
work situation of teachers deteriorating, the
unions adopted a more radical position. In 1977
the unions issued a joint policy calling for: a
system of direct negotiations on terms and
conditions of employment between the government and
the teachers' unions, a ratification process so
that agreements would become legally binding; an
agreed process of grievance settlement for breaches
of an agreement and a system of impasse resolution
of general disputes through conciliation and
voluntary, not compulsory, arbitration.

In the wider political arena, Victoria's poor
industrial relations record was causing embarrass-
ment to the government. It set out to reform the
Wages Board system making it more responsive to the
rhythm of local industrial conflict. A similar
approach in thinking was required in the state
education system, which remained beyond the reach
of the new state industrial relations system, or
beyond the reach of any modern industrial relations
system (Spaull, 1977).

By 1980 the teachers' strike was entrenched in
Victoria's educational and industrial life. It has
been this way since the mid-1960s, when Victoria
initiated the first wave of teacher strikes in
Australia. Of the 112 major teacher strikes in
Australia between 1965 and 1981, 74 occurred in
Victoria, although in actual teacher days lost,
Victoria only accounted for 58 per cent of the
total number. There have been many more other stoppages, in excess of 500, which have occurred for a
half day or day at individual schools in the same
period which are not recorded in this analysis.
The Victorian strikes should be seen against the
continuing international backdrop of teacher militancy, which also emerged in the 1960s, and this in
turn must be seen as part of the rise and growth of
white collar union militancy. There are also 'local' factors which help explain the growth and
incidence of teachers' strikes in Victoria. The
first is related to the existence of three separate
organizations which has made it easier for smaller,
more homogeneous groups of teachers to achieve
"shared experiences and shared goals", without
being excessively restrained by a centralized executive. A second factor results from Victoria's lack

of machinery for handling industrial disputes in education. The deficiency means that disputes flare out of control, particularly at the school level, and are only 'settled' by the heavy-handed use of sanctions which add further to teacher militancy. Finally Victoria's high and increasing incidence of teacher strikes in the last six years must be in part related to the prevalence of a 'teacher strike ideology' whereby the early industrial disputes were considered by teachers to be victories (Bessant and Spaull, 1972). That initial success has influenced the membership's pre-disposition towards later strikes, and convinced the VTU leadership and rank and file in the mid-1970s of the strike as the weapon of the last resort.

It was in this background context that the government replaced Lindsay Thompson as Minister for Education (May 1979) with Alan Hunt. A popular view was that Hunt was given the portfolio to 'clean up the mess' in the Education Department. He started with two large 'brooms': one directed towards the administrative re-organization of the Department, the other aimed at its teaching service. The Minister favoured the introduction of a direct negotiations system, except that compulsory arbitration not voluntary arbitration should be available when required and that all salaries matters should be determined by an arbitral process.[3] In November 1979 Hunt incorporated these arguments into a new proposal - a Victorian Teaching Service Conciliation and Arbitration Commission. This proposal was immediately rejected by the three teachers' unions; instead they called for a seminar on industrial relations in the Education Department. This was accepted by the Minister. The seminar recommended the establishment of a working party on industrial relations of principal parties in the education system. The Working Party presented its report (the Hince Report) in May 1981 (Hince and Spaull, 1984).

In major recommendations (which were to become the elements of the new industrial relation system) were:-
- The Education Department (through the Minister) should be the employer.
- The Department and unions should negotiate all claims, including salaries.
- A Teaching Service Conciliation and Arbitration Commission should be established, consisting of a President and other commissioners.
- Where no agreement is reached the parties

shall proceed to conciliation.
-   If no agreement is reached by negotiation and
    conciliation, the dispute shall be referred to
    arbitration if both parties agree.
The new system of industrial relations has significant advantages over the old arrangements. It forces the Education Department to become accountable
in its dealings with teachers' unions over teachers' conditions; it improves procedures for salaries determination, and it establishes machinery to
settle grievances and disputes. Like any industrial
relations system it cannot remove the source of
conflict or even prevent stoppages, but the character and incidence of stoppages may change.

A political dimension was introduced into the
reform of the system when Minister Hunt refused to
translate the Working Party's report into legislation. Cabinet and his party did not wish to be
seen as 'going soft' on teachers or encouraging
voluntary arbitration. In November 1981 the Minister rushed through Parliament the Education Services Act, a scrambled, ambiguous scheme, which
incorporated some elements of the Working Party's
report, including a Conciliation and Arbitration
Commission, but limited use of direct negotiations.
Immediate and categoric rejection was the reaction
of the unions. Despite their protests, the Bill
was proclaimed in March 1982, less than a month
before the state elections. A political solution
was now required if the unions were to obtain a
workable industrial relations system.

Limited Tenure Employment

The employment conditions of teachers was an
obvious area of government policy to reduce immediate and long-term public expenditures. The explo-
sion in the 1970s of white collar service employment, and accompanying unionization and industrial
militancy, was felt by conservative governments to
be a major source of Australia's high rate of
inflation. State education, with its prominent
position in state budgets, the increasing uncertainty of its product, and declining school popula-
tions, was singled out for special treatment.
Government policies comprehensively rationalized
teacher supply through: reductions in teacher
training intakes and facilities, reductions in in-
service, study leave and education research, and
the non-employment of trained teachers mainly married women teachers and new graduates from
teachers' colleges and universities.[4]

Victoria, which had prided itself on

progressive teacher recruitment and training since
the 1950s, was sensitive to the question of teacher
unemployment of new graduates. Moreover because of
the state-funded expansion of the private sector
the dimensions to the teacher surplus problem could
be concealed. Thus it was not such an obvious
political problem to the government until the late
1970s. With the interstate experience before it,
the state government opted for limited term contracts (and casual emergency teachers) almost as a
'wait and see' policy. New teachers would be offered employment for a short, defined period (one
term to six months) without formal guarantee of
further employment, or tenurable employment at a
future date. Limited tenure for 1000 teachers was
first proposed in February 1977, but was hastily
shelved, following union pressure. It was revived
in 1979 following the government's success at the
state elections, and increased pressure from the
Fraser 'new federalism' government. The Education
Department agreed only to fully employ teachers who
had been recruited by studentships, so that in 1980
all new teachers were to be offered a LTE contract.
The teachers' unions, who learnt of this from a
'leaked' official document, responded immediately.

They informed the Minister that such employment practice was not being applied to the state
public service or the police.[5] Their particular
objections were based on the loss of job security
for teachers - in an occupation where it has been
protected since 1883. This affected the morale of
new and experienced teachers, and the stability of
staffing levels of and needs in a school system
which already had a long history of staffing instability due to chronic teacher shortages. The unions also declared that if LTE was not withdrawn,
they would take industrial and political action to
prevent its implementation. This was something of a
gamble because the membership, the majority of whom
were in secure employment, had not been directly
consulted. Obviously there had to be some form of
union commitment to new members of the teaching
service. It could be seen by members as a threat
to the job security of other teachers. And yet
there was division on the best means of proceeding:
to demand tenurable contracts would possibly reduce
the overall number of teachers given any type of
future employment; to acquiesce on the notion of
short-term engagement of three or six months would
undermine staffing policies and fail to meet the
interests of a generation of young teachers.

In formulating a strategy, VTU officers conceded that it would be difficult to reverse the policy, not only because of the entrenched views of government MPs on public expenditure, but because of the attitudes of unemployed teachers, and the usual rank and file apathy. The policy therefore should be integrated into the ongoing three union campaign on staffing of schools. The target was to be local regional areas where political agitation and limited industrial action by "a showy burst of opposition could then be used to allow negotiation of acceptable conditions" for limited tenure teachers.

These strategies and targets were announced, following the meeting with the Minister for Education who quickly conceded that only new teachers not hired before the first day of the 1980 school year would be offered limited tenure. Sensing vacillation, the unions stepped up a campaign to bring the issues before local MPs (especially in suburban and country electorates) and school councils. At the same time a protest stoppage called for a general stoppage of teachers. In November 1979 over 20,000 teachers stopped work for a day, the first such occasion that the VTU had joined a VSTA-TTUV stoppage, thereby making it the largest teacher stoppage in Victoria, and as well, realizing the worst fears of departmental officials that government ineptitude would drive the large VTU into the militant post-primary camps. This was followed by further stoppages and threats of regional stoppages in 1980, which brought slight revisions in the scheme, and promises by the Minister to take the matter to the Cabinet and to establish a small departmental-union working group. Indeed union advice was that the Minister was seeking a way out if a suitable package could be negotiated, while still retaining flexibility in the future employment of new teachers. The unions, however, grew impatient and a series of general stoppages and regional rolling strikes between September and November 1980 forced the Minister's hand. Cabinet left the matter to him; he did so by introducing legislation to stand down teachers who continued to use the strike weapon, while refusing to negotiate any further on the LTE itself. He banked on the threat of direct penalties against militant teachers and the declining public interest on the issue of teacher employment. The unions claimed his actions had revived the issue amongst rank and file. Yet support for rolling strikes had fallen,

especially proposed industrial action late in 1980
and early 1981 while rank and file in the VTU were
becoming critical of the level of industrial stoppages, or as one regional VTU officer reported in
March 1981 "the organizer is now confronted by an
array of ostrich-like fundamental orifices". The
issue stalemated: the Minister was unwilling to
make any concessions. The unions resorted to publicity campaigns rather than direct industrial
action. As the VTU's draft report for the 1982
conference concluded: "The issue of limited tenure
employment of teachers drags on ... That this
entirely unnecessary start/stop approach to state
school staffing has not been forgotten. Neither
has the obdurate stance adopted by the Minister of
Education and the Victorian Government."[6]
     As with the question of reform of the
industrial relations system, limited tenure employment would not be resolved by negotiations or
disputation. It was now dependent on the outcome
of the unions' electoral action.

The Teachers' Unions and The Labour Movement: Trade Union Affiliation

     While trade unionism is not the same as wor-
king class consciousness, Australian teachers have
a long history of collective organization that was
a rudimentary form of trade unionism. This has been
the case in Victoria since the 1880s,although its
teacher collectivity has been blunted by the persistence of its organizational fragmentation. A
higher level of trade union consciousness in teachers can be found in their identification with the
labour movement: in the first phase, affiliation
with peak-councils, the state Trades Hall Councils
and through them with the Australian Council of
Trades Unions (ACTU), and the second phase, support
for the Australian Labor Party (ALP).
     Affiliation with the trade union movement has
been slow in developing among teachers' unions,
which may seem curious to outsiders, given the
strength and social acceptability of Australian
trade unionism. Yet trade union affiliation by
white collar unions can suggest two different sets
of motives. It can imply a class identification
with organized manual workers, or it can be an
alliance "which implies no more than a pragmatic
assessment that white collar goals can be achieved
with trade union support" (Thompson, 1977). In
Australia teachers' unions have been reticent to
formally join the trade union movement. Only the
NSW Teachers' Federation affiliated with a state

THC, and through it, with the ACTU, before the 1970s. Its 1941 decision was prompted by an ideological identification with the working class, as espoused by a radical-left leadership, who had come to power after the depression. Its continued affiliation after 1952, following the defeat of the left-wing, indicates that pragmatism was the operative factor.[7]

In Victoria the question of trade union affiliation has been an intermittent issue for many years. In the 1940s the VTU, a less radical, but more militant, union than the NSWTF, nearly voted to join both wings of the labour movement, as an expression of its frustration of being denied a teachers' tribunal. In the early 1970s, the TTUV as part of its ideological position would probably have affiliated with the local THC, but it remained outside in an expression of solidarity with the "Rebel 26 unions", the left-wing unions who had withdrawn from the THC. However in 1975 it affiliated, its decision being a modern example of the mixture of identification with the working class, and political and industrial pragmatism. The VSTA followed in 1977. In 1974 the VTU Council rejected a proposal of a conference resolution on THC affiliation. Between 1974 and 1980 it changed position largely out of pragmatic considerations: the other two unions were affiliates, and all three unions were moving closer through joint policies. More fundamental, however, was that it could see the advantages of such affiliation. At the state level, the trade union movement gave direct support to TTUV industrial disputes, or more general support when long service leave and workers' compensation provisions were threatened by conservative governments. At the national level the impact of the ACTU was decisive. It has undergone significant structural and functional changes (under the leadership of R.J. Hawke) which had increased the popularity of the trade union movement, as well as bringing into its ambit the white-collar peak organization, of which the VTU and ATF were members. Similarly the traditional, but unfounded teachers' arguments against affiliation: support for the ALP; political levies; direct involvement in other union's stoppages; fears of splitting a union where many members were not from trade union family backgrounds, did not carry the weight of earlier years. The arguments for affiliation on the VTU conference floor in 1980 reflected the pragmatism described above, as well as the emerging militancy in

industrial and political agitation. The mover of
the motion for affiliation argued:
> "... what can we achieve by being involved in
> the Victorian Trades Hall Council? One of the
> most important issues I think we as teachers
> must face when we talk about needs based staf-
> fing policies, limited tenure, needs in
> schools, building policies and so on, is that
> we do not have the support of the community at
> large, and we are fooling ourselves if we
> believe that the trade union movement supports
> us, because they don't even know what we're on
> about. Now I was on a sub-committee at the
> beginning of the needs based staffing campaign
> to work with other unions to explain what our
> policies and intentions were in staffing of
> schools; and we found it extremely difficult
> to move within the trades hall circle of which
> we were not a part, and get these trade union
> leaders to appreciate that education was an
> important issue."[8]

The Victorian teachers' affiliations with the
trade union movement proceeded without the internal
disputation that was predicted would happen to the
VTU in the 1940s, or probably would have occurred
in the early 1960s. Similar gradualist moves towards trade union affiliation have occurred in
other teacher unions in recent years, but the issue's potential divisiveness still exists, as evidenced by the eventual withdrawal from the ATF of
teachers' unions in South Australia and Tasmania,
following ATF's decision to affiliate with the ACTU
in 1978. The public debates and closeness in
teacher-referenda that ensued at the time, and as
the two unions have been coaxed back to the ATF,
indicate that large sections of Australian teachers
are still uneasy about their union's formal identification with the labour movement.

Being a member of the Victorian Trades Hall
Council has not been strategically beneficial, nor
conscious-raising for the Victorian teachers' union.[9] The weekly meetings of the THC, concerned as
they are with symbolic politics, gestures, procedures and information, have not been uplifting or
even educative. The TTUV Secretary warned teachers
of this, as early as 1975: such meetings were
'dead' and there was not widespread genuine interest in state education.[10] VTU delegates in 1981-82
were to find the interest in educational and teacher questions still on the periphery. Some also
found the THC to be tainted with sexism. One

delegate reported back to the VTU Council the 'reference to lounge suits only' on invitations to the Labour Day dinner. Another found the THC Secretary at council meetings to be autocratic.

There have also been the inevitable clashes of interests; the most obvious was the TTUV/VSTA's notice that they would support Australian Teachers' Federation policy opposing wage restraint, the official ACTU policy in 1982. On other occasions the teachers' unions have been overlooked, as when they were not invited to participate in a trade union programme in secondary schools. This oversight suggests that the gap between white collar and blue collar trade union perceptions is a two-way process, at least in the early stages of the teachers' presence in the trade union movement.

However as their presence has become more established and with the added weight of the VTU delegation, plus the influence of the Trade Union Training Authority schemes for teachers, and the increasing political mobilization, the THC has been much more receptive, even sympathetic, to the teachers' claims. Thus in the last two or three years an increased prominence has been given to teacher and education politics and industrial relations, both in the forum meetings and in committee works, while there has been continuing moral, even industrial support for striking teachers, such as during the Limited Tenure Employment campaign, 'stand down' legislation or official victimization of teachers.

Overall the teachers' unions have gained more from their affiliation with the trade union movement than they have contributed to that movement. Yet it is still early days in a dynamic relationship. Moreover the observable fact that trade union affiliation did not reap political havoc for the teachers' unions was important in imparting a conventional wisdom that teacher unionism is an established part of the modern labour movement and that at times, political strategies, similar to those of traditional trade unions should be adopted by teachers. Thus the trade union affiliation helped create a favourable climate for the unions, especially the VTU, to support the Australian Labor Party at the 1982 state elections and the 1983 federal elections.

The Teachers' Unions and the Labour Movement: The ALP

It is rare in a pluralistic system to find a teachers' union intervening, as distinct from protesting, in the electoral process. In Australia there have been examples of 'fringe' teachers' unions affiliating with the ALP.[11] Generally teachers have refrained from supporting these organizations, as they have refrained from supporting a political party at a general election, so as not to offend the rank and file, many of whom (in a compulsory voting system) vote for other parties. However Victoria's teachers have occasionally shown enterprise by campaigning to defeat Ministers for Education or a government. The most spectacular success was 1945 when the VTU helped defeat a government as a means of securing the Teachers' Tribunal (Bessant, 1977). Nearly thirty years later the teachers' unions would help defeat another conservative government to abolish the same tribunal. Yet the unions' role in the 1982 state elections was different to that of 1945: the unions' endorsement of the ALP was the first time in Australia that a teachers' union had intervened directly in electoral politics.

It was expected that the VSTA and TTUV would support the ALP, although radical factions in both unions were reluctant to be seen as too supportive of a moderate, reformist party. The VTU was the unknown variable and the real surprise in state electoral politics. The VTU leadership and senior staff were known to be sympathetic to the ALP, but not necessarily ALP members. The VTU president, Lester Rootsey, declared in November 1980 that it was time the VTU supported the party which endorsed the union's policies. In December 1980 the monthly Council meeting resolved that the ALP should be supported in some way as a protest against government policy. This was seen as a reasonable alternative to the union's continuation of strike action following the government's introduction of 'standdown' clauses. The VTU Council specified there should be withdrawal of the limited tenure and penal regulations against striking teachers and the acceptance of a reformed industrial relations system. In April 1981 the Executive canvassed the government and opposition parties on a list of specific policies. The government refused to agree to modify its policies, while the ALP responded with a set of identical or sympathetic education policies – which was not unexpected given the participation of teacher unionists, even ALP members, on the party's education committee and Shadow Minister's advisory group. This survey was reported to the annual conference in May 1981, and the

conference with the Council's December resolution
before it, resolved, "to determine the most effective way the VTU can assist in the election of an
ALP government at the next state elections".[12] The
debate was extremely short; the margin of the vote
"overwhelming". The leadership held its breath for
a grass roots reaction, which did not eventuate.
There were some 30 resignations from individual
members and protests and opposition from one branch
and 15 schools.

VSTA endorsement of the ALP followed at its
annual meeting in July, and the TTUV gave guarded
support in October, as it still required a clearer
statement from the ALP on union preference clauses,
a commitment to maintain junior technical schools
and central employment in the TAFE sector. All
three unions stated that the basis for the support
to the ALP flowed from the government's failure to
implement a worthwhile industrial relations system,
and its refusal to negotiate further on questions
like Limited Tenure, family leave provisions,
school staffing, etc. The unions' decision to
support the ALP was a bold, but not audacious
decision, although the force and direction of the
VTU conference decision took many commentators and
teachers by surprise. The 1979 state elections, the
Gallup polls and party's parliamentary performance
indicated that for the first time in over twenty
years the ALP had a real, but not certain, chance
to win power. In October 1981 there was a 'blood-
less coup' in its parliamentary leadership, but any
change of leadership must be seen as a gamble six
months before an election.

The unions' support for the ALP was $170,000,
of which $100,000 came from the VTU in a windfall
sale of shares in a local radio station. The VTU
also made a significant contribution to the ALP by
donating printing, clerical and research facilities, and above all else, by releasing its
several officers and all regional organizers to
work as liaison officers with ALP candidates in
marginal seats.[13] VTU-ALP offices were formed in
regional and provincial capitals, VTU officers
worked closely with ALP campaign committee, and
with the Shadow Minister for Education and his
staff. The targets were the general electorate
through ALP education, and primary education pamph-
lets paid for by the VTU, and by mobilizing teacher
and parents support at the school level through
visits and public meetings of the local candidates,
organized by the VTU regional office. In two outer

Melbourne seats a fully staffed VTU campaign office was operating six months before the election. The issues promoted by the ALP candidates at the VTU's request were the performance and broken promises of the conservative government; size of classes, buildings, tenure staff levels. Reform of the industrial relations system was not given prominence locally because of its technical complexity, and because of its obvious relationship to the sensitive area of the teacher strikes. Overall, the level and type of VTU support for the ALP was the most systematic organized attempt in state politics to bring an educational reform campaign before the electorate. It would also rank as one of the best examples of a sustained intervention by any interest group in Victorian politics. It succeeded in reviving public education as a major election issue - 'education' having become a tired, dispirited issue in the previous three elections. It was helped by conservative critics who accused the teachers' unions of 'buying a government' to gain such 'emotive' benefits as compulsory unionism, union domination of Labor administrations,'sweetheart' salaries deals, etc.

The influence of the unions' campaign on the final election result is difficult to assess. Labor would have won power, but in key 'education' seats the swing to the ALP was generally greater, while some 20 teachers joined the ALP caucus. Teachers took special delight in the local defeat of two Assistant Ministers for Education who had long records of teacher union bashing. The election result was deemed an outstanding success by the union leadership, while the new Minister for Education spoke in glowing respect for the electoral work of the VTU organizers. The euphoria and elation which greeted teachers on election night (and Monday morning at school) lingered for several months. VTU organizers reports from the regions contained phrases like - "teachers are noticeably more satisfied, interest in education and industrial issues is high in marked contrast to before"; "new confidence sense of professionalism"; "responding to educational and industrial concerns in very constructive relaxed and self assured manner". A year after the elections, one VSTA executive member bannered the first year of teacher unionism under a Labor government with 'Fruitful', 'Hectic' and 'Exciting'(Victorian Teacher, April 1983, p.7).

In its first six months of power the Labor government acknowledged the teachers' unions' support in a series of concessions, some of them symbolic gestures. These included: three salary rises (two revisions were overdue, before April 1982), repeal of stand-down and other penalties against the unions, abolition of limited tenure employment and corporal punishment, and promises to accept the family-leave agreement, teachers' rights including union preference, the appointment of union leaders to visible positions in the Teaching Service Conciliation and Arbitration Commission (the Teachers' Tribunal was abolished in August 1982), and the creation of a State Board of Education.

The significance of Victoria's intervention in the electoral process was not lost on the other states: the South Australian Institute of Teachers (1982) and Queensland Teachers Union (1983) considered supporting the ALP in their state elections, but ultimately they rejected the strategy in favour of more conventional 'education' campaigns. The success of Victoria also became a decisive factor in the ATF's decision to support, on a limited basis, the ALP at the 1983 elections. The decision however reflected the ambivalence within the ATF affiliates: Victoria was very anxious to emulate a 1982 election campaign, Western Australia in principle was reluctant to support a political party, Technical and Further Education Teachers Association did not wish to appear critical of the conservative federal government which had increased funds to TAFE, and the NSWTF was unwilling to support the ALP because of Labor's continuing 'state aid' policies. Thus the final resolution was worded "to oppose the unsatisfactory educational policies and practices of the government and support those aspects of ALP policy which constitute its greater commitment to public education".[14] The ATF donated $154,000 to its own national publicity campaign, not to the ALP, but the direction of this campaign changed dramatically in the sudden announcement of an early election in February 1983. The VTU wanted a more interventionist campaign in support of the ALP, but as it was not possible to reconvene ATF conference, it and the other Victorian unions went their own way. The VTU federal campaign was a miniature version of 1982: particularly in the use of regional officers in marginal conservative seats - all of which were to fall to Labor, and several Labor seats. Education was not a major issue - in a personalities' election, which saw the former ACTU president (R.J. Hawke), MP of less than three

years standing and the Labor leader of less than
one month, elected in a landslide ALP victory.
Moreover, the short election and the central control of electioneering, meant that the VTU campaign
in local electorates could not be effective as in
the state election.[15] Yet its visibility remained
high in these electorates. The contrast could be
found in NSW where the Teachers' Federation is
completely opposed to state aid. It allocated
$150,000 mainly for TV commercials, which produced
some excellent electoral material on education,
which implied support for the ALP, without actually
endorsing the party. It also worked in three marginal seats, but without the scale of operation of
the VTU. (Education, 28 March 1983).

The teachers' unions' role in the 1983 federal
elections have mobilized teachers into believing
that education can again become a major area of
national policy. However since then, the only
revival in educational politics has been the re-
emergence of the state aid issue, as a result of
Labor's first attempt to cut back the financial aid
to wealthy private schools. The teachers' unions in
Victoria and elsewhere must stand firm with the
Labor government (and the Minister, Senator Susan
Ryan) against the rising backlash from private
schools and 'education' Conservatives. The ATF's
functions are also likely to be scrutinized further
because of its poor showing in the 1983 elections,
and in its public campaign to defend the federal
government from the state aid backlash.[16] However
the ATF may be wary of future endorsements of
Labor, following Victoria's experience since mid-
1983.

The Victorian government continued to introduce new initiatives, re-opening negotiations or
fulfilling pre-election promises in areas of staffing levels, school government and industrial relations. Thus while the Teaching Service Bill to
formalize the new industrial relations system took
a year and a half to reach parliament (November
1983), it had been prepared with continuing consul-
tations and review by the teachers' unions' representatives, ALP education committee and ministerial
advices and industrial relations advice. The teachers' unions, however, were not prepared to wait
as long for the ratification of their new industrial agreements, these were reached in August 1982
after an industrial stoppage (TTUV, May 1983), and
threats of industrial stoppage by the VSTA.

The euphoria and optimism disappeared in the

same period, as the Minister announced (rather than by consultation), that there would be a two per cent reduction in education expenditures in the 1983-84 budget (August), consistent with government policies of an "unavoidable" reduction in government expenditures. The brunt of the educational cuts after August were in non-essential areas, but the subsequent reductions in emergency teachers, regional consultancies and special and normal support services to schools, was challenged by the teachers' unions. Their basic argument was that such reductions in school and TAFE expenditures would be unnecessary if the state government was prepared to take a tougher stand on aid to non-government schools. Old tensions between the post-primary and primary teachers' unions re-emerged when the VTU withdrew from a joint one-day protest stoppage on 25 October 1983, having secured certain concessions from the Minister. This isolated the other two unions and subjected them to public and Labor accusations, that their members were blinded by self-interest to the real educational achievements of the government. At this stage we must agree with a VTU vice-president that, "It is too early yet to determine whether it is the end of the honeymoon and the first step towards divorce proceedings" (Victorian Teacher, Oct. 1983, p.3). But the events since mid-1983 have silenced arguments that the teachers' unions should affiliate with the Labor Party.

. . . . .

In discussing the future of teachers' unions in a broad international setting, Roy Adam (1982: 202) suggested that during economic recession and declining public faith in state schooling, teachers' unions have been, and will be, "reduced to small holding operations with minimal support from their members or from the public". This has not been the case in Victoria, Australia, where its three teachers' unions have taken direct political action to secure certain policies which could not be attained by conventional industrial or political methods, including strike action. The Victorian unions have demonstrated to other teacher unions the value of intervention - even on a limited number of issues - in the political processes. Yet several basic questions remain. Was the interventionist strategy of 1982-83 merely an isolated event, born out of teachers' frustrations with state educational politics? Or will

interventionist politics be adopted as "a sophisti-
cated, coherent alternative" to the unions' knee-
jerk of the past? (P. Carswell, Victorian Teacher,
Dec. 1983: 34-35). Indeed, will intervention
become the unions' basic strategy in their attempts
to transform the school system, if not society?
These questions must become part of the Victorian
(and Australian) teachers' political agenda over
the next few years.

NOTES

* In preparing this chapter the authors are
   grateful to the Victorian Teachers' Union for
   permission to study its archives, current files
   and policy records. The VSTA and TTUV in the
   past have co-operated with the authors but
   because of the size of this chapter they were
   not approached for access to their archival
   records. The ATF records consulted are derived
   from reports of delegates to the VTU Council
   meetings.
1. For background on this statement see Bessant
   and Spaull (1972, 23-52). Currently there is
   an intense factional struggle in the NSWTF,
   which resulted in the right-wing factions organizing to defeat the president and deputy pre-
   sidents in the 1983 elections.
2. This is based on statistical information on
   working conditions from the ATF Biennial
   Surveys 1978-1982, articles and statements in
   the Victorian Teacher 1982-1983 and the
   authors' discussions with primary and secondary
   teachers.
3. From VTU files, 'Direct Negotiations' and
   'Deputations'.
4. In NSW, the NSWTF estimates that 10,000 teachers are unemployed in seeking full time employment as state school teachers. The number
   of registered unemployed teachers is around
   1,500. No figures are available for Victoria.
5. VTU file, 'Limited Tenure Employment'.
6. 1980 Minutes of VTU Council Meeting, 5 March
   1982.
7. N.B. The NSWTF is the second largest registered
   state union in NSW; also the NSW Trades Hall
   Council is composed largely of moderate to
   right wing unions.
8. Transcript of VTU Annual Conference, 1980, p.81.
9. From VTU file, Trade Hall Council.

10. Interview with Ron Dedman, TTUV Secretary in *Secondary Teacher* No. 7, 1975, p.3.
11. e.g. Between 1911-1915 there existed the NSW Teachers' Union, which was formed as a general teachers' union and affiliated with both wings of the NSW labour movement. In Victoria some ALP members in the VTU and other teachers' unions formed the Labour Teachers' Union in 1931. It remained affiliated with the ALP until 1955 when it became an anti-ALP union, as the Affiliated Teachers' Union. It remained and remains affiliated to the VTHC.
12. Transcript of VTU Annual Conference 1981, p.18-19.
13. VTU file 'State Elections 1982'.
14. VTU file 'Federal Elections 1983'.
15. Report to VTU Council of ATF Annual Conference 1983 (and correspondence) *Ibid*.
16. As a result of a 1983 High Court decision, the ATF has sought registration as a teachers' trade union within the coverage of the Commonwealth Conciliation and Arbitration Committee. At this stage it is not certain whether this will accelerate more towards a confederation or federation of teachers in Victoria (or even a new federal structure which will weaken the powers of state teachers' unions). What is known is that the Victorian teachers' unions, like those interstate, will be unwilling to relinquish real powers, although they will support the growth of a federal teachers' union which will have some industrial functions. Ironically Victoria's teacher union fragmentation left its imprint on ATF question: The VAT, which now calls itself Victorian Teachers Federation (in the hope of industrial recognition) added another badge to its disruptive influence, when it made the first application for federal registration in November 1983, as the Teachers' Association of Australia. The ATF formed the Australian Teachers Union in February 1984 for registration.

REFERENCES

Adam, R. (1982), 'The Future of Teachers' Unions' *Comparative Education*, *18*, 2: 202.
Bessant, B. (1977), 'The VTU and the 1945 election campaign' in A.D. Spaull (ed.)], *Australian Teachers*, Melbourne, Macmillan, 257-63.

Bessant, B. and Spaull, A.D. (1972), Teachers in Conflict, Carlton, Melbourne University Press.

Bessant, B. and Spaull, A.D. (1976), Politics of Schooling, Melbourne, Pitman.

Hince, K. and Spaull, A.D. (1984), 'A new industrial relations system for Victorian state teachers', Educational Administration Review, 2, 1, pp. 85-115.

Martin, R.M. (1975), Trade Unions in Australia, Ringwood, Penguin.

Spaull, A.D. (1977), 'Trends in Teacher Militancy' in A.D. Spaull (ed.) Australian Teachers (above), pp. 302-307.

Spaull, A.D. (1983a), 'The (New) Politics of Schooling', Proceedings of the Australian School Library Association National Conference 1983, Melbourne, 1983.

Spaull, A.D. (1983b), 'The Influence of Compulsory Arbitration on the Development of Teachers' Unionism in Australia', paper to American Education Research Association Conference, Montreal, April 1983.

Spaull, A.D. (1984a), 'The Origins and Formation of Teachers' Unions in Australia', in I. Palmer (ed.), Melbourne Studies in Education 1984, Carlton, Melbourne University Press, pp.134-68.

Spaull, A.D. (1984 b), 'Victoria's Teachers' Unions', in (P. Hay, ed.), Victorian Politics - A Reader, Melbourne Dove Publications (in press).

Stroud, A. (1982), 'An Analysis of Factors Influencing Males and Females in Their Aspirations in Administrative Positions in Primary Schools', M.Ed. Studies Project, Monash University.

Thompson, A. (1977), 'The Large and Generous View: The Debate on Labour Affiliation in the Canadian Civil Service 1918-28', Labour/Le Travailleur, 2, 2, p.137.

Chapter Two

THE APRIL REVOLUTION AND
TEACHER TRADE UNIONISM IN PORTUGAL

Stephen Stoer

The decade of the 1970s was one of considerable educational mobilization in Portugal.[1] During this decade, about half-way through it, the first organizations of a trade union character for teachers of Portuguese state schooling were formed since the closing down of all associations of public employees, including those of teachers, in the year 1933. To set the arena for a discussion of trade union organizations for teachers during and after the revolutionary period (1974-75), we would like to begin this paper with a brief mention of the birth of teachers' organizations at the beginning of the 20th century, followed by a brief characterization of teaching under the authoritarian Salazarist regime, the same regime which banned all teachers' organizations within the state system of education, and then, finally, re-engage teacher organizations as they reappeared first as resistance to the Salazarist regime and then as an official, and in fact, celebrated, trade union activity after the April revolution of 1974. It goes almost without saying that the orientation of teachers' trade unions in Portugal today, their conceptions of struggle and of the role of the teacher, their objectives and their relations with recent governments, are all very much tied up with the effects of the revolution of 1974 and with the reaction of teachers' organizations against the severely hard times of the Salazarist dictatorship.

One can perhaps distinguish three components of these effects and of this reaction: first, the particular strategies adopted by teachers as a result of (mainly) Salazarist state intervention, second, the explosive activity of the revolutionary period which included the formation of the first teachers' organizations in half a century, and third, the strategies adopted by teachers and their newly-formed organizations to deal with the 'normalization' period which followed the revolution. It is through the first and third components that professionalism as a teacher strategy made its first appearance in Portugal: first as a strategy by teachers to legitimate their struggle against Salazarism (in a particular conjuncture when a 'democratic' educational reform was proposed within the constraints of a non-democratic regime), and second, as a strategy by teachers to resist increasing state regulation of the school and classroom autonomy they gained during the revolutionary period.[2]

The first organization of Portuguese teachers came into being at the end of the 19th century in the form of the <u>Association of Mutual Aid for Portuguese Primary School Teachers.</u> According to trade union historian Gomes Bento, the inspiration underlying the movement of primary school teachers at the end of the 19th century was Republican in nature and consequently based on the belief that the school had the capacity, by itself, to transform Portuguese society:

> "Political thinking of the 19th century resulted in a pedagogism that made the school the backbone of harmonious economic progress inseparable from civic formation and which would make citizens more active and responsible for public things. The teacher was the . . . priest of democracy."[3]

In the early 1900s, primary school teachers took up, through their press,[4] positions showing the beginnings of their transformation into one of the most decisive sectors of the radical petty-bourgeoisie. They vigorously supported the ideological platform of Republicanism in the educational sector: free-thinking, laicism and anti-jesuitism. With the birth of Portugal's first Republic (October 5, 1910), a major reform of primary schooling was attempted. The main objectives of the 1911 reforms were the decentralization of primary schooling, the extension of primary education to the countryside, the general expansion of all sectors of education and increased salaries for teachers (who, as the force capable of achieving social change by

supplanting, or at least rivalling, the
traditional leadership of the local priest in
small communities, were central to Republican
education policy).[5] Unfortunately, a decade later
the Republic had still failed to institute the
reforms of 1911. This fact led in large part to
the radicalization of important sectors of primary
school teachers:

> ". . . historical conditions, including on
> the one hand the strength of the working
> class movement and on the other the non-
> resolution of socio-professional problems, at
> a time when the fast-rising cost of living
> and the failure of the Republican school in
> the development of popular education, led to
> the radicalization (to the left) of important
> sectors of primary school teachers and their
> attempt to identify themselves with the
> working class."[6]

Thus, the decade of the 1920s saw teachers'
organizations increasingly linked to the general
workers' struggle. Gradually, what was now called
the "pedagogic illusion of Republicanism" was
replaced with activity of a trade union-like
nature.[7] By 1925 the main teachers' organization
had grown to 7,000 members (out of a total figure
of 9,000 teachers). The last congress of primary
school teachers before the onset of Salazarism
(which began in 1928 and ended in 1974) was held
in Oporto in August 1926, hence only a few months
after the military coup of May 28, 1926 which put
an end to the experience of Portugal's first
Republic.[8] By 1930, with Salazarism hardening,
teachers were already being ordered to associate
only on pedagogic grounds. In response the most
active sectors disbanded their own organizations.

THE NEW STATE AND
THE REPRESSION OF TEACHER ORGANIZATION

In 1933 the Estado Novo ('New State')
published its Constitution. Promptly measures
were taken which aimed at the ideological control
of teachers, and at the division, devalorization
and artificial stratification of teachers,
including their isolation from other workers.
Censorship was introduced through Decree-Law 22
469. With the publication of Decree-Law 23 048,
article 39, of the 23rd September 1933, all
association of public employees was prohibited,
signalling the beginning of more than forty years

in the desert for any form of teacher organization.[9] Legislative repression in education reached its peak in the year of the Carneiro Pacheco Reform (1936). In addition to the portrait of the chief of state in every classroom and a crucifix behind every teacher's desk, all school curricula were to be based on principles indicating "ideas of fatherland, family and the love of birthplace".[10] The Carneiro Pacheco 'Reform' also shut down teacher training colleges, on the grounds that a training programme centred on "pedagogical objectives" for teachers of primary schools was a waste of time, money and intelligence, and ordered all teachers to sign a declaration of repudiation of communism and "of other subversive ideas".[11] In 1942 the teacher training colleges were reopened, but the course was reduced from three years to two years. In the meantime, <u>regentes escolares</u>, that is, 'teachers' with only primary school education (4 years of schooling), were called in to fill the places of trained teachers, thus ensuring an economic means of teacher supply.[12] The curricula of teachers training colleges which were approved in February 1942 remained in effect until October 1974.

The private lives of teachers were also affected. The Carneiro Pacheco Reform not only prevented, that is, prohibited, female primary school teachers from wearing make-up[13] but also required that they apply for permission to the Ministry in order to marry, such permission only being granted however under certain circumstances, namely: when "the potential spouse" had "good moral and civil behaviour" and had ". . earnings, or revenues - proven by possession of the appropriate documental evidence - equivalent to the earnings of a teacher".[14] These measures, and others like them, led Portuguese sociologist Filomena Mónica to remark:

> "For the New State, the ideal (female) teacher should not express her views, criticize, nor draw attention to any of her physical features and, if possible, should remain a virgin."[15]

Mónica also argues that the large number of women in the teaching profession, particularly in the primary sector, goes some way towards explaining the almost overnight transformation of the teacher from the "priest of democracy" under the Republic, to the teacher as "the moulder of souls" that he/she came to be under the New State.

From a position as "agent of transformation" and "missionary of modernity", the teacher moved very quickly to a position as "blind follower of tradition" and "missionary of anti-modernity". How was such a rapid transformation possible?[16] In the first place, there is no doubt that already before the arrival of the New State there was felt among teachers a general disenchantment with the First Republic.[17] Teacher expectations came to be frustrated as the Republic proved unable to live up to its rhetoric. Mónica suggests, in addition, that the large number of women in the profession, who made up the majority of the profession (67 per cent), "almost obliterated the function of the teacher as a former of opinions in provincial communities".[18] Women were considered ideal as teachers by Salazarism because they were "docile, cheap and politically conservative, as well as religious".[19]

By the second half of the 1940s, the nature of the demands on the Portuguese education system had begun to alter, with changes in the contribution the education system was required to make both to the maintenance of social order and to the support of economic development. Gradually the increasingly competitive nature of Portuguese society, particularly in the economic domain, but also in other areas sensitive to international contact – areas like education and the contact between Catholic organizations[20] – and the greater access to the Portuguese public to domestic and international news – mass television was introduced into Portugal in the mid-sixties – made it possible for the urban working class and the petty bourgeoisie to see education not only as a possible way to fulfil their social aspirations[21], but also as a means of gaining entry into the political system. Slowly a new emphasis on educational planning and policy oriented towards economic goals became evident. Education came to mean, in terms of national development, economic growth, and increasingly, with the advent of popular mobilization – resulting from the corporatist regime's inability to capture, organize and articulate the demands of civil society – equality of opportunity in education. The Veiga Simão Reform in education in the early seventies brought together these different but related notions of national development.[22]

Veiga Simão, Minister of Education to the Caetano government, proposed a radical reform of

national education, at the beginning of 1971, and
for the first time in the history of the
corporatist regime, invited a national debate and
criticism of the Reform. With the incapacitation
of Salazar in 1968, Marcello Caetano, Salazar's
successor, had initiated, in 1969, a process which
came to be known as 'liberalization'. Although
lasting only a few years (already by the end of
1971 Caetano's 'liberalization' was hopelessly
compromised by conservative elements of the ruling
coalition), this process allowed a revival of
overt trade unionism among certain sectors of the
working class and gave a measure of voice, through
the Veiga Simão Reform, to demands for greater
access to education. The education reforms
outlined by the Caetano government initially
stated as their objective "the democratization of
education" and were, indeed, far-reaching in
scope. In the end, however, these reforms found
themselves politically neutralized and reduced to
a shadow of their former selves. Indeed, the
Veiga Simão Reform never really had any hope
of effectively implementing democracy in
Portuguese education. For this reason it met, and
even provoked, considerable opposition. One of
the chief focal points of opposition to the Reform
was a group of secondary and preparatory school
teachers who constituted in the last years of the
Salazarist regime

". . . the only organized and progressive
pro-associative movement of Portuguese
teachers in defense of their interests and
rights, professional and civic, and for a
real democratization of schooling and
education in Portugal (known as the GEPDESP,
Grupos de Estudo, here referred to as the
'Study Groups')."[23]

A study of the history of the Study Groups
reveals some of the contradictions that arise when
the democratization of schooling is attempted
within a political dictatorship! Their basic
demand, made in the first years of the seventies,
was simply that teachers should have the right to
hold meetings in educational establishments. At a
more general level, they aimed at mobilizing
teachers on issues related to professional conduct
and integrity in order to combat what had been a
long period of social devaluation of the teaching
profession. In addition to what has already been
said above about the situation of teachers under
Salazar, it should be pointed out that by the year

45

1970 about 80 per cent of preparatory and
secondary school teachers were either provisional
or untenured. As a result they were paid during
only ten months of the year, they received no
holiday pay, had no guarantee of returning for the
following school year, no rights to social
assistance, pensions or of moving up the pay scale
and were subject to immediate dismissal. Thus,
they had become in the secondary sector what the
'regentes escolares' were in the primary sector:
cheap labour for the Ministry of National
Education.

At the VIth Congress of lyceum education held
in Aveiro during the month of April, 1971, the
Study Groups argued for the need to create
"legislation allowing for the reorganization of
teacher associative life".[24] Effectively, the
Study Groups were out to test the limits of the
regime, to see just how far it was prepared to go
in its proclaimed "battle" for the democratization
of education.[25] Already in 1971 they were arguing
that democratization included participation in the
structures that decide school life. The following
is a paragraph of a proposal sent by the Study
Groups of the North of Portugal[26] to the Ministry
of National Education on March 29th, 1971:

"It is proposed that the right to participate
in decision-making processes, in that which
concerns the management of school
establishments, namely the School Councils
(Conselho Escolar), which shall in the future
have the function of choosing the Director or
Rector of such establishment, be guaranteed
to all teachers."[27]

By the first few months of 1974, and after
all dialogue had broken down between the Study
Groups and the Ministry of Education, it became
increasingly apparent that "a noose was tightening
around the Study Groups' neck".[28] The Ministry of
National Education's attitude towards the Groups
can be summed up in the following dispatch, issued
in February 1974 (a mere two months before the
April revolution) by the Secretary of State for
Instruction:

". . . the constitution of an association of
teachers as a social collectivity - with the
objectives indicated above (that is, to make
teachers aware of their position in society;
to defend professional, individual, and
collective interests of its members) give it
a notoriously trade union-like character,

(which is) in flagrant violation of constitutional and legal imperatives (that is, public functionaries are prohibited by article 39 of the National Work Statutes of DL 23 048 of 23 September 1933 from organizing themselves in private unions and from joining corporatist organizations)."[29]

THE FORMATION OF A TRADE UNION FOR TEACHERS

The revolution of April 1974, including the captains' coup d'etat and the vast popular response which accompanied it, made possible the realization of the blocked objectives of the 'Grupo de Estudos'. The immediate demand of teachers at the start of the revolutionary period was holiday payment for all teachers. This demand was met, amid much publicity, by the Ministry of Education. From October of the same year, negotiations were initiated with the, by then, IIIrd Provisional Government to obtain an adjustment in 'letter' on the scale of public employees' earnings. These negotiations also included reducing the range of the scale, bringing teachers' salaries into line with public employees with the same qualifications, and giving priority to the demands of primary school teachers. Finally, after the events of the 11th March, 1975,[30] the teachers' proposal was accepted by the IVth Provisional Government. There then took place the largest pay increase for teachers, especially primary school teachers, in dozens of years.

With the April revolution there occurred, virtually overnight, a shift of power from the Ministry of Education to the schools, from the Directors of the schools and the traditional teaching staff to progressive teachers and the student body. Local initiative after the 25th April, that is initiative at the level of the school population, commanded events, at least for the first six months of the revolution, and for much longer in terms of enduring effects.[31] The schools were to all intents and purposes occupied after the 25th April - by their own students and teachers:

". . . and thus occurred . . . 'the taking of power' of the management of the schools, substituting old directive bodies with commissions of students and teachers . .".[32]

And further,

"Immediately after the military coup and when the popular revolutionary torrent imposed a massive participation on all things Portuguese, school management structured under fascism fell roundly, and in its place arose, alternatively, the marvellous spontaneity that was democratic management in its early days."[33]

Thus, essential creative energy among teachers and students immediately after the 25th April was located in schools. And it was in the schools that the process of building a teachers' trade union movement began.

On the 2nd May, 1974, 5000 teachers participated in the election of an installation committee for a trade union of teachers in Lisbon.[34] In hundreds of schools elections were held for trade union delegates. Inevitably there was considerable continuity between the action and demands of the Study Groups of the period 1971-4 and the formation of a trade union of teachers after the 25 April coup d'etat. More precisely, Portuguese educator Rui Grácio has suggested that such continuity existed in the following ways: a) in terms of its leaders; b) in terms of the regional definition of the nascent trade union structure; c) in terms of the predominance of teachers from preparatory and secondary education; d) in terms of the objectives of the new leaders of the trade union, that is, the defense and promotion of professional interests of teachers, and participation in the definition and application of a national policy of schooling; and e) in terms of political outlook:

"Leaders and activists of the Study Groups, in the declining phase of Caetanism located themselves without exception among the ranks of the political opposition to the regime; some were even ideologically close to, or even attached to (or would become attached to after the 25th April), organizations or simple political currents of varying inspiration: liberal, socialist, communist, trotskyist, maoist, etc. As the Portuguese Communist Party was, and is, the most important and most structured political organization within the world of work, before and after the military coup, it is no surprise to verify that the provisional trade union structure of teachers appeared, generally and in a first phase, hegemonized by elements of

that party, or under its influence."[35]
Right from the beginning, however, there was considerable resistance to the conception of trade union structure and struggle promoted by the Portuguese Communist Party. One can perhaps systematize in a first phase (i.e. during the revolutionary period 1974-75) the tensions that existed between different conceptions of political project and expression among the agents of the revolution in schools, and throughout the education system generally, through the use of two mobilizing currents with conflicting solutions for resolving the problem of the revolution in Portugal: 'alfabetização' (mass literacy) and 'poder popular' (popular, or people's, power). Breines, in a recent work,[36] has referred to the distinction between 'strategic' and 'prefigurative' politics. While the latter is essentially anti-organization, anti-hierarchical and based on participatory democracy, the former is committed to building organization in order to achieve power to produce structural changes in the political, economic and social orders. In Breines' terminology, 'alfabetização' employed a 'strategic' conception of politics, while 'poder popular' put at the top of its agenda the condemnation of the class nature of the 'capitalist' school, in a capitalist Portugal, and its replacement through the immediate creation of the 'socialist' school (the school would thus become a counter-institution based on participatory, direct democracy). 'Alfabetização' had as its priority the immediate expansion of the school to the whole of the Portuguese community. In the meantime it would set about the concretization of a central revolutionary power to be eventually capable of orienting the school as an aid to the construction of the socialist society.

Below, we shall return to look in greater detail at the actual structure and programme of the main trade union organization that still claims the Study Groups as part of its heritage. For the moment it should be made clear that during the revolutionary period (1974-75) there became active two 'revolutionary' strategies of social transformation synonymous with the mobilizing currents we have termed 'alfabetização' and 'poder popular'. Both of these strategies manifested themselves, with varying degrees of support, within the 'motor of the revolution', that is, within the 'Armed Forces Movement' (the MFA). One strategy aimed at taking over, or dominating, the state apparatuses, on providing a centralized direction of the revolution with the MFA acting as the vanguard force linking the state apparatuses and the government to the people. The main task of central power would be to interpret and to put into action (to organize) the demands of civil society on the basis of two main criteria: bringing previously excluded groups into the political system and changing the political culture of the country. The other strategy was based on the notion of a social movement autonomous from the state, on notions of dual power, of setting up a revolutionary alternative through the locally-based organs of 'poder popular'. Thus, for this strategy, the situation was defined as 'pre-revolutionary', it being considered that the MFA, another 'important site of class struggle', could be important to the social movement only to the extent that it could manage to protect and promote the occupation and local control of schools, factories, houses and land by the elements of the social movement themselves.

Opposing both these strategies eventually[37] were the 'bourgeois' political parties (particularly the Socialist Party and the Popular Democratic Party, which later became known as the Social Democratic Party). These parties countered the more radical demands of 'alfabetização' and 'poder popular' with a demand for the institutionalization of pluralist representative democracy, on Western lines, particularly after the massive legitimation boost they received from the Constituent Assembly elections of April 15, 1975. Effectively, they called for the dissolution of the MFA and the return of the soldiers and their officers to the barracks.

As a result of its preoccupations with calculated organized struggle in order to achieve and consolidate new categories of power, 'alfabetização' found itself most effective in centralized mobilization activities (such as literacy campaigns and the MFA Cultural 'Dynamization' Campaign). 'Poder popular', on the other hand, with its concern for the pedagogy of the revolution, that is, with the process, the means, the participation and the dialogue of the revolution, was the logically dominant category of the spontaneous movement in the schools which culminated in the creation of the democratic management of the schools (<u>Gestão Democrática</u>).

At the level of the schools, the current of 'poder popular' argued that there was more than one way to build a trade union for teachers in Portugal. In opposition to what was termed the 'centralized machine', "dependent on numerous functionaries, governing teachers by way of circulars and negotiations with friends in the Ministry of Education"[38], 'poder popular' proposed the "decentralized and democratic" union, with power centred as much as possible on teachers in schools, thus "privileging the workplace and giving strength to the social movement of teachers". The model proposed by 'alfabetização', 'poder popular' claimed, would imply instituting permanent posts (not linked to work in schools) and would reduce trade union delegates to mere followers of the orders of the leadership, thus putting in jeopardy their role as spokesmen for the grassroots (frequently bypassing regional processes). In addition, this model was called a 'conciliatory political project', refusing a clear anti-capitalist alternative. The net result of any such trade union model would be the use of the union as a prop for political party interests leading to the 'regimentation' of teachers so that they defended interests other than those democratically adopted by the teachers' trade union.

For 'alfabetização', on the other hand, the crucial question was considered to be the question of 'divisionism', or, in terms of its opposite number, trade union unity. The severe repression suffered by Portuguese teachers under Salazarism had split their ranks. Some teachers had had some form of teacher training, most hadn't. Some teachers had tenured positions, most were untenured. Primary school teachers were separated from the rest as a result of tight ideological control over their classrooms and, indeed, as we have seen, over their private lives. In addition, teachers complained that the public was unaware of the poor working conditions of teachers.[39] 'Alfabetização' also reacted strongly against what were called the 'divisionist tactics' of 'poder popular'.

An important agreement among trade union organizations already existing (in a semi-clandestine state) at the time of the revolution, and later among those about to embark on the construction of a trade union, was that divisions within the movement would be fought tooth and nail (in addition to the 'nightmare' experience of the First Republic and conceptual opposition to the 'spontaneist' politics of 'poder popular', the spectre of a sudden return to 'fascism' haunted the movement, and the defeat of Salvador Allende's Popular Unity in Chile the year before the revolution in Portugal confirmed such fears). The trade unions called for the building of a single trade union confederation (and within the education sector, for the building of 'one trade union for all teachers') that would centre on the already existing confederation organization 'Intersindical'. Intersindical came into being in 1970 at the height of Marcello Caetano's attempts to 'liberalize' the Salazarist dictatorship:

> "On 28 September 1970 representatives of four trade unions of Lisbon (metal workers, wool, banks and commerce) met and decided ... to convocate other trade unions for a joint meeting which came to take place on 11 October with thirteen trade unions represented. The official date of the meeting, the first public and open act of the coordinated action of the trade unions is considered the founding date of Intersindical."[40]

During the first nine months of the revolution an apparent unity existed among the Socialist Party, the Communist Party and the Armed Forces Movement (making possible the minimum coherence needed for political practice at government level). As the dynamic of the revolution deepened this apparent unity came under increasing strain. It was finally shattered during the month of January, 1975. The shattering point was reached as a result of the favourable passage by the Provisional Government (in spite of Socialist Party opposition) of the law on 'unicidade sindical'. As a consequence, the Socialist Party accused the Communist Party publicly, for the first time since the 25th April 1974, of being anti-democratic and of acting against the programme of the MFA. It also accused the MFA of being overly influenced by the Communist Party.

'Unicidade sindical' was, for the Communist Party particularly, and for a good deal of the Armed Forces Movement too (committed to defending the organization of all workers as a group so that

they might defend their own interests in the wake
of a crumbling dictatorship), the logical solution
for trade union unity in the climate of
revolutionary Portugal. It meant the extension of
Intersindical into a single general trade union
confederation allowing only one union per branch
or per professional category. According to he
<u>Bulletin</u> of the Armed Forces Movement, 'unicidade
sindical' recognized:

> ". . . free will as expressed by workers in
> their meetings, which permits the exercise of
> trade union activity within firms, allowing
> for the existence of trade union
> representatives, trade union propaganda and
> the carrying out of meetings within firms;
> the law prohibits the state and employers
> from intervening in trade union life; the
> law does not permit the existence of more
> than one union for each sector of activity or
> professional category within the same
> geographic sphere, that is, the law does not
> permit parallel trade unions."[41]

The same <u>Bulletin</u> asked (somewhat rhetorically),
"Does this law limit the freedom of unions? Would
not a law to the contrary lead to the control of
the unions by political party interests acting in
the interest of employers?"[42] Alvaro Cunhal,
Secretary General of the Portuguese Communist
Party and also its chief theoretician, was to
later term the law, "an important victory of the
workers and consecration of trade union liberty in
the specific conditions existing at the time in
our country.[43]

For the Socialist Party the basic problem was
that a single trade union confederation could,
indeed, be controlled by a single political party:

> ". . . in January 1975, a bitter conflict
> broke out over a Portuguese Communist Party
> attempt to sanctify in law the monopoly role
> already exercised by the Party in the trade
> union world. The 'PCP' aimed to make the
> Communist-dominated Intersindical the only
> permissible trade union confederation."[44]

Thus, it was claimed that

> "Mário Soares demanded a pluralist union
> framework that would prevent Portuguese trade
> unionism being turned into a mere conveyor-
> belt for party directives"[45] (obviously
> Communist Party 'directives').

The Constitution of 1976 did not, in fact,
come to consecrate the principles of 'unicidade

sindical'.[46] When the dust of the revolutionary period had settled, the socialist Party found itself elected to power. Its project was, by this time, the establishment of pluralist democracy in Portugal, at least in terms of the functioning of its institutions. The alternative project, of 'Portugal in transition to socialism', expressed in different ways by 'alfabetização' and 'poder popular', was thus gradually excluded, at least those forms and contents symbolizing it to the greatest degree were excluded from the realm of the state. Former Prime Minister Vasco Gonçalves, reflecting on his experience as head of four provisional governments during the revolutionary period (the 2nd, 3rd, 4th and 5th), and hence as chief spokesman for a possible version of the 'alternative project', expressed the fading of the 'socialist' project in the following manner:

"The experience of the Provisional Governments (except for the VIth) showed that it was possible for Portugal to practise a policy of national independence (Article 7 of the Constitution foresees the abolition of all forms of imperialism and the creation of an international order capable of securing peace and justice in relations between peoples; Article 9, section a, says the state is to guarantee national independence and create the conditions - political, economic and social - necessary for it). The profound transformations that occurred in the socio-economic structure prove that this was so, as do the decolonization process, and the opening and development of relations between Portugal and the socialist countries and the countries of the Third World. Proof is also found, negatively, in the fact that the governments of Western Europe, and of the U.S.A., of the countries of the EEC and EFTA, only came to consider political conditions favourable for agreements with the Portuguese government after the fall of the Vth Provisional Government."[47]

Of course, the project of a pluralist Portugal was based on an alternative conception of national independence, one centering on the strengthening of Western-style democratic institutions:

"At a time when Portugal is engaged in a profound crisis of identity provoked by five hundred years of colonial frustrations and long periods of political obscurantism, the integration of the country into the European Community as a full member is much more than a path leading to economic growth. It is a venture capable of uniting the democratic forces in the task of preparing a future which will be freer and more prosperous for all Portuguese."[48]

It is in the light of these two 'projects' and conflicting alternative conceptions of national independence that one has to consider the formation of a trade union for teachers since the end of the revolutionary period.

To sum up this section so far, we began by saying that the building of a trade union for teachers in Portugal after the coup d'etat of 25 April 1974 started in the schools themselves in continuity with the activity and organization of the Study Groups during the first part of the decade of the seventies. Such activity and organization was hegemonized by the mobilizing current we have termed 'alfabetização'. At the same time, however, 'poder popular' quickly established itself as the dominant category of mobilization activity within the schools. 'Poder popular' produced a virulent critique of what was described the excessive centralizing tendency of 'alfabetização' – a tendency originating in the objective of occupying power rather than constructing it. To accomplish the latter, 'poder popular' set about delimiting the objectives and action of the 'socialist school'. Partly in response to 'poder popular', and partly as a result of its own logic, 'alfabetização' concentrated its activity on the consolidation of the transformative gains brought about by the captains' coup and the huge popular response that greeted it. This led it to conceive its activity mainly in terms of assuming, or at a minimum, of influencing, central policy-making powers.

With the end of the revolutionary period and the fading of the project that was 'Portugal in transition to socialism', a period of 'normalization' ensued.[49] The victors of the revolutionary period, that is, the political parties championing Western-style pluralist democracy, set out to re-establish the power of the state at all levels and in all sectors of state institutions. This process led to the complete marginalization of 'poder popular' (already a spent force by the end of the revolutionary period) and, as a reaction against 'normalization', to the consolidation in the education sector of 'alfabetizaçāo' domination in the main teachers' trade union organizations.

The reduction of the authority of the state in education during the revolutionary period had led to increased autonomy for teachers over teaching activities (concretised, for example, in the new regime of democratic management of schools[50]). As a response to normalization, and its attempts to regulate teacher autonomy, teachers adopted through their main union organizations a strategy of 'professionalism', that is, they began to stress the importance of specialist knowledge particularly in teacher training and in school management. This strategy aimed at legitimating their newly-gained autonomy and at refuting the accusations showered upon them by the orchestrators of normalization.[51] The preoccupation of the democratic regime with the re-establishment of state authority had the effect of negating teacher professionalism as a possible ideology of the state. In this sense, one might argue that a major effect of normalization, and its blame-the-teacher-for-the-excesses-of-the-revolution discourse, was to close the ranks of at least a significant portion of Portugal's most active (militant) primary and secondary school teachers in opposition to the state. Naturally this strategy of professionalism as oppositional state activity was centred in the trade union organization(s) adopting the heritage of the Study Groups.

CONSOLIDATING TEACHERS' TRADE UNION ORGANIZATION: THE SPGL AND SINDEP

The first elections held in Lisbon for providing the teacher trade union movement with a provisional and directive leadership (called the Commissāo Directiva Provisória), held in July, 1974, accounted for almost 65 per cent of the entire teaching body, in spite of the fact that many teachers were already on holiday.

For these first elections, all teachers, except for those excessively compromised with the former regime, comprised the voting electorate (membership cards, the payment of dues, etc., only came into effect from the end of 1974). The winning list was closely associated with the Portuguese Communist Party (and representative of the Study Groups), although from the viewpoint of 'poder popular' groups:

> "The result of the first elections for a
> trade union for teachers was based on a
> 'misunderstanding': the winning group was a
> miscellaneous pack of voters who wanted order
> instead of school assemblies, were against
> long hair, drugs and free love and who wanted
> the order of the 'alliance MFA-people' and
> 'Portuguese democracy in transition to
> socialism'."[52]

In the following elections, held in March in
Lisbon and in April in Oporto, the list loosely
associated with the Socialist Party was the
winner. Although there was a drop in the number
of teachers participating in these elections,
still more than 50 per cent of the entire teaching
body participated in the voting act (more than 75
per cent of teachers holding union cards).
Disputes among the leadership elected in 1976 led
to new elections in June, 1977. In these
elections the Portuguese Communist Party list
regained control of the leadership of the union
movement. The situation has remained the same
since then.

In spite of the efforts made to avoid
'divisionism' among teachers in the years
following the revolution by the mobilizing current
'alfabetização', conflicting strategies, directly
tied to alternative conceptions of national
independence, on how to confront 'normalization'
led, in 1978, to a split in the teachers' trade
union movement. In 1978, the appearance of what
was termed 'Carta Aberta' (Open Letter) - later to
become the 'General Union of Workers' (UGT),
supported and sponsored by the Socialist and
Social-Democratic parties largely to confront
Communist Party domination within the General
Portuguese Confederation of Workers (CGPT-IN) -
and protests over the results of the elections of
that year, produced the first hints of the
formation of an alternative trade union for
teachers. These hints were concretized in 1980
with the setting up of a commission under the
leadership of the breakaway 'Trade Union of
Teachers of the Northern Zone' which led to the
formation of the 'Independent Trade Union Movement
of Teachers of Greater Lisbon', and which shortly
thereafter became the present-day 'Democratic
Trade Union of Teachers' (SINDEP), which operates
mainly in the Lisbon and southern regions of
Portugal.[53] In what follows we shall present a

brief account of the basic political commitments
and educational priorities of what are now in
Portugal, in the world of teaching, the two major
representatives of the two 'projects' for national
independence referred to above: on the one hand,
the project still very much tied to socialist
notions developed during Portugal's revolutionary
period (although the goal now is defending the
very existence and debate of these notions, rather
than hope for their implementation) articulated by
the SPGL, and on the other, the project oriented
towards the EEC whose spokesman in the teaching
world is SINDEP.

The SPGL is, without any room for doubt, the
main trade union for teachers in Portugal. It has
since 1974, and even before through the influence
exercised by members of the Study Groups, been the
main leader and definer of trade union policy for
teachers, either in conjunction with other 'zones'
or 'areas' sympathetic to its leadership and
policy, or as a pole of opposition in relation to
which other potential unions could begin to define
their own positions. It has consistently set the
tone for all trade union debates on education
since its conception, has shown on several
occasions its capacity to mobilize fairly
effectively large numbers of teachers and has gone
some way towards not only criticizing but also
influencing policy-making decisions at the level
of central government[54].

What are the major objectives of the SPGL in
Portuguese education? A document based on an
account of the First Trade Union Congress of
Teachers of Greater Lisbon held in March, 1981[55],
gives us some idea of the union's major
preoccupations and goals. The three priority
areas for the union are: 1) the democratization
of the Portuguese school and an increase in the
quality of schooling; 2) enhancing the value of
the teaching profession; and 3) reinforcing
teachers' capacity to carry out trade union
action. All three of these areas, whose wider
implications are dependent on the historical and
political contexts that we have pointed to
throughout this paper, are given a framework in
the statement of principles which oriented the
Congress of 1981:

> "The existence of the teachers' trade union
> movement is an expression of the right to
> free association conquered and made possible
> with the 25th April (revolution). The action

of the SPGL is indissolubly linked to the complex process of struggle for the betterment of living and working conditions of teachers and of their professional situation, for a better and more democratic schooling and for the defense of liberty and democracy in our country. The First Congress of the SPGL . . . constitutes a moment of great meaning for teachers and for schooling, and an important expression of the development of teachers' trade unionism in democratic Portugal. After four days of sessions, preceded by preparation in schools of all levels and sectors of education in the zone of Greater Lisbon, the Congress proclaims itself in favour of the development of trade union action in defense of the democratization of the school and the raising of the quality of education and in defense of enhancing the value of the teaching profession."[56]

More generally, the SPGL argues that education in Portugal is a sector in 'global crisis'. The hopes raised by the revolution have not been fulfilled. This is because a) there has been a deficient expansion of the school system (20 per cent of youth still do not finish the compulsory six years of schooling - the lowest compulsory schooling figure in Europe - and 45 per cent do not complete the ninth year of schooling); because b) the Portuguese education system is poorly adjusted to the economic and social developmental needs of the country (67 per cent of youth do not carry on their studies beyond the ninth year and there is no/very little professional training - in addition, only eight to ten per cent go on to some form of higher education); and because c) school failure rates are extremely high.

The reasons for the crisis, according to the SPGL, are Salazarism, almost fifty years of it -
("The absence of liberty had sharp repercussions in the profession working against the very nature of the educational act, which is essentially liberating and creative")[57]
plus left-over disturbances and unfulfilled goals from the revolutionary period, and most importantly, what is termed "a containing, authoritarian and incompetent education policy", initiated by the first education ministry of the

new constitutional regime headed by Socialist
Party member, Sottomayor Cardia, and continued by
education ministers thereafter[58]. As evidence of
this 'negative policy' the SPGL quotes figures on
spending on education in Portugal (at a time of
accords with international organizations like the
World Bank and the IMF) which show a decrease on
educational spending from 19 per cent of the 1976
budget to 13 per cent of the 1978 budget.[59]

Finally, to counteract conservative education
policy, the SPGL calls on the teacher as an
'active intervener' in the education system. The
teacher, in other words, should be devoted and
militant, particularly to defend the conquests of
the revolution (the most important conquest of
which, apart from free association, is considered
to be the democratic management of schools). In
sum, the SPGL defends a type of trade union
organization guaranteed to promote the highest
degree possible of 'direct democracy' and 'high
teacher participation': it is based on the
existence of a Directing Committee, a General
Assembly and an Association of Delegates, elected
in all schools, zones or 'concelhos' (in the case
of primary schooling).

The alternative trade union project for
teachers, based largely on the Lisbon-based
organization SINDEP, stresses above all else its
'democratic' nature, in opposition to the
'undemocratic' and 'Communist-dominated' SPGL. It
is claimed that whereas SINDEP openly declares its
affiliation to the UGT (presumably a 'democratic'
trade union confederation), the SPGL tries to
disguise its de facto affiliation to the CGPT-IN.

The general concerns underlying SINDEP's
activity as a trade union for teachers are claimed
to be: 1) problems with national identity
resulting from the end of the 'colonial epoch'
(and, as we have seen, entry of Portugal into the
EEC as a solution to this problem); 2)
subordination of economic to political power, and
of political power to the voting act (trade union
activity based on individual rights); 3) a social
pact with the government (respecting the conventions of the International Labour Organization
that recognize workers' organizations as
bargaining agents); 4) reform of the social
security system (including the proper functioning
of a national health system); 5) acceptance and
defence of the principle of choice in education;
and 6) ecological preoccupations.[60] SINDEP, like

the SPGL, considers enhancing the dignity and prestige of teachers an immediate and fundamental objective. With respect to this objective, SINDEP argues that the non-recognition of the fact that there do indeed exist two conflicting viewpoints and practices of teacher trade unionism in Portugal has consistently weakened the bargaining power of teachers in the years since the revolution.[61]

The Constitution of 1976 recognizes the role of trade unions to defend the rights and promote the interests of the workers they represent. Further, it recognizes the role of trade unions in policy making.[62] Both the SPGL and SINDEP have been recognized, albeit unofficially,[63] as legitimate interlocutors of teachers. In the case of the SPGL this has occurred because of the organizational force of the union and because of the undeniable influence of the union among teachers (that is, the union packs real muscle), while with SINDEP it has been more the similarity of societal project adopted by the union with the Government's own project that has led to its acceptance as representative of a certain sector of teacher opinion. The problem for SINDEP is that both the process and the context of the relation between the Portuguese state and the education system favour the militant oppositional activity of the SPGL. In a period of economic stagnation, with the education system in an apparent state of contraction, the demand for modernization implicit in a programme that calls for Portugal's entry into the Common Market encounters great difficulty finding some response. In addition, the permanent tension that exists between the state apparatus for education and the substance of its practice[64] is exacerbated by a seemingly endless 'normalization' process (Portugal celebrates this year the 10th anniversary of the revolution) that stresses the bureaucratic control of teachers. The resistance of teachers to this process characterizes very clearly the activity of the SPGL. SINDEP, on the other hand, finds itself caught in the contradiction of aiding and abetting the normalization process while at the same time claiming to represent teacher resistance to encroaching state regulation.

NOTES

1. This theme is developed in detail in Stephen
    R. Stoer (1983), 'The April Revolution and
    the Contribution of Education to Changing
    "Portuguese Realities"', Ph.D. thesis in
    Sociology of Education, The Open University.
2. We are indebted to Helena Araujo for a number
    of insights on Portuguese teachers and
    strategies of professionalism. Most of them
    can be found in Helena Araujo (1982),
    'Towards an Analysis of Social Class and
    Ideologies in Portuguese Teachers', M.A.
    Dissertation, Institute of Education,
    University of London.
3. See Gomes Bento (1978), <u>O Movimento Sindical
    dos Professores   -   finais da Monarquia e a
    Primiera República</u>, Lisbon: Editorial
    Caminho, p. 16.
4. Which included the two major periodicals
    <u>Educação Nacional</u> (conservative) and
    <u>A Federação Escolar</u> (progressive).
5. See Stephen R. Stoer (1981), 'Democracy and
    Socialism in Education in Portugal', in
    Dale, R., Esland, G., Fergusson, R. and
    MacDonald, M. (eds.), <u>Education and the
    State: Volume 1, Schooling and the National
    Interest</u>, Lewes: Falmer Press.
6. Gomes Bento, op.cit., p.94.
7. A satisfactory account of teachers and their
    organizations during this period would, of
    course, attempt to contextualize their
    struggle within the Portuguese workers'
    movement of the 1920s.   For works that
    contribute to this project, see Gomes Bento,
    ibid.;   António Candeias (1981), 'Movimento
    Operário Português e Educação (1900-1926)',
    <u>Análise Psicológica</u>, ii (1), July/August/
    September;   M.F. Mónica (1980), 'Ler e Poder:
    debate sobre a educaçcão popular nas
    primeiras décadas do século XX', <u>Análise
    Social</u>, no. 63;   and Aurea Adão (1981), 'La
    Condition des Instituteurs Portugais, 1901-
    1951', Doctorat de Troisième Cycle thesis in
    Educational Sciences, University of Bordeaux
    II.
8. Portuguese historians have referred to the
    Ist Republic (1910-1926) as both the
    "decadence of the liberal political system
    initiated in 1820", that is, "not the
    beginning of something structurally new but

. . . rather tha last phase of something which had started much before", and as the "elevated capacity of a society to rethink itself and to act". (The first quote is from leading Portuguese historian Oliveira Marques, quoted in Douglas L. Wheeler (1978), Republican Portugal : A Political History 1910-1926, London and Madison: University of Wisconsin Press, p.254; the second from Manual Villaverde Cabral in an article written for the newspaper Diário de Notícias, 26 October 1982). There appears to be no doubt, however, that the Republic's sixteen years were stormy ones. D.L. Wheeler has termed the Republican period "a kind of uninterrupted civil war on a small scale". To emphasize his point Wheeler refers to the fact that ". . . for some time (in France) the chaos of Lisbon politics . . . led to the coinage of the verb 'to Portugalize', which was meant to mean 'bring chaos to a political situation'". (See D.L. Wheeler, 'A República Pesadelo (1910-1926)', Diário de Notícias, 13 July 1982).

9. The private sector was authorized after 1933 to organize 'national syndicates', but even here unions were to obey the rules of corporatist organization. According to author Howard Wiarda, these included complete government control over trade unionism and collective bargaining procedures. This meant all funds for unions originated in the state, that union elections were controlled, union leaders were appointed, wages were set by the government, etc. See H. Wiarda (1977), Corporatism and Development: the Portuguese Experience, Amherst: University of Massachusetts, pp. 260-269.

10. Principles set out by the União Nacional, the only legal political party, in 1934.

11. See M.F. Mónica (1978), Educação e Sociedade no Portugal de Salazar, Lisbon: Presença, p.180.

12. By 1940 the regentes escolares represented 18 per cent of the entire primary school teaching force. They earned less than school caretakers.

13. Mónica, op.cit., p.186.

14. Luisa Cortesão (1982), Escola, Sociedade, Que Relação?, Oporto: Edições Afrontamento, pp. 85-86.

15. Mónica, op.cit.
16. Very little physical or legal action was taken by the Salazarist regime against teachers acting as leaders of trade union organizations after the overthrow of the Republic. Nor was there any large-scale replacement of teachers in schools.
17. Mónica suggests this in op.cit.
18. Ibid. By "former of opinions", Mónica is obviously referring to the Republican notion of the teacher as a 'missionary of modernity'.
19. Not that women fared any better under the Republicans, according to Mónica (ibid.) – here they were considered inappropriate for their "temperament and physical constitution did not allow them to propagate new ideas, combat vice and prejudice and stimulate local life". (Ibid., pp.209-10). Mónica does not challenge the evidence for the "naturally conservative nature of women" during this period; her argument is based mainly on documented male attitudes of the period.
20. In addition, the regime was <u>forced</u> to compete with an increasingly vocal, although mostly clandestine or semi-clandestine, opposition.
21. Although the argument is too complex to be dealt with here, it has been suggested that the increase in school population between 1960 and 1970 was largely due to changes in the Portuguese class structure.
22. The changes in Portuguese corporatism, the effects of the African wars and the relation of education to the state during the fifties and sixties are treated in a variety of Poretuguese works. Some of them are brought together in S.R. Stoer, 1983, op.cit.
23. A. Reis Monteiro (w/d), <u>Educaçāo, Acto Político</u>, Lisbon: Livros Horizonte, p.167.
24. From the document of the First Congress of Trade union for Teachers of Greater Lisbon (<u>SPGL</u>), 'A Escola e os Professores na Sociedade Portuguesa: Resoluçāo', March 1981.
25. The chief mobilizing slogan for the Veiga Simāo Reform was 'The Battle in Education'.
26. The Study Groups had a well-organized and extensive network – two factors which upset the regime considerably.
27. Quoted in A. Reis Monteiro, op.cit., p.175 (emphasis in the original).

28. R. Gràcio, op.cit., pp.49-50.
29. See Monteiro, op.cit., p.211.
30. The 11th March marks the date of the second 'mini-coup' that took place during the revolutionary period. On this date, right-wing forces led by former President Antònio de Spìnola were easily defeated after a coup attempt, Spìnola being forced to flee the country. The event enabled Vasco Conçalves, Prime Minister at the time, to take radical measures such as the nationalization of the banks and insurance companies.
31. See, for example, Stephen R. Stoer, 1983, op.cit., especially Appendix IV, which documents this process and also other intense activity at school level during the first three months of the revolutionary period.
32. M.E. Brederode Santos (1981), 'Inovação Educacional', in M. Silva and M.I. Tamen (eds.), Sistema de Ensino em Portugal, Lisbon: Fundação Calouste Gulbenkian, p.395.
33. Manuel Leite (1980), 'Em Defesa da Gestão Democràtica', A Escola, p.5.
34. According to Cadernos: Educação 'Os Sindicatos de Professores: uma conquista de Abril, Document of the Portuguese Communist Party, 1977.
35. Rui Gràcio, op.cit., pp.53-54; p.60.
36. Wini Breines (1980), 'Community and Organization: The New Left and Michels' "Iron Law"', Social Problems, Vol. 27, no. 4, Abril.
37. 'Eventually', for during the first year of the revolution there was considerable support, particularly among sectors of the Socialist Party, for modified versions of 'alfabetização' and/or 'poder popular'.
38. 'Against the Capitalist School' '(1978), A Polìtica na Escola, Lisbon: O Armazem das Letras, pp. 56-58.
39. Cadernos: Educação..., op.cit.
40. Alvaro Cunhal (1976), A Revolução Portuguesa: o Passado e o Futuro, Lisbon: Edições Avante. For the state of trade union activity during the Salazarist regime and particularly during its last decade, see Màrio Pinto and Carlos Moura (1972), 'Estruturas Sindicais Portuguesas: Contributo para o seu Estudo', Anàlise Social, vol. 9, no. 33, pp.140-190; also Howard Wiarda, op.cit.

41. Serafim Ferreira (ed.) (1975), MFA, Motor da Revolução Portuguesa, Lisbon: Diabril, pp.305-308.
42. Ibid.
43. A. Cunhal, op.cit., p.66.
44. Tom Gallagher (1983), Portugal: a twentieth-century interpretation, Manchester: Manchester University Press, pp.208-209.
45. Mário Soares was at the time, and still is, leader of the Socialist Party. See Gallagher, Ibid., p.209.
46. See Appendix I to this article for all clauses of the 1976 Constitution dealing with trade unions.
47. Vasco Gonçalves (1977), Discursos, Conferências de Imprensa, Entrevistas, Lisbon: Seara Nova, p.41.
48. Carlos Rosa Fernandes (1978), 'Portugal and the Economic Community: some reflections on the Free Trade Agreements', Principal Assistant, Secretariat for European Integration, in the EFTA Bulletin. Jaime Gama, M.P. for the Socialist Party declared in Parliament: "the construction of Europe is the aim of the democratic forces of this country, and only those currents which, through manifest obscurantism, do not believe in the democratic and European future of our country, oppose it." See J. Cândido de Azevedo (1978), Adesão de Portugal a C.E.E., Lisbon: Editorial Império, pp.282-3.
49. 'Normalization' is discussed in greater depth in S.R. Stoer, 1983, op.cit.
50. See S.R. Stoer, ibid., especially Chapter 3.
51. H. Araujo develops this argument in op.cit. The crux of the argument is that state employees "may use specific elements of professionalism (as an ideology) with aims other than the legitimation of a given social structure".
52. 'Against the Capitalist School', op.cit., p.58. Both the slogans cited in the quotation originated in the MFA and were taken up by 'alfabetização' currents (which largely explains 'poder popular' opposition to them).
53. In spite of claims of 20,000 members in the Lisbon area and in southern Portugal, absolutely no evidence or precise statistics were presented by SINDEP in the course of research for this paper, in spite of repeated

requests. SINDEP now forms part of what is called the 'Federation of Portuguese Teachers Unions' (FNSP), which includes other trade unions for teachers of a similar tendency (for example, the SPZN - 'Teachers Union of the Northern Zone'). It is, in fact, very difficult to get information or statistics on teacher trade union activity outside the Lisbon area, which accounts for the Lisbon bias of this article. The following statistics were presented by SPGL (with regard to the alternative 'federation' FENPROF) (see also Appendix II for a further breakdown of statistics with regard to the SPGL).

FENPROF:

SPA - Azores - founded 1978 - no. of teachers area: 2500 - no. of teachers paid up: 1400; SPE - Europe - founded 1980 - no. of teachers area: 700 - no. of teachers paid up: 350; SPM - Madeira - founded 1975 - no. of teachers area: 2350 - no. paid up: 1245; SPRC - Coimbra/Centre - founded 1974-1982 ('reorganized') - no. of teachers area: 15000 - no. of teachers paid up: 2980. (The northern zone was recently 'reorganized' and no numbers are presented).

54. The SPGL called its members out on strike during the months of February and March 1978, and April and May 1980. In both cases the majority of members responded to the strike call and governmental policy was affected. Less successful was the union's participation in the 'General Strike', called by CGPT-Intersindical, in February 1982.

55. See SPGL document . . . Resolução, op.cit.

56. Ibid., p.3. Interesting to note is that in all SPGL documents there is persistent reference to the split 'workers' (i.e. teachers and others) - 'patronato' (i.e. bosses, and more specifically, Ministry of Education).

57. Ibid., p.17.

58. The SPGL claimed in 1978 that the Education Ministry actually tried to put at risk (in addition to all other 'anti-democratic' actions carried out) teachers' right to strike (through Dispatch 9/78 of 31 January). The strike referred to above, in February and March 1978 (see note 54), the first strike by teachers for more than half a century, was

the teachers' - SPGL's - reply.
59. SPGL document . . . Resolução, op.cit., p.6.
60. See O Jornal do Primeiro Congresso do SINDEP, April 1982, 'Declaration of Principles', p.2.
61. SINDEP is referring here to the refusal of the SPGL, the CGPT-IN, and the Portuguese Communist Party to recognize, or take seriously, first 'Carta Aberta', then the UGT and SINDEP itself.
62. Constitution of the Portuguese Republic, 1976 Article 58, see Appendix I to this article.
63. According to spokesmen for both unions, governments in Portugal have still not recognized, that is 'regularized', the adoption of the collective bargaining statutes of the International Labour Organization. See Article 58, Constitution in Appendix I.
64. For an analysis of this tension see Roger Dale (1982) 'Education and the Capitalist State: Contributions and Contradictions', in M. Apple (ed.) Culture and Economic Reproduction in Education, London: Routledge and Kegan Paul.

BIBLIOGRAPHY (additional)

Benavente, Ana and Correia, M. Adelaide Pinto (1981), Obstáculos ao Sucesso na Escola Primária, Lisboa, 1980, Instituto de Estudos para o Desenvolvimento, Lisbon.
Grácio, Rui (1973) Os Professores e a Reforma do Ensino, Lisbon: Livros Horizonte.
Lawn, Martin and Ozga, Jenny (1981), 'The Educational Worker? A Reassessment of Teachers', in L. Barton and S. Walker (eds.), Schools, Teachers and Teaching, The Falmer Press.
Martins, Hermínio (1971), 'Portugal - 2', in M. Archer and S. Giner (eds.), Contemporary Europe, Class, Status and Power, London: Weidenfeld and Nicolson.
Pinto, Cabral (1977) Escolas do Magistério, Reforma e Contra-Reforma, Cadernos O Professor 6.
Sampaio, J. Salvado (1977), O Ensino Primário 1911-1969, Contribuição Monográfica, Vols. I, II, III, I.G.C. (C.I.P.), Lisbon: Fundação Calouste Gulbenkian.
Stoer, Stephen R. (1982), Educação, Estado e Desenvolvimento em Portugal, Lisbon: Livros Horizonte.

APPENDIX A

The Constitution of the Portuguese Republic

1976

Preamble:
"On 25 April 1974 the Armed Forces Movement, setting the seal on the Portuguese people's long resistance and interpreting its deep-seated feelings, overthrew the Fascist Regime.
The liberation of Portugal from dictatorship, oppression and colonialism represented a revolutionary change and an historic new beginning in Portuguese society.
The Revolution restored fundamental rights and freedoms to the people of Portugal . . ."

Article 1:
"Portugal is a sovereign Republic based on the dignity of the human person and the will of the people and committed to its own transformation into a classless society."

Article 2:
"The Portuguese Republic is a democratic state based on the sovereignty of the people, on respect for and the safeguarding of fundamental rights and freedoms and on plurality of democratic expression and democratic political organization, whose object is to ensure the transition to socialism by creating the conditions for democratic exercise of power by the working classes."

Article 9:
"The basic tasks of the state shall be:
a) To safeguard national independence and create the political, economic, social and cultural conditions to it;
b) To secure organized participation by the people in solving of national problems, to defend political democracy and to ensure respect for democratic legality;
c) To socialise the means of production and wealth, in forms appropriate to the characteristics of the present period of history, to create conditions permitting the promotion of the people's welfare and quality of life, especially those of the working classes, and to abolish exploitation and oppression of man by man."

Article 57:

1. Workers shall be free to form trade unions, a condition and safeguard for the building of their unity in defence of their rights and interests.

2. In the exercise of trade union freedom the following freedoms shall be safeguarded for workers without discrimination:

   a) freedom to set up trade union associations at all levels;

   b) freedom of membership, no worker being required to pay dues to a trade union of which he is not a member;

   c) freedom in the organization and internal regulations of trade union organization;

   d) the right to engage in trade union activity within the enterprise.

3. Trade union associations shall be governed by the principles of democratic organization and management, based on regular elections to their governing bodies by secret ballot. They shall not be subject to any authorization or recognition, their foundation being active participation by the workers in all aspects of trade union activity.

4. Trade union associations shall be independent of employers, the state, religious denominations. Adequate safeguards for such independence shall be laid down by law as the foundation of the unity of the working classes.

5. In order to ensure unity and dialogue among the various currents of opinion which may exist in the trade unions, workers shall enjoy secure exercise of the right to different tendencies in the unions, in cases and forms laid down in their statutes.

6. Trade union associations shall have the right to establish relations with or to join international trade union organizations."

Article 58:

"1. The trade union associations shall be competent to defend, and promote the defence of, the rights and interests of the workers they represent.

2. Trade union associations shall have the right to participate in:

   a) the preparation of labour legislation;

   b) the management of social security institutions and other bodies whose aim is to satisfy the interests of the working classes;

c) the supervision of implementation of economic and social plans.

3. Trade union associations shall be competent to exercise the right of concluding collective agreements.

4. The rules governing competence to conclude collective labour agreements and the scope of their provisions shall be laid down by law."

Article 59:

"1. The right to strike shall be safeguarded.

2. Workers shall be entitled to decide what interests are to be protected by means of strikes. The sphere of such interests shall not be restricted by law."

Article 60:

"'Lock-outs' shall be prohibited."

APPENDIX B

SPGL: 'Sindicate dos Professores da Grande Lisboa'

A. Total number of members (initially – 1975) = 35,960
B. Total number of members (up to September 1983) = 35,106

(A. and B. include all persons having taken out membership with the union. Many of them (40 to 50%) have not paid regularly their union dues. See note 53 above.)

Breakdown according to sector of schooling:

			%
1.	Primary	7475	21.3
2.	Preparatory	7929	22.6
3.	Secondary	11652	33.2
4.	Higher	1934	5.5
5.	Others	688	2.0
6.	Private	4194	11.8
7.	Unknown	1234	3.5

Notes:
'Others' = teachers in long-distance learning, etc.
'Unknown' = teachers who have changed their professional situation and who have not made their new position known to the SPGL.
'Primary' = includes nursery school teachers.
'Private' = also includes nursery school teachers, plus teachers of the primary, preparatory and secondary sectors.

Chapter Three

TEACHER UNIONS AND EDUCATIONAL POLICY IN FRANCE

Roger Duclaud-Williams

INTRODUCTION

It seems convenient to divide this paper into
three parts. In the first I shall provide a
necessary minimum of factual information about the
most important teacher unions, the political
positions which they defend, and the relationships
among them and between the unions and the
political parties. It will also be possible in
this first part of the paper to present some
information about the size and density of union
membership.

The object of the second section of the paper
will be to defend the proposition that teachers
and their unions play a more important part in
national politics in France than is typically the
case elsewhere. Evidence in support of this
proposition can be found in the opinions of those
directly involved in educational politics but it
is particularly interesting to examine in addition
the influence which teachers' unions have had on
reform proposals in education both before and
after May 1981, the date at which the Left
captured the all important office of president,
subsequently also succeeding in winning a
comfortable majority in the National Assembly.

Finally, I shall seek to answer the question
of how it is that teachers and their unions have,
in France, come to occupy a position of such
peculiar political importance. The explanation of
the high profile adopted by teachers' unions, in
educational questions and in relation to political
questions not related to education, requires at
least a brief excursion into the historical
origins of the educational system and will also
lay considerable emphasis on a particular aspect

of the historical legacy - educational
centralisation.

UNIONS, PARTIES AND TENDENCIES

The logical starting point for any
description of the teachers' unions in France must
be the FEN (Fédération de l'Education Nationale).[1]
At its most recent congress in February 1982 the
FEN declared 493,000 members and 47 constituent
unions.[2] The FEN then is exactly what its name
would suggest - the federation of all the most
important teacher unions. The logic which
underlies the decision of constituent unions to
join such a federation is simple and compelling,
particularly in its application to the smaller
unions. Such small unions gain administrative
support and can profit from the access to those in
positions of power which the FEN possesses but
which they would never be able to obtain acting
alone. For the larger unions the calculation of
advantage is less obvious and we shall return to
this question later when considering some of these
unions.

The exact delimitation of responsibilities
between the FEN and constituent unions is not
always an easy matter and at least one observer
believes that the FEN has tended in recent years
to assume greater responsibilities at the expense
of member unions.[3] In the crucial sphere of
salary negotiations however, the assignment of
tasks is not too complicated. All those employed
by the Ministry of Education, whether teachers or
not, are civil servants. The FEN therefore
represents the world of education in the general
civil service pay negotiations from which all
categories of teacher benefit once an agreed
annual percentage has been fixed. This means that
member unions are simply left, as far as salaries
are concerned, with claims designed to alter the
position of their members on the grid which fixes
the differentials for the whole of the civil
service. This leaves the dominant role in salary
negotiations for the FEN but from time to time the
government reluctantly agrees to modify the grid
system at the request of a member union, and this
has happened very recently when the position of
the primary school teacher was slightly improved
after long and arduous negotiations between their
union, the SNI-PEGC and the government.[4]

Before mentioning the principal member

unions, it is necessary to say something about factional divisions within the FEN and this in turn requires a brief discussion of the emergence of the FEN in the late 1940s. Communist and non-communist elements were able to co-operate reasonably effectively within the trade union movement in France in the period from 1944 to 1947 when the Communist Party was represented within the governing coalition. However, with the expulsion of the Communist Party from government in the spring of 1947, and growing tension between East and West, this unity within the trade union movement came to an end.

The teachers' unions were in a difficult situation faced with the awkward choice between a communist-controlled trade union confederation and a confederation controlled by anti-communists close to the Socialist Party. The largest member union of the FEN organised a referendum of its members at this time which showed majorities against joining the communist-controlled CGT (Confédération Générale du Travail), by 62% as against 38%, and an even larger majority opposed to joining FO (Fédération Ouvrière) 75% to 25%.[5] If the views of the primary school teachers expressed in this referendum were typical of those of other categories of teacher represented in the FEN, the only course open to the Federation in these circumstances and the one which was adopted, was that of remaining outside the two major trade union confederations.

Although this avoided splits within and between teachers' unions which would have substantially weakened the teachers when confronting their single employer, the Ministry of Education, it had certain disadvantages. In the first place it meant the break with the pre-war tradition which had united the major teacher unions with the most representative unions within the working class movement. Secondly, it meant that currents of opinion, soon organised in tendencies which were broadly sympathetic to the communist and socialist parties, now had to be contained within the FEN. This, briefly, is how the FEN came to possess the developed and occasionally cantankerous internal political life which it exhibits today.

The interesting thing, for a student of politics, is that organised factional life exists not only within the FEN itself, but within the most important of the constituent unions as well.

At the 1982 Congress of the FEN, support for the two major factions was distributed as follows: Unité, Indépendance et Démocratie (UID) 61%, Unité et Action (UA) 34%. The five per cent of remaining votes were shared between three revolutionary anti-communist far-left tendencies.[6] UID, the tendency close to the Socialist Party, has controlled the FEN since its foundation. Whilst UID has always been in a controlling position within the FEN and within most of the member unions, opposition organised by UA, most of whose members are sympathetic to the communist party, has generally tended to grow in strength in the post-war period. The most notable step along this upward path was reached in 1966 when UA won majority control of the secondary school teachers' unions, SNES (Syndicat National des Enseignants du Second Degré). At the SNES Congress in March 1983, the controlling UA tendency received the vote of 63% of the delegates.[7]

Most unions within the FEN are extremely small and do not possess the developed factional internal political rivalry that the larger unions can boast. Most of these smaller unions are sympathetic to UID. UA controls the secondary school teachers' union SNES, the union of university teachers, the PE teachers' union and the union of teachers in colleges of education. Factional rivalry within the FEN has sometimes prevented the Federation from adopting a clear line on matters where there is strong division between UID and UA, but UID control has never been seriously threatened and therefore the FEN has been able to grow and to act powerfully in the defence of its members without being too seriously handicapped by internal divisions. But before going any further we must say something about what UID and UA stand for in educational and political terms.

In most recent years the major difference between these two tendencies has been one of style and tone and tactics rather than one of objective. UA's militancy often means a greater readiness to support occupations, demonstrations and other more or less spectacular activities designed to draw the plight of the educational service to the attention of a wider public. UID, even when its political opponents, the Right, were in power, as between 1958 and 1981, was more inclined to see virtue in negotiation and discussion. There have been numerous occasions when UA and the unions which it controls have called national one day or half day strikes and these have been denounced by UID as provocative and damaging to the interests of teachers. On a broader political plane the relations between the two tendencies tend to fluctuate very much as the relations between communist and socialist parties have oscillated between conflict and co-operation. What we see here then is the importing of non-educational conflicts into the world of education but it should not be forgotten that the arguments between UA and UID can never reproduce exactly the arguments taking place outside the educational world between Communists and Socialists. This is because both tendencies, whatever their disagreements, are committed to continued support for the FEN and a dialogue and democratic competition between these two tendencies within a single federation continues, however bad relations become outside the educational world between communist and socialist parties. This is something of which the FEN is justly proud. Nor should it be forgotten that, whatever general political differences may exist, there are agreements on more specifically educational matters, notably the defence and expansion of the education budget, greater security of employment for temporary teachers, the inclusion of all educational activities within the responsibility of the minister of Education, and the integration of the private Catholic schools into a state system. Shared hostility towards the governments of the right in power before 1981 and a shared sympathy for President Mitterand and his government since then have also helped to promote co-operation between these two rival tendencies. But if there is much which unites both tendencies in defence of agreed educational policies, there are certain specifically educational differences between UID and UA which derive from the close relationship between the UID tendency and the primary school teachers, and the equally close relationship between UA and the secondary school teachers. The character of these arguments can best be understood by describing the educational platforms defended respectively by the primary school teachers' union, SNI-PEGC and the secondary school teachers' union, SNES.

The SNI-PEGC (Syndicat National des Instituteurs et des Professeurs de l'Enseignement Général des Collèges) recruits the bulk of its members from teachers in the nursery and primary schools. If membership was confined entirely to this sector, then differences of view between the SNI-PEGC and the SNES would not have arisen. No such clear delimitation of territory has however been possible since 1963 when, in the first step towards the unification of secondary education, the Minister created the lower secondary school or CES (Collège d'Enseignement Secondaire) which gathered under one roof forms of secondary and higher primary education which had previously been provided in distinct establishments.[8] As a matter of course those primary school teachers who had previously been working in the extension classes of primary schools began working in the lower secondary school and today the SNI-PEGC and SNES can claim roughly equivalent membership and support within the lower secondary school. Hence, both unions have a right to official consultation when policy is framed for the lower secondary school and their conflicting views acquire a particular importance.

The SNI-PEGC's view about the organisation of 10 years of compulsory schooling which stretch from 6-16 are embodied in its proposal for what is called the basic school or 'Ecole Fondamentale'. The philosophy underlying the proposal for the basic school is that there are certain fundamental educational requirements which are relevant to all children between the ages of 6 and 16 regardless of their social origins or academic potential. The SNI-PEGC does not see any fundamental difference between the form which education should take for the 6-11 year olds and the form it should take in what has traditionally been described as the lower secondary sector. In particular they do not see the need for specialist subject teachers in the lower secondary school and feel that the emphasis on subject specialisation in traditional secondary education is inappropriate now that all 11-15 year olds attend the same school and are to be offered the same educational opportunities.

The basic school is also specifically designed to deal with a problem which the SNI-PEGC regards as critical, namely the present difficulties encountered by some children in moving from the primary to the secondary school. The union feels that as long as a different ethos and philosophy prevail in primary and secondary education, co-operation between these two institutions will be difficult and there will be a lack of necessary continuity. The concept of the basic school is also designed to insist on the fact that, although some degree of academic specialisation, not streaming, may be desirable for children behond the ages of 13, no children should be permitted at this stage to leave the basic school for vocationally oriented education or training in a technical school. A further crucial element in the basic school proposal is that the relationship which ought ideally to exist between teacher and pupil throughout this school ought to be a personal one rather than a relationship purely instrumental to the communication of knowledge. Thus the SNI-PEGC insists that the forms of training which are appropriate for those teachers intending to concentrate on the 11-15 year old age range must not place too much emphasis on mere academic achievement in one or two special subjects. In the union's view, the priority here, as in the training of primary school teachers, should be on the development of pedagogic skills, and any sharp separation of theory and practice is to be avoided.

The SNES, on behalf of secondary school teachers, sees considerable dangers in the basic school proposals as outlined by its rival, the SNI-PEGC. They feel that the traditional distinction between the ethos and purposes of primary and secondary education needs to be maintained and that the basic school proposals contain the danger of what is sometimes called, rather unattractively, primarisation. In order to understand the position of the SNES on this matter it is necessary to bear in mind that, although the two unions are in one sense rivals, they are not rivals in the recruitment of members within the lower secondary school. This school is at present staffed by two categories of teachers, the PEGCs (Professeurs de l'Enseignement Général des Collèges), who are recruited by the SNI-PEGC, and the certificated teachers (Certifiés) who are recruited by the SNES. The certificated teachers recruited by the SNES possess a university qualification in the subject in which they are specialists. Many, although not all, of the PEGCs who are recruited by the SNI-PEGC do not possess a university qualification and are regarded as specialists in two subjects, although their initial training may have been in a college of education without particular subject specialisation. One can readily understand why the SNES sees primarisation as representing a refusal to recognise the specialised expertise of their certificated members. They feel that if some form of compromise is worked out concerning the training which is to be received by teachers employed in future in the lower secondary school, this will involve a loss of a quality of education in the secondary sector which was once only offered to a privileged minority but which ought now to be generally available. Another aspect of the objections raised by the SNES to the SNI-PEGC proposals is that it would be loath to lose the advantages which it possesses at present of having a foot in both the lower secondary school and the lycée (the lycée now takes all those pupils who decide at the age of about 15 to continue to pursue their academic studies rather than either leaving school or enrolling in a vocational course in some technical establishment).

In comparing the principles of trade union and political action to which the SNI-PEGC and SNES are committed it is important to avoid the misplaced application of models drawn from English or American experience. Whilst it is true that the SNI-PEGC and the FEN and other unions controlled by or sympathetic to the UID tendency are great believers in the virtues of negotiation and dialogue, and place a high priority on the protection of the material interests of their members, their approach is not to be assimilated to that of moderate unions in Britain and America. These French unions have never believed that they could or should avoid involvement in the political life of the nation. These unions and the FEN itself claim, and are granted, a right to be officially consulted on a full range of decisions taken in relation to education whether they affect the terms and conditions of service of teachers or not. But more than this, they frequently issue statements of common purpose signed with political parties of the Left on a wide range of matters of general concern and, for example, editorials in the SNI-PEGC's weekly 'Ecole Libératrice' make general comments about political developments which have nothing to do with education. Both the SNI and the SNES played a prominent part alongside the socialist and communist parties in campaigning and demonstrating against those aspects of Giscard d'Estaing policies of which the Left disapproved.

But there are still real disagreements

between the SNI and the SNES, or if one prefers, between the UID tendency and the UA tendency, about the appropriate degree of involvement in politics for a trade union. Before the Left's victory at the polls in 1981, the SNES frequently argued that those with UID sympathies exaggerated the advantages to be won through negotiation. At times SNES spokesmen could be heard arguing that no significant improvement in the operation of the educational system could be expected whilst a reactionary government remained in power, or in a more radical formulation, whilst a capitalist system continued to operate.[9] It was often stressed that such minor improvements as could be extracted from those in office could only be won by a show of political force and to this end the SNES and UA were more frequently to be found organising demonstrations and meetings and acting in collaboration with parties and unions quite outside the educational system. A typical illustration of the sort of differences referred to here was seen in the campaign leading up to the legislative elections of 1973 when the SNES endorsed officially the common programme of government agreed between socialist and communist parties whilst the SNI and the FEN declined to offer specific advice to their members, although they were publicly on record as hoping for a Left victory.

The next union about which it is necessary to say a few words is the SGEN-CFDT. It draws members from all parts of the educational system, from primary to higher education, and is mainly distinguished from other unions on the Left by its enthusiasm for decentralisation and its tendency to attach more importance to qualitative than quantitative changes.

We have now identified the major trade unions and may proceed to examine the basic data on membership levels. Table 1 summarises the information which has been presented already for greater convenience. Several general points are worth underlining. Despite small inroads by the SGEN, the SNI has the enormous advantage over other unions of enjoying mass support upon which it can count, with little fear of membership drifting away. Berger writes of the primary school teacher of the early 60s: "The good primary school teacher feels it his duty to join a union"[10]. The SNI also enjoys an advantage in terms of sheer numbers since it has more than three times as many members as its nearest rival. The political significance of this numerical strength is increased by the fact that, as long as the UID tendency continues to control the SNI, then it will also control the FEN and in this way preserve its predominant position within the educational world from all challenge from the communist and non-communist Left. It is also particularly worth noting that, even when teachers are offered a full range of political possibilities, their political sentiments in France are anchored firmly to the Left of Centre, although not on the extreme Left.

A 1977 poll of teachers in public and private schools showed the overall level of union membership to be 72% with this figure rising to 79% for teachers in the public sector.[11] Such high density is unusual by comparative standards and even more striking in France where it is generally estimated that the density of union membership in the working population as a whole is hardly above 20%. Since high membership levels are an important element in the successful exercise of political influence by teacher unions, which we shall be examining later, it is worth pausing to ask here how the unions have been so successful in this respect. The first point to be noted by way of explanation is as simple as it is important. We are dealing here with the public, not the private sector, and, until very recently in France, the major obstacle to the development of high levels of union membership in the private sector has been marked managerial hostility to union activity of any sort. In the public sector, generally, these difficulties have long ceased to exist.[12]

A second factor helping to explain this exceptionally high union membership is the ability of unions to supervise the process of appointments. The 'Comités Administratifs Paritaires', advisory commissions composed of equal numbers of union delegates and officials, use a variety of points schemes to make recommendations on appointments. But these recommendations are rarely challenged. A survey of secondary schoolteachers in the early 1970s showed clearly that many teachers feared the consequences of arbitrary administrative decisions and considered the administration to be inaccessible.[13]

Low union membership in much of the private

sector in France seems to result from destructive competition between politically rival unions. The relative political homogeneity of teachers in the public sector (see Table 2) greatly reduces the possible negative impact of such competition. Even when teacher unions go beyond the defence of shared economic interests to raise more contentious political issues, these can be unifying as the example of 'laïcité' so forcefully demonstrates.

Nor should it be forgotten that competition between teachers' unions often takes a more organised and less destructive form than competition between unions within the private sector in France. All unions which are members of the FEN sign non-aggression pacts and recruit only within the territory allocated to them. Thus, although both the SNI-PEGC and the SNES have members in the lower secondary school, the SNI confines its recruitment to the PEGCs and the SNES recruits certificated teachers. This means that genuine competition for members only occurs when there is a challenge by a union not in the FEN as is the case with the SGEN and the SNALC. But, as we have already made clear, the FEN unions occupy dominant positions in all educational sectors and therefore the damaging effects of inter-union competition are substantially reduced. It seems safe to conclude therefore, that whilst competition between unions and even more the involvement of unions in political controversy are sometimes objected to by significant minorities of teachers, the unity of teachers on other political matters, the limits on competition, and the strong desire of teachers to defend themselves against the administration and its supposed arbitrary tendencies, more than offset these difficulties and help to explain the exceptionally high levels of union membership within the teaching profession in France.

THE POLITICAL POWER OF THE UNIONS

The aim in this section of the paper is to demonstrate the importance of the teachers' unions as influences on the development of the educational system. We shall see, in our examination of the Legrand proposals for the lower secondary school and their reception, that the unions have had an important influence on the direction and pace of educational change.

The Lower Secondary School and the Legrand Report

The question of the unification of the separate forms of educational provision for pupils in the first four years of secondary education has been on the political agenda since at least 1936 when the Popular Front Government chose the Radical Jean Zay as Minister of Education. Many accounts of the numerous unsuccessful attempts at reform in the succeeding forty years have stressed the important part played by the unions in complicating the task of would-be reformers.[14] At the cost of some simplification, it is possible to divide the period since 1936 into two. Until 1966, when the Left in the guise of the UA tendency took control of the SNES, one could say that the battle for reform could reasonably be described in terms of Left advocacy and Right opposition. In this first period the primary school teachers and their allies in the Socialist and Radical parties, and the Communists, argued for unification. They were opposed by the parties of the Right and the secondary school teachers.

Since 1966 the position has been much more complicated. The SNI-PEGC on behalf of primary school teachers, and the SNES, on behalf of the secondary school teachers, were from now on in agreement with the principle of unification at the level of rhetoric. Therefore the left-right division seemed to retain its significance, but, when the unions reacted to particular reform proposals, conflicting views often emerged within the Left wing coalition. These disagreements between the SNI-PEGC and the SNES were often related to the Government's intentions regarding what kind of teacher should be employed in the lower secondary school. If primary school teachers were to be allowed to win promotion to the lower secondary school, then the chances were that the SNI-PEGC would be sympathetic to the reform and the SNES would oppose it. The problem for Ministers throughout this period arose because of the impossibility of dissociating changes in the structure of the school system from policies affecting the future of clearly identifiable categories of teachers.

When the Left came to power in 1981 streaming had been abolished in the lower secondary school. Paradoxically this step had been strongly opposed by the unions and the parties of the Left. In these circumstances there was no obvious way forward for the new Socialist Minister. Some initiative was expected because his party and its allies had condemned all recent developments. His almost inevitable course of action was to ask for the preparation of a report dealing specifically with the lower secondary school. We cannot concern ourselves with all aspects of the Legrand report.[15] The purpose of the following brief discussion is therefore to underline the fact that the character of the relations between Government and unions remains, even in the changed political circumstances since 1981, crucial to the success or failure of Government policy. We can best make this point by extracting from the Legrand report those recommendations and arguments which have the greatest effect on the conditions of employment of secondary school teachers, and describing the reaction of the teachers' unions to these proposals.

One of the problems to which Legrand devoted particular attention was the failure of the French school to become an educational community. His diagnosis, and that of many others, pointed to the tendency of teachers to restrict their commitment to the school to the purely academic realm as one of the major causes of this difficulty. The obligations of the French teacher to the educational service are expressed primarily in terms of teaching hours. When a teacher has no timetabled periods he is under no obligation to remain in the school. In addition, many teachers successfully persuade their Heads to group their teaching periods so as to give them a free half day or whole day off during the school week.

Legrand suggests in his report that teachers would be encouraged to view their responsibilities in a new light if their obligations were no longer defined in terms of hours of teaching but instead in terms of hours of presence in the school. He suggests that teachers working in the lower secondary school, regardless of the category into which they fall, and the form of training which they have received, should be obliged to spend 22 hours in the school per week. Of these hours 16 should be devoted to teaching, three hours to counselling and contact with those pupils for whom the teacher has a personal responsibility, and three hours to meetings with other members of staff, parents and the like. If adopted, the Legrand proposals would alter the amount of teaching which people were required to carry out, the form of their obligations to the educational service, and in addition would standardise teachers' obligations according to the type of school in which they taught, rather than allowing them to vary according to the level of the teacher's qualifications as is the case at present.

The SNI-PEGC and the SGEN have welcomed the Legrand report and hope to see it implemented.[16] But predictably, what is acceptable to one body of teachers, in this case the PEGCs and their representatives, seems unacceptable to the SNES speaking on behalf of the better qualified secondary school certificated teachers. At present SNI-PEGC members must provide the state with 21 hours of teaching per week whereas SNES members are only under an obligation to provide 18 hours. The calculation is not a difficult one. If implemented, Legrand would mean, for existing PEGC teachers, a substantial improvement in their terms of employment because in exchange for only one additional hour of obligatory presence in the school they would be exempted from five hours of traditional teaching - these five hours to be spent in future in counselling pupils and in discussions with staff and parents. This looks like a good deal.

The position for SNES members teaching in the same lower secondary school is much less favourable. If employed on the terms suggested by Legrand they would be obliged to spend four hours more per week in school and in return their teaching load would fall by only two hours from 18 to 16 hours.

The initial reaction in January 1983 of the SNES leadership to the Legrand proposals was mixed. Whilst the union was sympathetic to many of the fundamental principles to which the report was attached, it sought negotiation on certain matters. This attitude of guarded acceptance seems to have stiffened as a result of pressure from the rank and file, some of it coming from within the UA tendency. At a special two day conference called late in January to discuss the Legrand proposals, attended by all the most important teacher and parent organizations concerned, rank and file doubts were strongly expressed.[17] When speakers at the rostrum mentioned Legrand, boos and whistles were often to be heard. The same kind of rank and file doubts about Legrand and other aspects of Government policy were expressed at the National Congress of the SNES which was held in March of the same year.[18] The leadership's motion on the Legrand proposals still received the approval of 63% of delegates but there was some pressure to organize a 24 hour strike in protest at Government policy.

It should not be imagined that the increase in required hours of presence in school from 18 to 22 per week was the only cause of SNES doubts about the Legrand proposals. Some teachers were evidently worried by the proposal that the practice of requiring pupils to repeat a year should be confined in future to the final year of the lower secondary school only. The same kind of doubts existed about the proposal that separate provision for those with learning difficulties be progressively reduced. Finally, there was out and out opposition from the SNES officially to the proposal that teachers accept responsibility for guiding and counselling a small group of pupils who would be attached to them individually. The union's official spokesman argued, in terms which echo the traditionalism sometimes clearly visible in this union, that to accept such responsibilities would be to usurp the proper role of parents.

SNES doubts were not without political repercussions. The Minister made clear his views on the report early in February.[19] He accepted most of the report's proposals including the key proposition which suggests dividing each class into different ability levels for maths, French, and modern languages, whilst retaining the mixed ability class for all other subjects, that is 62.5% of the suggested curriculum. But on the questions which were clearly most crucial to teachers and their unions, the Minister reserved judgement. Whilst accepting the report's proposals that harmonisation of teachers' obligations within the lower secondary school was a desirable objective, the Minister rejected the particular formula of 22 hours presence in school and 16 hours of class teaching advocated in the report. On the question of teachers' obligations to their employer, the State, the Minister felt that more negotiation was required before a final decision could be taken. He was clearly hostile to what he conceived to have been the practice of many of his predecessors in imposing reforms which were unacceptable to the teaching profession. Describing the manner in which he wished his reforms to be implemented, he spoke of "an approach which will be progressive and decentralised and each stage of which will be explained and discussed with all those concerned, above all representative organisations".[20]

Our examination of the Legrand proposals and their reception enables us to compare the situation in 1983 with that which existed during the 1970s, and in this way to come to some conclusions about the role of the teachers' unions now that a Left-wing Government has come to power. It would seem that, so far at least, as a result of the co-operative attitude of the Communist Party to the Mitterand-led Government, the purely partisan element in relations between the unions and relations between unions and government has ceased to be important. This has meant that discussions which before May 1981 were often strident and emotional are now always friendly, even if the unions still adopt a firm tone from time to time. But a dramatic change in the tone and style of union/government relations has not brought a change in substance of the same importance. Although both the Minister and Legrand are convinced that a harmonisation and an extension of teachers' obligations into a new realm are an important part of the reform, there is no guarantee at present that the Government will be able to produce any significant change in this area. The educational traditionalism of the SNES and the disagreements between the SNES and the SNI, even if they are now more educational than political, remain a significant obstacle in the Minister's path. But we must not forget that, though the process of harmonisation and the broadening of teacher responsibilities have been, until now, blocked by SNES hostility, none of the unions have opposed those crucial aspects of the report which concern the character of the curriculum and the organisation of teaching in the lower secondary school. We must therefore conclude that a reforming Minister in a Left-wing coalition has no easy task but that the difficulties which he must overcome are certainly less formidable than those encountered by his Right of Centre predecessors. We may now move on to ask how it is that the teachers' unions have acquired the exceptional degree of influence which they undoubtedly possess.

EXPLAINING TEACHER POWER

The first characteristic of the educational system to which it is necessary to give our attention in explaining the extent of the influence of teachers' unions is its highly centralised character. It is important to be clear at the outset about what is meant by centralisation in this context. When we say that the French educational system is highly centralised, we are not necessarily asserting that the Minister and his immediate entourage possess a high concentration of power which they may use as they see fit. If the system was centralised in this sense it would have little room for the exercise of significant influence by those not at the summit of the bureaucratic structure. The aspect of centralisation to which we wish to draw attention here is in some ways formal rather than real. The system is formally centralised in the sense that change can only be brought about by a process whose culmination is new legislation, or more often, the issuing of a new decree under the Minister's signature. To put the same point in a negative sense, centralisation in this formal sense means that particular localities and educational institutions are deprived of the capacity to innovate with respect to their own practice.

Whilst it is perfectly legitimate to characterise one educational system as more or less centralised than another, for our purposes it is important to pinpoint the areas of decision-making in which the interests of teachers are most directly affected. In the definition of the curriculum, the qualifications and terms of employment of teachers, and the definition of the educational structure in the sense of the rules governing the flow of pupils within and between institutions, are handled centrally. How then does centralisation in this sense amplify the impact of the teachers' unions on educational policy?

It seems to me that centralisation increases union power in a number of very different ways. We must first take account of the fact that, however well endowed a union may be in money and manpower, it is infinitely poorer than its adversary, the Minister and his bureaucracy. In this position of relative poverty, it is particularly important for a union to concentrate its resources at one level and on one point of access. If, for example, the French system were to operate in a manner more closely resembling the English, with discretion in some matters being left to the individual headmaster, it would be much more difficult for the union to protect its members.

The SNI-PEGC and the SNES are aware of the danger represented by any increase in the power of headmasters. This is particularly so because within the French system there is a considerable contrast between the minor role of Heads in primary schools and the much more developed administrative role of Heads in secondary establishments. Much of the close collaboration between local bureaucracy and the SNI-PEGC depends upon the administration's need for channels of contact with the teacher in the classroom. This union has successfully prevented the development of the head in the primary school as an alternative line of communication between bureaucracy and teachers, and in this way made itself indispensable to both teachers and bureaucracy. For a variety of reasons the unions which are active in the secondary sector have not been so successful in this task.[21] The point I am making here is simply that observation of the way in which their own system works makes quite clear to the French unions the dangers which they may run into in any more decentralised system of administration and policy-making.

But centralisation assists the unions in other ways. One of the difficulties faced by unions in other liberal democracies wishing to challenge decisions to which they are opposed is that of dealing with the argument that the union is introducing politics into education. In systems which are more decentralised than the French, it is quite often possible to legitimate local decisions, or the decisions of headmasters, principally in educational terms. Any union wishing to challenge such decisions faces the obvious difficulty that, in the popular mind, the union is identified as a political and partisan actor in a way in which the headmaster, or perhaps the local chief education officer, is not. Centralisation in France means that the French teacher unions do not run into this particular difficulty. The Minister and his appointees in the regions and departments are frequently involved in the defence of politically controversial educational decisions. No one on the Right or the Left can pretend that managing the educational system is anything other than one of the most important governmental responsibilities. Thus the teachers' unions do not have to bear the responsibility for bringing politics into education. French educational policy-making has always been highly politicised and it is difficult to find anyone in France who imagines that it could or should be otherwise.

Finally, centralisation is important because of the way in which it facilitates the development of neo-corporatist relations between the bureaucracy and the teaching unions. Much of the general literature on European corporatism stresses the existence of a high degree of centralisation as a necessary condition for the development of corporatist relations between interest groups and the State.[22] In the closing decades of the 19th century it was still possible for French Ministers of Education to legitimate their decisions simply by pointing to the fact that they were members of a Government which enjoyed the support of a majority in the National Assembly. Twentieth century European Governments have not felt it politically wise or technically desirable to limit the forms of interaction between Government and people in this way to the electoral process. The political and technical need to develop alternative forms of consultation and additional sources of information is all the greater when the level of centralisation is high. The Minister's need to be seen to be consulting, and winning consent, might, of course, have benefitted other interests than those of the teachers, but the principal rivals to the teachers, parents, have been slow to organise and, until recently, the largest representative organisation of parents in France was very closely linked to the SNI-PEGC.[23] Evidence that Ministers have felt the need to be seen to be consulting the organised interests exists in the extensive system of formal representative advisory bodies at national, regional and departmental levels.

No account of the factors which assist or handicap the teachers' unions in the exercise of influence would be complete without some discussion of the impact of the economic crisis. Tapper and Salter have recently argued, with respect to England and Wales, that, during the period of the Great Debate and again in the period since 1979, the teachers' unions have been unable to mount effective resistance to the policies of tighter central control and cuts in educational spending.[24] In their view, the teachers' unions have not yet found the kind of language or the kinds of arguments which could provide an effective answer to policies which are legitimated in terms of increased efficiency. They argue that it has been possible for those in positions of authority to take advantage of the atmosphere of austerity created by economic difficulties to break out of the cosy triangular relationship which once existed between the Department, the local authorities and the teachers. Ministers and their officials in England have succeeded in drawing into the educational debate the representatives of interests who were previously excluded. This applies particularly to parents and employers. In this way the Department has obtained greater freedom of manoeuvre and substantially reduced union influence.

Developments in France have not followed a parallel course. French economic difficulties since 1973 have been real enough but the coming to power of a new Government in 1981, committed to a policy of expansion, has meant that public discussion has taken place in a climate of greater confidence and less panic than has often been the case in the UK recently. The educational budget for 1982 was substantially higher than that of the previous year, and, although early optimism has subsequently been tempered, educational policy has not yet come to be dominated by purely economic considerations in the way so familiar to observers of the English scene. Arguments about preparation for the world of work are still largely confined to vocational and pre-vocational education.

It may be useful to give two brief examples of the way in which recent decisions about the curriculum in France have tended in quite the opposite direction to that apparent in England. One of the proposals of the Legrand report which the Minister has accepted is that the traditional core of the curriculum, maths, French, and the first modern language, should be accorded less teaching time in future and, for example, only take up three-eighths of the weekly timetable. This squeezing of the traditional core of the curriculum is occurring in order to allow previously rather underprivileged subjects such as art, sport and manual work, a more important place.

The second example which points in the same direction concerns the place of maths in the lycée. Much criticism of the lycée curriculum and its relation to the baccaleauréat in recent years has concentrated on the over-emphasis on mathematical ability. The importance of mathematics in the 'C' stream of the baccalauréat has given candidates with a 'C' baccalauréat an advantage over other candidates and this has had the effect of encouraging many students to enter the 'C' stream and spend many hours on mathematics although they have no intention of pursuing later a career or further studies in which this mathematical knowledge would be relevant. Steps have already been taken since 1981 to reduce to some degree the amount of weight given to mathematical ability in the 'C' stream and to prevent the choice of baccalauréat stream depending as exclusively as it has in the past upon a pupil's mathematical ability.

It would appear that, to date, the impact of the economic crisis on decision-making within the educational system has been less in France than in England, that educational decisions are still taken and justified primarily in educational terms, and that the French unions are therefore not handicapped in the same way as their English counterparts.

In this discussion of the way in which normally relatively unimportant political actors – teachers' unions – have come in France to assume a prominent role on the Left and within the educational system, it is necessary to pay some attention to certain characteristics of French political culture which have tightened the links between the teaching unions and their members. A number of students of French society and politics have pointed to the French fear of being subject to arbitrary authority. Crozier in particular has pointed to the way in which those subject to the decisions of superior authorities have, in France, often succeeded in surrounding the exercise of discretion with rules.[25] The object of these rules is to confine discretion as narrowly as possible and hence give subordinates the maximum of security and certainty with respect to decisions that affect them. Crozier's general model of France as a bureaucratic society was almost certainly developed at least in part as a result of the observation of the behaviour of teaching and other unions in the public sector. Whether the model is capable of application by extension to the whole of French society need not detain us here, but it is certainly relevant when describing relations between the educational bureaucracy and individual teachers.

The French teacher of the early decades of the twentieth century clearly resented his dependence on the administration and saw in his trade union the instrument with which to confine administrative discretion. Now that the rules have been elaborated the union still has the crucial task of overseeing, jointly with the administration, their detailed application to individual cases. With the passage of time those in positions of authority have become almost as convinced as their subordinates that it is desirable to control the exercise of discretion in this way. This acceptance legitimates much union activity and contact between bureaucracy and unions. It gives the unions regular access to administrators at all levels and provides for them a foundation on which influence over a wider range of educational decisions can be built.

It remains in this section of the chapter to elucidate a paradox to which reference has not so far been made. There is general agreement that, among the liberal democracies of the West, France is one of the least corporatist. Yet it would not be an exaggeration to suggest that the French educational system exhibits some highly corporatist features. Since the term corporatism has been used in so many different ways, it may be wise to specify to which features of the system I wish to attach this label. The most crucial of these is a de facto, although not widely advertised, acceptance on the part of policy-makers that decisions over a wide range of matters can only be taken jointly by the Ministry and the teachers' unions. Secondly, and arising necessarily out of the first characteristic, the system shows a strong tendency to reject as inadmissible, demands coming from actors outside the close relationship between bureaucracy and teachers' unions. Thirdly, this closeness of relation between the bureaucracy and a particular organised interest gives educational policy at least a degree of immunity from the consequences of changes in party control.

Such a neo-corporatist relationship between a particular Ministry and its clientèle is not unknown in other policy arenas in France. The existence of something similar has been observed, for example, in the sphere of agricultural policy, but it remains true that such a close relationship is more the exception than the rule. In explaining the lack of development in a corporatist direction many observers of French politics have pointed to the obstacles represented by a highly ideological style of political debate. Typical here are the divisions within the organised working-class movement between Communist-controlled unions, Socialist unions, and unions of a more traditional character. Such very real division within the organised and unorganised working-class makes any degree of corporatist development, in this sphere at least, extremely unlikely.[26] We must ask then how it has been possible for the teachers' unions, working in a country whose electorate is deeply divided, to produce a degree of cohesion in organisation which permits the exercise of considerable influence.

The first element in any explanation must be the organisation along extremely democratic lines of the internal factional life of each of the major unions. Dissidents within the unions are not obliged to leave to found a rival union or accept the undignified position of a permanent minority. Union practice encourages and permits them to organise as a tendency and to compete with other tendencies in union elections. In addition, a minority tendency within any union may well succeed in capturing the departmental union federation even while failing to win a majority at the national level, hence the rewards of office and a limited degree of local influence are open to representatives of minority tendencies. Exactly the same principles of organised democratic factional competition operate within the FEN.

But it is also true that the political opinions of French teachers are substantially skewed towards the Left end of the political spectrum and that this makes unity easier to maintain. Tables 2 and 3 contrast the voting intentions of teachers in the public and private schools with those of the French population in general as polled in December 1977. As the tables quite clearly show, the Leftward skew is very pronounced although it works to the advantage of the Socialist party and not the Communists. The figures presented here refer to teachers in public and private schools and the total of 70% intending to vote for Left or extreme-Left candidates on the first ballot would rise to 79% if the private schools were excluded. Even more striking as evidence of the extent of the skew are the results shown in reply to the question asking how teachers would vote on the second round if there was a contest between a Socialist and a Right-wing candidate. The split here for teachers in the public sector is 91% to 9% in favour of the Left. When asked whether they agree with, or are opposed to, public financial assistance for the private school, teachers in the public sector reply in the negative by a margin of 73% to 16%. The importance of these figures for our purposes is that they make clear how it is possible for the teachers' unions to retain large memberships and at the same time involve themselves in partisan political activity which, in other sections of the economy, would almost certainly cost them large numbers of members. The kind of diversity of political opinion, which normally prevents unions from combining political activity with a large membership, does not exist within the state educational system and it is this, in combination with a number of other factors discussed here, which permits the development of well supported unions which can take a stand on a wide range of educational and political issues.

CONCLUSION

This chapter has sought to provide an overview of the teachers' unions in France and some assessment of their impact on the evolution of educational policy. In the final section of the chapter, I have pointed to the centralisation of the educational system, the political reactions in France to the onset of the economic crisis in 1973, and the political opinions of individual teachers, in order to explain how it is that the teachers' unions have been able to exercise such a degree of influence. On a more speculative note, I shall conclude by asking whether it is possible to detect any tendencies at work which may, in the long run, produce a change in the relationships which I have described.

The most likely immediate threat to existing arrangements lies in the commitment of the newly elected Socialist Government to decentralisation. The logic of the argument which has already been developed suggests that, if the educational system were substantially decentralised, the strong defensive position of the unions might be undermined, at least to some extent. Such a course of events seems highly unlikely. Educational decentralisation has only occurred in areas of decision making of relatively little interest to the unions.[27] The exact location of schools, and their size and design, are often of interest to local politicians in France, but the teaching unions are more concerned with how well endowed these schools are in posts and in what goes on inside them. Very little change in these areas seems likely, and if there is any, it will probably simply take the form of what the French call deconcentration, that is a shift of responsibility from one administrative level to a lower level without any implication that locally elected politicians should be allowed to assume responsibilities previously exercised by officials. Limited further deconcentration represents less of a danger to the unions than decentralisation in favour of the local authorities.

One salutary lesson from the recent past also suggests that change only comes slowly and is difficult to predict. Writers in the 1960s were struck by the rapidity with which the profession of primary school teachers was becoming a female preserve. Dire warnings were issued about the lower level of involvement of women in political and union questions and the consequences their arrival in larger numbers would have for the degree of support which the unions would enjoy in the future.[28] It remains the case that women teachers are less interested in politics, are somewhat more likely to practise their religion, and have political opinions less skewed towards the Left end of the spectrum, but the increase in their numbers has not so far had any perceptible impact on the unions' activities. Until very recently the SNI-PEGC was involved in promoting practices designed to set higher entrance requirements for young girls wishing to become primary school teachers so as to slow down the rate of feminisation of the profession.[29]

Perhaps the present Minister, Alain Savary, from his position as manager rather than observer of the system, has come to conclusions very similar to those defended in this chapter. Change will come but slowly and only with the consent or acquiescence of those most directly concerned.

Table 1:   Teachers' Unions in France
          Summary of Main Characteristics

Unions	Characteristics			
	Membership Claimed	Political Character	Affiliation	Area of Rec/ment
FEN	493,000 (Feb 82)	UID Control	None	All levels of education
SNI-PEGC	260,000 (1983)	UID Control	FEN	Nursery, primary & lower secondary
SNES	71,000 (1983)	UA Control	FEN	Lycèe & lower secondary
SGEN	60,000* (1983)	Left	Confèd. Française Dèmocratique du Travail (CFDT)	All levels of education
SNC	37,000 (1982)	Moderate (unpolitical)	None	Lower secondary
SNALC	15,000 (1984)	Right	None	Lycèe & lower secondary

*Some non-teachers

Source: Figures supplied by Unions.

Table 2:   First Round Voting Intentions as Percen-
           tages of Votes Cast (no response: 25%)

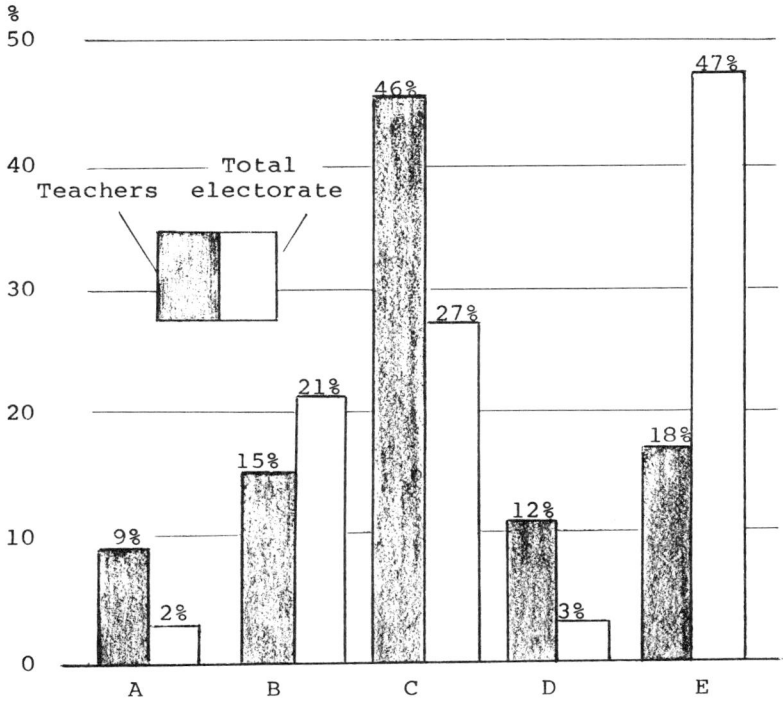

Code: A: Extreme Left United Socialist Party
      B: Communist Party
      C: Socialist Party
      D: Ecologists
      E: The Majority (Parties of the Right)

Table 3:   Second Round Voting Intentions as
            Percentages of Votes Cast

	All Teachers	State Education	Private Education
Communist versus Right-Wing Majority Contest			
Communist Party:	61	74	11
R-W Majority:	39	26	89
Socialist versus Right-Wing Majority Contest			
Socialist Party:	81	91	37
R-W Majority:	19	9	63

Source: Le Monde de l'Education, Feb 1978, p.11.

NOTES

1. One study of the FEN exists in English
    although it is now rather outdated:
    J.M. Clark (1967), Teachers and Politics in
    France: A Pressure Group Study of the FEN,
    Syracuse University Press.
2. Le Monde, 2.2.1982.
3. See concluding chapter in R. Cheramy (1974),
    La Fédération de l'Education Nationale,
    Editions de l'Epi.
4. Le Monde, 11.3.1982.
5. R. Cheramy (1974), Chapter 1.
6. Le Monde, 5.2.1982.
7. Le Monde, 29.3.1983.
8. A particularly clear account of this reform
    and other developments in the 1960s can be
    found in J. Fournier (1971), Politique de
    l'Education, Editions du Seuil.
9. L'Humanité, 13.2.1976.
10. I. Berger and R. Benjamin (1964), L'Univers
    des Instituteurs, Editions de Minuit, p.16.
    This study has subsequently been updated as
    I. Berger (1979), Les Instituteurs - D'une

Génération à l'autre, Presses Universitaires de France.

11. Le Monde de l'Education, February 1978.

12. A. Prost (1968), L'Enseignement en France - 1800-1967, Armand Colin, Chapter 15.

13. Les Enseignants du Second Degré - Etude Psychosociologique (1973), La Documentation Française, Collection Travaux et Recherches, No. 26, Chapter 2.

14. F.G. Dreyfus, 'Un Groupe de Pression en Action - Les Syndicats Universitaires devant le Projet Billères de Réforme de l'Enseignement', Revue Française de Science Politique, Vol. XV, No. 2.
J.M. Donegani and M. Sadoun, 'La Réforme de l'Enseignement Secondaire en France depuis 1945', Revue Française de Science Politique, Vol. 26, No. 6.
R. Duclaud-Williams, 'Centralization and Incremental Change in France: The Case of the Haby Educational Reform', British Journal of Political Science, Vol. 13, pp. 71-91.
R. Haby (1981), Combat pour les Jeunes Français, Julliard.

15. A detailed summary can be found in Le Monde, 7.2.1983.

16. Le Monde, 8.1.1983.

17. Le Monde, 23.1.1983.

18. Le Monde, 29.3.1983

19. Le Monde, 2nd and 3rd February 1983.

20. Le Monde, 2.2.1983.

21. R. Duclaud-Williams, 'Local Politics in a Centralized System: The Case of French Education', European Journal of Political Research, forthcoming.

22. G.Lehmbruch and P. Schmitter, Trends Toward Corporatist Intermediation, Sage, 1979.
G. Lehmbruch and P. Schmitter, (eds.), Patterns of Corporatist Policy-Making, Sage, 1982.

23. This organisation is the Fédération des Conseils de Parents d'Elèves de l'Enseignement Public (FCPEEP).

24. B. Salter and T. Tapper, Education, Politics and the State: The Theory and Practice of Educational Change, Grant McIntyre, 1981.

25. M. Crozier, The Bureaucratic Phenomenon, Tavistock Publications, 1964.
M. Crozier, The Stalled Society, The Viking Press, 1973.
W. Schonfeld, Obedience and Revolt: French

        Behaviour Towards Authority, Sage, 1976.
26. V. Lorwin, The French Labor Movement, Harvard
     U.P., 1954.
27. Law of 22.7.1983.
28. I. Berger and R. Benjamin (1964).
29. Le Monde, 30.8.1978.

Chapter Four

POLITICAL TEACHER UNIONISM IN JAPAN

Haruo Ota

Every facet of Japanese society was changed after she lost World War II. Education was no exception. Under the slogan of 'democratise education', the educational system was reformed. One of the most notable phenomena in the drastic change in post-war education was the emergence and development of large scale teacher unionisation.

Prior to the war, a teacher was assigned the role of "an obedient servant of the state, subject to the closest scrutiny of his personal life and placed at the lowest rung [of] the civil service hierarchy" (Levine, 1969: 148-149). Although there were some efforts to unionise the teaching force, those efforts were sporadic and isolated and, therefore, never successful in attracting the majority of teachers.

Shortly after the war, the dream of pre-war teacher union activists came true; the Nihon Kyoshukuin Kumiai (Japan Teachers' Union), better known as Nikkyoso, was formed, which organised almost all of the nation's elementary and secondary school teachers at that time. Since then, Nikkyoso has been a major educational and political force affecting not only the welfare of its members but also the governance and control of Japanese education.

There has been persistant antagonistic rivalry between Nikkyoso and the Ministry of Education, which holds the responsibility of implementing the policies of the conservative ruling government. The Ministry of Education has consistently insisted on strong governmental control over education. On the other hand, Nikkyoso, supporting the opposition Socialist party, contends that education should not be controlled by the government, but by the people.

This rivalry, which has exacerbated conflicts and confrontations between the two forces over virtually every facet of education, is a manifestation of the state of post-war Japanese education. It is for this reason that a study of Nikkyoso[1] is "the key to an understanding of developments within post-war Japanese education" (Duke, 1973: xiii).

MODELS OF TEACHER ORGANISATIONS

Teachers form different kinds of organisations with varied motivations, interests, and goals. Here we shall briefly examine three models of teacher organisations which may serve to give us a theoretical framework for an analysis of Nikkyoso.[2]

Professional Associations

Teachers can organise themselves based on their professional concerns. The identification of professional attributes has long been one of the most controversial issues of academic interest, especially among sociologists. There are many ways of defining 'profession'; however, it appears that the following six attributes are commonly accepted by experts as the cadre of the professional value system:

1. Expertise, normally stemming from prolonged specialised training in a body of abstract knowledge.
2. Autonomy, a perceived right to make choices which concern both means and ends.
3. Commitment to the work and the profession.
4. Identification with the profession and fellow professionals.
5. Ethics, a felt obligation to render service without concern for self-interest and without becoming emotionally involved with the client.
6. Collegial maintenance of standards, a perceived commitment to help police the conduct of fellow professionals (Kerr, et al., 1977: 332).

Professional associations are basically designed to enforce and maintain these characteristics. Particularly, they are concerned with maintaining the high quality of services to the public and the high standards of professional practice of their members in order to preserve public esteem and professional autonomy (Lieberman, 1956: 258).

Teaching is usually not classified as a full

profession but as a semi- or quasi-profession.[3]
Because of this, professionally oriented teacher
organisations tend to attempt to develop the
'professionalism' of teachers. For such
organisations, teachers' professional knowledge
and skills are of primary importance. Improvement
of teachers' professional activity and maintenance
of better service to students and to the public at
large are their central concern in order to
promote the quality of education and, in turn, to
establish teaching as a 'profession'.

Some observers point out the narrow interests
and apolitical nature of professional
associations. As Kevin Harris puts it:

> "[professional associations] are usually
> narrow in scope and are relatively
> apolitical. Their main concerns appear to be
> promoting the 'professionalism' of teachers,
> looking after narrow sectional interests, and
> publishing journals mainly with classroom
> issues . . . "
>
> (Harris, 1982: 150).

Moreover, professional associations usually
do not recognise any group conflict within the
profession. Unity is emphasised among all those
engaged in the profession. They argue that
teachers, for instance, have the same interests as
administrators in terms of achieving educational
goals and that there should not be conflicts
between them.

Economic Unions

In contrast to professional associations,
which have the purpose of promoting and
maintaining the professional quality and conduct
of its members, there is another type of teacher
organisation primarily devoted to promoting the
welfare of its members. The main and probably
most clearly recognisable purpose of such an
organisation is to "provide (primarily economic)
benefits for members" (Tannenbaum, 1965: 710).
This economically oriented organisation may best
be labelled 'economic union'.

The economic union seeks its ends through
collective bargaining with the management. The
theory and practice of bargaining are based on the
assumption of inherent conflicts of interest
between employees and employers and on the
assumption that there is a strong community of
interest within the employee group regarding
certain items and areas of judgement (Wildman and
Perry, 1966: 245). The conflicts are limited,

however, because the economic union depends on a given corporation's existence - it cannot survive and achieve its goals without the survival and goal attainment of the corporate body. The union may therefore share common goals with the corporate body in some areas of mutual concern (Tannenbaum, 1965: 710; Kochan, 1980: 19).

While on the one hand, the economic union's strength stems from collective bargaining; on the other hand, the bargaining power is effective only within the existing system. We can see the strength and limits of the economic union most clearly in the American labour movement:

"[The American labour movement] has always seen itself as an integral part of the economy and social system, seeking to make its gains for workers within the system rather than trying to control the means of production . . . Its main incentive has been to raise wage rates and welfare benefits, improving the conditions of work and winning for the employee a great sense of economic security, dignity, and social status"

(Owen, 1976: 36).

The economic union is more or less conservative in the sense that it does not bargain for control over the enterprise; rather, it bargains for union recognition, wages, fringe benefits, acceptable working conditions, and participation in decision-making, at most.

Political Unions

The third variety of organisation for teachers may be called the 'political union'. As has been mentioned, economic unions exist primarily to benefit their members economically. On the other hand, political unions manifest an interest in the overall welfare of the workers. In this sense, as Robert F. Hoxie points out, political unions are 'class-conscious' rather than 'trade-conscious' (1966: 48). While economic unions recognise only limited conflict between employees and employers, political unions see the conflict as divisive; they disapprove of the prevailing system and especially of the employers' control of the means of production and the wage system.

The activities of political unions are usually based on socialism, and especially on Marxist theory, which provides counter paradigms to economically oriented unionism. According to Marxism, the interests of workers cannot be

advanced until the basic structures of the prevailing system, in which only the narrow interests of the ruling class are served, are changed (Harris, 1982: 143). Marxist assumptions concerning trade unions can be described this way:
"First, workers should not be required to live with the consequences of the market economy. Second, a conflict of interest based on class difference [exists] in a capitalistic society. Third, negotiations with employers [can] only provide short-term and temporary benefits to workers . . . Fourth, trade unions [are] viewed as a means for achieving short-term economic improvements within the existing system, but more importantly, as vehicles for the overthrow of that system"
(Kochan, 1980: 4).

There is no doubt that political unions of teachers tend to be radical or even revolutionary. Their primary concern is with "the ideology of the school" (Harris, 1982: 150). From the political union's view, schooling under government control does not build a new social order, but only reinforces the existing social order for the ruling class. It is, therefore, not surprising that political teachers' unions get deeply involved in politics and in the struggle against the government for the power to control schooling. Thus, school governance or control becomes the most critical theme for the political teachers' union.

PROFESSIONALISM IN NIKKYOSO

Nikkyoso is certainly not a professional association. This is not, however, to say that Nikkyoso has been unconcerned with the 'professionalism' of teachers or the quality of education. Indeed, from the beginning, Nikkyoso has been interested in professional aspects of teaching and Japanese education. Nikkyoso's platform, adopted as basic policy at its inaugural meeting, clearly states that its objectives are to establish democratic education and freedom of research as well as to raise the economic, social, and political status of its members and to contribute to the construction of a democratic nation devoted to peace and freedom (Nikkyoso, 1977: 41).

To encourage democratic education and freedom

of research, Nikkyoso has conducted various activities, among them the National Education Research Conference (Kyoiku Kenkyu Zenkoku Shukai), generally known as Kyoken. As one observer put it: "This is an attempt by Nikkyoso as a professional organisation of educators to organise educational research systematically in order to develop democratic education" (Yuasa, 1982: 70). The first conference was held in November 1951 with the theme of education for peace under the slogan, 'Never send our students to the battlefield again'. Over 3,000 teachers attended the three-day conference and discussed in eleven sectional meetings topics such as efficiency of the newly introduced 6-3 school system, the decline in student achievement, special education, kindergarten programmes, the conetents of textbooks, and the development of peace education.

Today, Kyoken has become established as a permanent and important part of Nikkyoso, attended by nearly twenty thousand teachers with over twenty sectional meetings. The conference is open not only to teachers but also to parents and the general public. Scholars sympathetic to Nikkyoso make significant contributions to the conference. They give lectures and serve at sectional meetings as advisors. The tradition of inviting a group of scholars who share Nikkyoso's ideals lends "a certain degree of academic respectability to Nikkyoso's entire movement" (Duke, 1973: 108).

There is no doubt that Kyoken has provided the opportunity for classroom teachers to examine and study the problems they encounter in their day-to-day activities and, consequently, to promote quality in teaching. However, it is important to note here that the goal of Kyoken is not to promote teachers' research activities merely for the sake of research, but, as the basic policy of Kyoken states,

> "to understand educational problems as they correlate with political, economic, and social problems, to democratically promote educational research activities in connection with the advancement of the lifelihood and rights of teachers, and to establish an educational environment devoted to the freedom of the worker"
>
> (Nikkyoso, 1977: 52).

ECONOMIC UNIONISM IN NIKKYOSO

Under the current legal system in Japan, public employees, including teachers, do not enjoy the basic rights of workers to bargain collectively and to strike. This lack of fundamental rights for public employees has been a controversial issue in trade unionism in general and in teacher unionism in particular in post-war Japan.

During the early post-war years, the legal status of teachers was much different from what it is today. The policy toward labour unionisation that was established during the American Occupation was very liberal for that period; the Occupation authorities encouraged the labour movement in order to advance their major goals of demilitarisation and democratisation of the Japanese society. The newly adopted constitution guaranteed "the right of workers to organise and to bargain and act collectively" (Article 28). Moreover, the new Trade Union Law granted even the right to strike to employees in both the private and the public sectors. It was during this liberal period that teachers established Nikkyoso to take advantage of the Occupation authorities' liberal attitude toward labour unions and of the new constitution and law.

This liberal period, however, was very short lived. With its perception of both the international and internal communist threat and the relationship of Japan's union leadership to communism, the Occupation authorities drastically altered their policy, moving from a pro-labour to an anti-labour position (Cummings, 1980; Duke, 1973).

After General MacArthur's intervention in a general strike, a series of legislative acts, intended to restrict public employees' right to bargain collectively and to strike, were drawn up by the Japanese government. Among these acts was the Local Public Service Law (LPSL: Chiho Komuin Ho) of 1950, which is one of the most important acts for teachers because it defines their legal status.

Under the provisions of this law, teachers have been classified as local public servants, and their basic rights as workers, guaranteed by the constitution, have been restricted. Under the law, teachers can form organisations "whose purpose is to promote improvement of working conditions" (Article 52). Such organisations, however, may be formed only at the prefectural and/or local level where the teachers are employed (Article 53).

Teachers can still negotiate with the local government; however, there are some restrictions. First, the scope of negotiations is very narrow; only wages, hours, and other working conditions are negotiable. Other concerns, especially managerial issues, are non-negotiable. Second, the term 'negotiations' as used in the LPSL is different from the term 'collective bargaining' used in labour relations in the private sector:

> "'negotiation' does not include the 'right of collective agreement' . . . but only the right to conclude a 'written agreement' . . . The Japanese government has stated that a 'written agreement' is not the same thing as a 'collective agreement' between labour and management of private industry . . . This implies that a 'written agreement' is less binding than a 'collective agreement'"
> (Thurston, 1973: 181-182).

Thirdly, teacher organisations cannot strike in the event that an impasse is reached in negotiations. Without the right of striking, which is the most effective bargain lever available to any employee organisation, a public employee union is a relatively weak 'negotiator'.

The implication of the Local Public Service Law (LPSL) for Nikkyoso is of great significance. Nikkyoso is not a national union but a federation of prefectural "personnel organisations" (Shokuin Dantai) of teachers. More precisely speaking, Nikkyoso is merely a voluntary organisation which is not recognised by any law. As has previously been mentioned, teacher unions are public employee organisations that must be organised within the prefectures in order to be allowed to negotiate with the government. Thus Nikkyoso, legally speaking, is not eligible to negotiate with the national government since teachers are hired by the prefectural government. Only prefectural and local teacher organisations can negotiate with the government:

> "Beyond [the prefectural] level it is not unlawful for teachers' organisations to form nationwide confederations, but such nationwide teachers' confederations are de facto bodies only and are nowhere guaranteed by the LPSL or any other law the right to

negotiate with national public bodies"
(Thurston, 1973:181).

The chief problem Nikkyoso has been facing as an economic union is as to how, without the critical right to bargain collectively and to strike, it can improve the economic condition of its members. We can identify three major approaches Nikkyoso has employed to cope with the problem. The first and most novel approach has been to appeal to international organisations, including the International Labour Organisation (ILO), in an effort to win broad-based support. Nikkyoso began a strong campaign to "restore the fundamental rights of workers" on the stage of the ILO in 1960 immediately after an Education Minister's refusal to hold consultative meetings with them.[4] Nikkyoso submitted a list of complaints to the ILO charging that: (1) the Japanese government defies trade union rights by denying public employees the right to strike; (2) the Japanese government interferes with Nikkyoso's organisation and administration by discriminating against full-time union officials and union members; and (3) the Ministry of Education refuses to meet Nikkyoso representatives. Nikkyoso also requested that the ILO recommend that the Japanese government recognise Nikkyoso as a representative bargaining organisation for teachers (Nikkyoso, 1977: 219).

In its testimony before a fact-finding commission appointed by the ILO, Nikkyoso explained why the union could not negotiate with the government at either the national or the local level. At the national level, Nikkyoso contended, the Ministry of Education had refused negotiations with the union on the ground that, under the LPSL, no national union could be recognised as a bargaining unit for teachers because they were local public servants appointed by local or prefectural school boards. Nikkyoso further charged that at the local level the school boards refused to negotiate with the local teacher unions, claiming that budgets, salaries, working conditions, class sizes, and so forth were decided by the Ministry of Education and that they had nothing to do with those matters. Thus Nikkyoso concluded that "there was no one with whom the union could negotiate" (Duke, 1973: 169).

Following hearings and direct investigations in Japan, the Commission published its report. While it did not advocate that the teachers be granted the right to strike, it did conclude that "the maintenance of the absolute prohibition to strike [is] unrealistic". The report also recommended that the government "decide as a matter of policy whether it prefers central or local negotiations in respect to the employment of teachers" (Duke, 1973: 171).

In the meantime, the government ratified a controversial resolution, Convention 87 of the ILO[5], and adopted several amendments to domestic labour laws[6]. However, the government did not alter its basic position on public employee unions even after hearing the recommendations of the Commission. The Ministry of Education resumed consultative meetings with Nikkyoso in 1965 but Nikkyoso still did not have the right to enter into negotiations. Even after the Commission's report, Nikkyoso has continually complained about the unfair labour regulations of the Japanese government to international organisations such as ILO, UNESCO, WCOTP[7], and IFFTU[8]. Although Nikkyoso has been successful in obtaining international support for the restoration of the fundamental rights of workers in Japan, it has not been successful enough to get the Japanese government to recognise it as a labour union.

Nikkyoso's second approach to developing economic unionism has been through a wage struggle within the prevailing system. While on the one hand, the LPSL deprived teachers of the right to bargain collectively and to strike, on the other hand, it established the National Personnel Authority (NPA: jinji-in), whose duty is to make recommendations to the cabinet to bring the wages of public employees in line with wages earned in private industry. The cabinet, the ruling party in the government, then establishes the national wage scale for public employees, taking into account the NPA's recommendations. However, since the recommendations do not have binding power, the cabinet has the prerogative to adjust or even to ignore the recommendations. Once the national salary scale for teachers is set up in this way by the cabinet, it becomes a guideline for teachers' salaries throughout the country (The Special Law for Educational Personnel, Article 25; Duke, 1973: 166). Consequently, the salaries of public school teachers do not vary much among different prefectures.

Under the NPA's system for determining teacher salaries, the major tactics used in

Nikkyoso's wage struggle have been to demand that the NPA submit an acceptable wage adjustment recommendation to the cabinet and to petition the cabinet to totally accept the NPA's recommendations. To this end, Nikkyoso have engaged in relatively peaceful rallies such as sit-ins and demonstrations in the NPA building and around the Diet (Japan's Parliament) to put pressure on the NPA and the cabinet. In 1966, for example, Nikkyoso called mass vacations[9] to demand from the government full implementation of the NPA's recommendations for a 6.9 per cent salary increase in April, the first month of the budgetary year[10]. With the overwhelming approval of the action by the union members, over 130,000 teachers in twenty-three prefectures walked out of their classrooms for either half a day or two hours (Duke, 1973: 182-183). This collective action was not strong enough to persuade the government to implement salary increases retroactively to April, but it was the greatest direct action taken by Nikkyoso in the wage struggle in its history to that point.

Thereafter, Nikkyoso used similar tactics almost every year and, year by year, it made progress toward its goal of obtaining full implementation of the NPA's recommendation within the present system. Finally, in 1971, the government agreed to implement the salary increases of public employees retroactively to April.

Through its successful wage struggle within the NPA system, Nikkyoso has come to realise the necessity of taking a more radical approach for the advancement of economic unionism. At its national convention in 1970, Nikkyoso re-examined the wage struggle within the NPA system and set forth a new approach aimed at replacing the present system of determining wages with direct negotiations with the government, and restoring the basic rights of workers to bargain collectively and to strike. To develop this approach, Nikkyoso emphasised strike action under the slogan "Restore the right to strike by strikes" (Nikkyoso, 1977: 339-340). In April 1974, for example, Nikkyoso went out on a one-day strike along with workers in other parts of the public sector, to press for their demands for restoration of their right to strike as well as for large wage increases. Approximately 330,000 teachers in thirty-four of Japan's forty-seven prefectures participated in the strike, which left 24,000 elementary and secondary schools disrupted and classes for 12 million students suspended. This strike was of great significance for two reasons. First, it was the first one-day strike in Nikkyoso's history. Since the foundation of Nikkyoso, teachers had never failed to show up for work for a full day because of strike action. Second, the strike was undertaken under the slogan, "Restore the right to strike by strikes". And that, Nikkyoso claimed, made teachers convinced of the necessity of the restoration of their right to strike.

However, this strike-oriented approach was not without problems. It was countered by strong attacks and criticism from both within the union and from outside. On the same day of the strike, the police took action, investigating the union's headquarters, the prefectural headquarters, and the leaders' houses in nearly 900 different locations in 12 prefectures for evidence related to so-called "strike for the right to strike". Over 15,000 teachers were summoned by the police for investigation. One day later, the union's chairman Makieda was arrested in Tokyo (Japan Quarterly, 1974: 330). Moreover, the new approach has been subject to criticism by the union's minority group, who support the Communist party. Its contention, to be discussed shortly, is that teachers must realise that people have a high expectation for teachers and that teachers have an obligation to serve all the people as they educate students. The group has urged teachers to reconsider Nikkyoso's strike-oriented approach and to establish a new policy which is not contrary to the people's expectation for teachers (Egawa, 1977: 159).

In spite of government pressure and criticism by the minority group, Nikkyoso has maintained its strike-oriented approach to developing economic unionisation. However, the final goal of its struggle to "restore the fundamental rights of workers" is still far from being realised.

POLITICAL UNIONISM IN NIKKYOSO

It can be said that the history of education in post-war Japan is a history of confrontation between the Conservative government and Nikkyoso struggling for control over education. From its beginning, Nikkyoso has been under the control of people closely associated with Marxist-oriented left-wing political forces such as the Socialist and Communist parties. Under their leadership, Nikkyoso has been concerned not only with the economic affairs of its members and their rights, but also with Japanese education in the political, social, and cultural contexts. We can see Nikkyoso's broad concerns beyond economic unionism in its 'Code of Ethics', adopted in 1952 as "the basic ethical lines which teachers should follow" (Miyahara, 1963: 104).

1. Teachers shall work with the youth of the country in fulfilling the tasks of society.
2. Teachers shall fight for equal opportunity in education.
3. Teachers shall protect peace.
4. Teachers shall act on behalf of scientific truth.
5. Teachers shall allow no infringements on freedom in education.
6. Teachers shall seek after proper government.
7. Teachers shall fight side by side with parents against corruption in society and shall create a new culture.
8. Teachers are labourers.
9. Teachers shall defend their right to maintain a minimum standard of living.
10. Teachers shall unite.

The code also spells out some Marxist-oriented ideology that expresses such revolutionary concepts as the following:

"Upon our shoulders have been laid the historical tasks of protecting peace . . . and realising a society free from exploitation, poverty, and unemployment . . . [Such a society] cannot be attained without a high degree of autonomous growth toward maturity on the part of the labouring class . . . The realisation of a new society of mankind . . . which respects fundamental human rights . . . is possible only through the power of the working masses whose nucleus is the labouring class."

Based on such left-wing ideology, Nikkyoso's major educational goal has been to establish 'democratic education'. According to the union, democratic education is education for the people that aims for peace and truth in the world, based on the spirit of the Fundamental Law of Education[11] (Saito, 1980: 41). A former chairman, Makieda extended the concept of democratic education relying upon the law:

> "It is education that is not controlled by any existing government or by the particular political party that happens to possess the reins of government. Democratic education is education that is controlled by the people and not by the bureaucracy"
>
> (Thurston, 1973: 93-94).

To Nikkyoso, strong governmental control of education means education controlled by the Conservative party and a bureaucracy which is backed by monopolistic, capitalistic organisations. Such education is dangerous because it could lead the nation to war, as the pre-war authoritarian educational system did.

Given such extreme ideology and the objectives of Nikkyoso, it is not surprising that the union has expended its energy mostly on the struggle with the government, especially with the Ministry of Education, for control over education. There have been numerous confrontations and conflicts between the Ministry of Education and Nikkyoso. Here, let us examine some particular confrontations which are of great significance in the development of post-war educational policy in Japan.

As was the case with labour union policy, the American Occupation took a very liberal position on educational policy. The Occupation put a great deal of emphasis upon educational reform to accomplish its major goals of demilitarisation and democratisation of Japanese society. To this end, the Occupation tried to reform Japan's highly centralised educational system, in which the Ministry of Education had monopolistic power over almost every facet of education such as curricula, textbooks, methods of instruction, teaching personnel, and the like. The Occupation thought this traditional mode of school governance was responsible for the indoctrination of the nation's youth before and during the war. Decentralisation of the school system, therefore, was the most fundamental theme of the Occupation's reforms. Complying with the Occupation's policy, the Japanese government attempted to decentralise its system with the establishment of American-style locally elected school boards and curtailment of the power of the Ministry of Education. Behind the Occupation's educational reforms was the idea that it could take control away from the central government and turn it over to the people (U.S.

Education Mission to Japan, 1946). During the Occupation, confrontations between the Ministry of Education and Nikkyoso did not take place. As Makeida put it:

"[During that period] Nikkyoso and the Ministry of Education worked together to promote the cause of education aimed at establishing peace and democracy. Thus there were no conflicts or confrontations between them concerning educational policy. In those days, Nikkyoso was struggling with the problem of establishing various conditions conducive to the cause of education. Another problem it faced was the advancement of the economic, social, and political status of its members. The Ministry of Education rather co-operated with Nikkyoso by promoting its movement"

(Makeida, 1982: 21).

The honeymoon period of Nikkyoso and the Ministry of Education came to an end in the early 1950s, just after Japan regained her independence with the signing of the San Francisco Peace Treaty, when the Japanese government began to revise the post-war educational system developed under the Occupation. The first attempted revision of the reformed educational system was to change the selection process of school board members from election to appointment. The government proposed a new law which would empower the prefectural governor and the local mayor to appoint the members of the board of education with the approval of the prefectural and local assemblies. The law also provided that the Ministry of Education would have the power of approval over the appointments of the prefectural superintendents of schools, and that the Ministry of Education and the prefectural school boards would have the veto power over local board decisions (Ota, 1978: 258).

The Conservative government rationalised the new system on the grounds that it would "insure the political neutrality of education, build a harmonious relationship between educational administration and local government and . . . consolidate educational administration into one body consisting of the national, prefectural, and local educational agencies for more efficient administration of education" (Duke, 1973: 130). Among these reasons, the 'political neutrality of education' was the most controversial issue.

Under the old system, since teachers were allowed to be board members, many Nikkyoso-supported candidates were elected and, in some cases, they dominated the boards. The Conservative government came to realise that this development could pose a threat to their control over education because, under the elective board system, Nikkyoso, supported by the Socialist and Communist parties, could have great influence in local school governance. The government needed a system that would prevent these political factions from gaining power over school governance and that could preserve the "political neutrality of education".

From Nikkyoso's point of view, however, the proposed appointed school board system was not only an attempt to decrease the influence of Nikkyoso in school boards, but also an increase of political interference in education by the Conservative government. An observer sympathetic to Nikkyoso described the implications of the appointed system this way:

> "More than half the members of prefectural assemblies belong to the Liberal Democratic Party, and . . . from eighty-five to ninety-six per cent of the members of city, town and village assemblies are Conservative . . . With this kind of political distribution on the local political scene, it is clear which party will be victorious in political matters. Through the new appointive system . . . the political designs of the ruling Liberal Democratic Party can better penetrate eduational administrative circles at the local level"
>
> (Mochida, 1963: 44).

Nikkyoso organised nationwide rallies against the new system with the claim that school boards would become "just a channel through which the directions and orders of the Education Ministry are transmitted" (Duke, 1973: 131). In Tokyo, it held mass demostrations with 29 other organisations, including the National Association of the Board of Education, the Japanese PTA, and the Federation of Housewives (Nikkyoso, 1977: 93). However, the appointed school board system eventually replaced the elective system in 1956, when the Conservative government succeeded in passing the law which authorised the new system, taking advantage of their majority in the Diet.

Coupled with the debate over the school board

system was the so-called Teacher's Efficiency Rating System (Kinmu Hyotei). While the revision of the school board was a controversy over control in local school governance, the institution of the rating system was a controversy over control in the school. In 1956, the Ehime Prefecture Board of Education decided to implement the rating plan in order to reduce its financial deficit. Under the plan principals would rate the efficiency of teachers without consulting with them, and only those teachers with high ratings would receive annual pay increases. One year later, the Ministry of Education proposed an extension of the system throughout the country. The Ministry of Education urged each prefecture to adopt the rating system for salary increases, promotion, and other administrative matters pertaining to teachers. It also developed an evaluation form which included such rating criteria as classroom management, lesson guidance, disposition of school duties, love of education, sincerity, sense of responsibility, impartiality, knowledge, ability, skills and the like (Duke, 1973: 141-142). The Ministry of Education argued that administrative decisions taken on teachers should be based on their performance and capabilities because the seniority-based system was unjust in that it treated competent and incompetent teachers equally. The Ministry of Education also contended that the rating system would provide a rational basis for personnel administration.

Nikkyoso quickly responded with the issue of a statement of "Warning to the Ministry of Education" in which was expressed its strong determination to fight against the rating system. In the statement, Nikkyoso gave the reasons for its opposition as follows:

"First, [the rating system] would prevent teachers from establishing education for the people which encourages children to develop their independence and academic ability. Second, it is impossible to implement the ratings scientifically and objectively in schools due to the nature of education. Third, the rating system might be misused as a means of conducting unfair promotions, transfers, and discharges."

The 'Warning' further analysed the underlying idea behind the rating system:

"The main purposes of the system are to establish a school system that the Ministry of Education can control as it did in pre-war Japan, to implement the educational policies of the ruling government, to restrict teachers' autonomous behaviours, and to undermine the teachers' union movement" (Nikkyoso, 1977: 113).

Following Nikkyoso's widespread and defiant struggle, which included a series of nationwide mass vacations and demonstrations, the rating system was eventually implemented in all but two prefectures. However, the system did not function as originally intended; the rating results were not employed as the basis for determining salary increases and promotions. For one thing, school boards were reluctant to use the ratings for personnel administration due to the almost certain turmoil which would result from the ratings and the invalidity of the evaluation form (Duke, 1973: 153). For another thing, Nikkyoso was successful in rendering the system meaningless. In one instance, teachers in Kanagawa prefecture undermined the system by getting their principals to give similarly favourable ratings to all of them (Thurston, 1973: 208).

A related and recent issue in personnel administration was the government's attempt to institute the appointment of 'head teachers' (shunin) in the school. The issue arose in 1971 in a final report prepared by the Central Council for Education - an advisory body to the Ministry of Education. The report recommended that there be established a well organised intra-school administrative system so that educational activities could be developed under the leadership and responsibility of the principal. To this end, the report recommended the creation of managerial positions wihtin the faculty (Nikkyoso, 1977: 577). Following the report, the Ministry of Education issued an ordinance which authorised the position of 'head teachers' and provided that "Under the supervision of the principal, the head teachers will engage in liaison and co-ordination work and will also give guidance and advice on the formulation of educational plans and other school affairs" (Nikkyoso, 1977: 616). The Ministry of Education stressed the monetary and educational benefits of 'head teachers' and de-emphasised the managerial characteristics.

Nikkoyoso was opposed to the Ministry's action, claiming that since 'head teachers' were to be appointed by school boards and receive allowances, the position of 'head teachers' would crystallise the hierarchical power structure in schools, and that it would disrupt the unity of teachers and their union membership and strength. Although Nikkyoso was unsuccessful in preventing the institution of the plan, it has been trying to make the position of 'head teacher' less attractive and less managerial by urging appointed head teachers to donate all or part of their allowances to the union so that it could use the money for the purchase of instructional aids and equipment. The exact effect at this writing is not ascertainable, but a recent study indicates that the donation rates have been decreasing and that the position of 'head teachers' has been gradually institutionalised as a managerial position in schools (Shinohara, 1978b).

Still another major issue in the confrontation between Nikkyoso and the Ministry of Education concerns the curriculum and textbooks, that is, the content of education. Nikkyoso has been claiming that the Ministry of Education should not be concerned with the content of education but only with 'external matters' of education, such as the physical facilities of schools. If the government interferes with the content of education, it violates a provision of the Fundamental Law of Education by exercising "improper control" (Thurston, 1973: 96). Accordingly, the formation of school curricula and selection of textbooks, Nikkyoso contends, ought to be entrusted to those who are greatly concerned with the learning and growth of children, most of all, then, to teachers.

Uner the current system, the basic framework for school curricula, including the objectives and standard contents to be taught in each subject, is outlined in the 'Course of Study', prepared by the Ministry of Education. The controversy is as to whether the 'Course of Study' is merely a guideline for the formation of each school's own curriculum or if it is to be the standard curriculum for all of the nation's schools. Under the former interpretation, individual schools and teachers have the right to develop their own curriculum. But under the latter, schools and teachers are required to comply with the standard curriculum. Although Nikkyoso has interpreted the 'Course of Study' as a guideline, the Ministry of Education has increasingly gained greater power over the contents of education, claiming the right to standardise school curricula.

As for textbooks, the Ministry of Education has established a textbook authorisation system under which all the textbooks to be published for official use in the elementary and secondary schools are subject to examination by the Ministry. On some occasions, the Ministry of Education has required authors to revise their drafts in order to secure its approval. In recent years, the Ministry's increasing demands for revision have been highly controversial, especially in such subjects as history and social studies. Under the present system, textbooks are adopted by the local school board with the guidance and advice of the prefectural board of education. Recently, however, the Central Council for Education issued a report which recommended that a more centralised procedure for textbook adoption be implemented (The Textbook Sub-Committee of the Central Council for Education, 1983).

The underlying concepts of the current system for the selection of school curricula and textbooks assume that it would enforce and improve uniform educational standards, guarantee equal opportunity in education, maintain the appropriate contents of education, and insure the political neutrality of education. However, there is no doubt that the system also decreases the influence of the teacher unions on the contents of education. In the eyes of Nikkyoso, therefore, the 'Course of Study' and the textbook authorisation system are obvious attempts by the Ministry of Education to mould the contents of education in accordance with governmental policies (Makieda, 1976: 68).

Nikkyoso has not only been claiming that the system of textbook authorisation and the standardisation of the 'Course of Study' should be abolished, but has also been promoting a campaign urging teachers to formulate their own curriculum and to prepare their own teaching materials. In Hiroshima, for example, the unionised teachers edited reading material for peace education entitled 'Hiroshima'. It has been widely used in the prefecture as additional reading material in social studies.

Evaluating the outcome of this campaign would require more time and further study; however, it is sufficient to point out here that the campaign represents a new approach by the union. As we have seen, and as some other observers have also pointed out, it has always been the Ministry of Education that has initiated new policies and plans, while Nikkyoso on the other hand, has always taken a negative position on these plans. Nikkyoso has never before developed positive and constructive counterproposals. Thus, this campaign is of great significance in that Nikkyoso is initiating its own positive policy for the improvement of the quality of education.

CURRENT MAJOR PROBLEMS FACING NIKKYOSO

In recent years there has been a general acknowledgement that Nikkyoso is at risk. We can describe three major problems for the union: (1) declining membership - despite the increasing number of members, the membership rate has steadily declined; (2) bitter internal rivalry - recent serious confrontations between the Socialist and Communist factions have threatened a break up of Nikkyoso; and (3) the sharp rise in concern among the public about the general deterioration of education, and increasing pressure upon Nikkyoso to bear the responsibility for the problem.

Size and membership are often used as indicators of union power. As far as the size of membership is concerned, Nikkyoso, as it approaches 600,000 members[12], is Japan's largest teachers' union[13] and her second largest national union[14]. The number of members in Nikkyoso has been increasing over the last decade. Absolute membership in a union, however, does not necessarily provide accurate information about the union's power; gains in absolute membership may simply indicate an expanding work force and the maintenance by a union of its share of that work force (Cresswell et al., 1980: 106). This is the case with Nikkyoso. When founded in 1947, Nikkyoso claimed that it had organised nearly all of the nation's school teachers. Today, however, only a little over half of all personnel in elementary and secondary schools remain members of Nikkyoso. Gradually, and sometimes drastically, year by year, the rate of membership has steadily declined. According to statistics compiled by the Ministry of Education, the decline in membership has occurred as follows: 86.3 per cent of all educational personnel were members in 1958; 74.0

per cent in 1962; 63.3 per cent in 1965; 56.2 per cent in 1970; 55.9 per cent in 1975; 52.0 per cent in 1980; and 51.1 per cent in 1982. These figures, showing an evident decline in membership, are rather misleading; the numbers indicate the percentage of the Nikkyoso's membership in the total work force in elementary and secondary schools, including principals, vice-principals and other non-instructional staff. Accordingly, Nikkyoso claims that figures indicating membership as a percentage of the non-supervisory, instructional work force provide a better indication of the organisational leverage of the union. According to Nikkyoso, in 1978, for example, the rate of membership was 73 per cent, nearly 20 per cent higher than indicated in the Ministry of Education's survey. Moreover, the union contends that in 1980 approximately two-thirds of 47 prefectural unions maintained a membership of over 70 per cent of their elementary and secondary school teachers.

Nevertheless, it cannot be denied that there has been a downward trend in the enrolment of those eligible for membership. A number of factors have consistently been cited to account for this decline. The fierce struggles against the government and the compulsory withdrawal of principals and vice-principals from the union are probably two major factors responsible for the declining membership rate of the 1950s and 1960s. During its struggle against the Teachers' Efficiency Rating System, for example, Nikkyoso lost eighty thousand members between 1957 and 1960 (Duke, 1973: 153). In Ehime prefecture alone, where the rating system was initiated, the union lost two thousand members a year during that period, and at present only a small percentage of the prefectural teachers remain in Nikkyoso. Donald R. Thurston speculated about the varying reasons for the teachers' withdrawal from the union after its severe clashes with the government as follows:

"After participating in these struggles, teachers left the union for a variety of reasons: dissatisfaction over the use of violent tactics that disrupted classrooms, capitulation to pressures from boards of education to leave the union, and frustration from the excessive concern of union leaders with national and international politics while slighting the more immediate concerns

of teachers with education and their own welfare"
(1973: 122).

In addition, new revisions in the National Public Service Law in 1966 forced principals and vice-principals to withdraw from the union. Some forty thousand supervisory members gave up their membership in Nikkyoso after the implementation of the revisions (Duke, 1973: 181). Until forced to withdraw, about 40 per cent of the principals and over 60 per cent of the vice-principals had remained members of Nikkyoso, despite various attempts by the government to discourage them from retaining their membership in the union.

A more important factor in the contemporary decline in membership is the significant decrease in the number of new teachers who have joined Nikkyoso in the last decade. In 1970, 51.2 per cent of all new teachers joined the union, while in 1982 only 35.7 per cent did. Nikkyoso here again claims that the statistics of the Ministry of Education are misleading because they are compiled at the beginning of the academic year when some new teachers have not yet decided whether to join the union or not, and because some new teachers are required by school boards not to join the union when they are hired.

However, a recent survey, conducted by Nikkyoso itself, confirmed the trend among new teachers of standing off from the union. Nikkyoso's survey of 3,391 new educational personnel, from 20 to 24 years of age, revealed that most of the teachers surveyed were not sufficiently motivated to get involved in union activities (Nikkyoso, 1979). Although eight out of ten recognised the necessity of teachers' unions, they did not feel they had serious enough problems to seek help from unions, nor did they feel they would look to unions for help even if they did. Five of ten were satisfied with their salaries and fringe benefits, and four of ten had no complaints about their working conditions or rights. Among those who were dissatisfied with salaries and working conditions, very few took their grievances to unions. In addition, only three of ten had negative attitudes toward the educational policies of the government, which Nikkyoso has always opposed. The survey also documented apathetic attitudes among new teachers toward union activities; four out of ten did not have any opinion about Nikkyoso before entering the teaching profession because of their indifference to the union. Even after joining the union, two out of ten remained unconcerned with union activities. It might be said that the trend among new young teachers to avoid union activities is only part of the general trend among young people in the country who are reluctant to get involved in anything outside their own private concerns. However, some observers point out that the union organisations within the school are not functioning well enough to attract and recruit new teachers. This trend among young teachers, Nikkyoso admits, is becoming a serious problem which cannot be neglected if the union is to survive.

There has been persistent internal rivalry in Nikkyoso between the groups which support the Japan Socialist Party (JSP) and the Japan Communist Party (JCP). The rivalry extends back to the early post-war period before Nikkyoso was formed, and has become so bitter in recent years as to threaten the very existence of the union.

Probably the most bitter controversy involving these two political groups has been over the issue of formal affiliation with political parties. The political activism of labour unions in Japan is well known; Japanese unions have overtly supported particular political parties, including the JSP and JCP. Close relationships with political parties have provided "the instruments through which unions have been able to participate in government, albeit as part of the opposition" (Thurston, 1973: 222). Nikkyoso, being no exception to this, had given support to both the JSP and JCP up until the early 1960s. That policy was changed at the 1961 annual convention. Taking over the union's national leadership from the Communist group, the Socialists proposed a motion to give exclusive support to the JSP on the ground that the JSP had broad support from the working class. The proposal, vigorously opposed by the Communists, threw the convention into confusion:

"Amid shouting, filibustering, and general confusion, a vote was taken . . . When the vote was about to be taken on the matter concerning association only with the Socialist party, opposition radicals surrounded the chairman of the subcommittee, thrusting the convention into total chaos as fighting broke out. The convention was abruptly adjourned. The spectacle was given much publicity."

(Duke, 1973: 158).

The motion to support only the Socialist party was eventually adopted one month later, but the issue has still remained controversial. Since that time, the Communist faction has proposed a motion at every annual convention that the policy of exclusive support for the Socialist party should be amended to one of support for both the Socialist and the Communist parties. Although the motion has failed to be adopted to date, the margin of the vote has been getting as narrow as one-third in favour of the motion. The narrower the margin, the bitterer the dispute between the two factions. It is not unusual that a bitter debate on political affiliation dominates the union's annual convention.

The bitter rivalry between the two forces also can be seen in their disagreements about strike action and the definition of 'teacher'. The latter controversy stems from the JCP's announcement of a new definition of 'teacher' immediately after Nikkyoso's unified one-day strike in April, 1974. In the announcement, the JCP contended that it was wrong to define teachers merely as labourers, and thus neglect a professional and sacred aspect of their role. The announcement was extremely controversial because it was an affirmation of the concept of the 'holiness' of teaching, which Nikkyoso has traditionally denied because that concept has been used by the government in its attacks on Nikkyoso. As Makieda put it:

"Using the concept of the 'holiness' of teachers, the Conservative government has denied teachers the right to strike, prohibited teachers from involving themselves in political activities, and deprived teachers freedom of education and research . . . Therefore, it is important to relate this concept of the 'holiness' of teachers to our struggles for freedom of political action as educational labourers, the freedom to strike, and freedom of education and research. Thus, it can be said that the history of Nikkyoso is the history of the struggle against the label of 'holy occupation' and also the struggle to change the perception of teachers who accept this concept."

(Nikkyoso, 1977: 375).

The main point of the announcement by the JCP was to emphasise the 'holy' responsibiilities of teachers. It states that "teachers, with professional knowledge, skills, and experiences in education, have obligations and responsibilities to the people in helping children learn basic knowledge and skills" (Nikkyoso, 1977: 373). This view of teaching offers a remarkable contrast to Nikkyoso's traditional view, according to which teachers are defined as labourers or educational labourers, and much emphasis is put on their rights, such as the right to strike and even the right to make decisions on educational policies.

This theoretical difference carries over to the debate on strike tactics. As has already been mentioned, since 1970 Nikkyoso has adopted strike action as an important means of promoting its concerns. The Socialist faction, the majority in the union, supports and promotes the policy on the grounds that the strike is the most effective weapon labourers can use to win concessions from the government. On the other hand, the Communist faction, stressing the professional aspects of teaching, proposes an alternative strike policy which they believe could be supported not only by teachers, but also by principals and parents. Only limited strike action is acceptable to this faction. In 1973 the Tokyo Prefectural Union, under the leadership of the Communists, went on strike. During the strike action, the union let some teachers stay at each school to supervise the children. This action was taken because the union thought that teachers should not ignore their responsibilities to children and parents even while on strike. Although the Communists have remained a minority faction in Nikkyoso, their negative attitude toward strikes has had great impact on the union's strike policy. Since the historical one-day strike of 1974, Nikkyoso has been unsuccessful in going on nationwide unified strikes due to the opposition of Communist groups in several prefectures. It seems that the internal conflicts between the two factions, having stemmed from the debate on the definition of 'teacher', have now weakened the leverage of the union, and perhaps threatened to destroy the union itself.

Another problem Nikkyoso is facing stems from the general deterioration in education which is sweeping over the whole of the country. In recent years, Japanese education has gained a high reputation internationally. Many people claim that the nation's astonishing economic growth since World War II is mostly the result of the high quality of Japanese education. There is some evidence to support the claim. Illiteracy, for example, is virtually non-existent in Japan; it is estimated that less than one per cent of the Japanese are unable to read and write. Over 90 per cent of Japanese students graduate from high school and one third of those go on to post-secondary education. The academic performance of Japanese students in such subjects as mathematics and science consistently ranks above those of other industrialised countries.

These findings, however, tell us only about the bright not the dark side of Japanese education. Probably the most serious problem of Japanese education today is the highly competitive testing system, called 'shiken jigoku' (which literally means 'examination hell'). Under this system, students must take entrance examinations for admission to high school and college. Some children even take entrance examinations to enter kindergarten and/or elementary school, if they seek to enter the elite private institutions. These in turn supply many students to the prestigious high schools and universities. Many Japanese fervently believe that success in life greatly depends upon success in entrance examinations, especially at the college level. Actually, however, entering a college does not guarantee job security, since major firms recruit from only a handful of first-rate universities, like Tokyo and Kyoto Universities. Thus, from the time they first enter school, all Japanese children embark on a highly competitive test-taking race aimed at success and survival in life. As an American observer put it:

"No single event, with the possible exception of marriage, determines the course of a young man's life as much as entrance examinations; and nothing, including marriage, requires so many years of planning and hard work."

(Ezra Vogel, quoted in Beauchamp, 1982: 28).

It might be true that the "high quality of Japanese education" results from the highly competitive testing system. But the system is not without problems. It produces deleterious effects on schools and children:

"The devastating effects on the curricula of

high schools which results from their
preoccupation with preparing for the entrance
examinations; the backwash into the middle
schools, preoccupied with preparing students
for the entrance examinations for the 'best'
high schools - those which have the best
record for getting students into the top
universities; the backwash into the primary
schools arising from the entrance
examinations to the private middle schools -
and so back to the pre-pre-kindergarten which
was reported in 1970 to have failed to devise
adequate tests for 2 year olds and decided to
test their mother instead."
(Dore, 1976: 49).
Education preoccupied with examinations places
great emphasis on memorisation and rote learning
of concepts and facts rather than on analytical,
critical, and creative thinking. As a high school
student put it: "For the tests you only memorise,
which you forget as soon as the exams are over"
(McGrath, 1982).

Since the competition for respected high
schools and prestigious universities is so fierce,
Japanese children often attend supplementary cram
schools, called 'juku' in Japanese. The vast
majority of these schools have been developed with
the single objective of helping children pass the
entrance examinations of their desired school or
schools. A recent survey by the Ministry of
Education showed that six of every ten junior high
school students in urban areas were enrolled in
some kind of cram school. Thus, it is not unusual
for Japanese children to spend seven hours in
regular classes, two hours in 'juku', four hours
doing homework, and only five or six hours
sleeping a day.

While schooling under the examination system
might make sense to those who are doing well in
school, for the ones who fail or who are low
achievers it is extremely hard to tolerate. Some
of these disappointed youths resort to suicide.
Although the suicide rate among Japanese youth is
not so high in comparison with that of their
counterparts in the West, it is unique in that
most of the cases seem to be a result of the
intense academic pressure to do well in school and
to prepare for the highly competitive entrance
examinations.

Recently, 'school violence' has received a
good deal of publicity. Violence in schools is

not a new phenomenon in Japan; violence among students and vandalism have been commonly seen in schools. What is sensational about recent 'school violence' is that the victims have been teachers for the most part. In 1982, junior high school teachers were victims of 1,404 physical attacks, which was twice as many as in the previous year.[15] In one instance, a gang of 20 students surrounded a group of teachers in the school courtyard, accused them of inflicting pain on one of their number and began to beat them up. It took 20 patrolmen to subdue the boys, but not before ten teachers had been injured (McGrath, 1982). Obviously, some students are beginning to choose open 'rebellion' against the examination system and teachers, who work for the system, rather than the ultimate 'escapism' of suicide.

Until very recently, Nikkyoso had argued that these educational problems, called, in general terms, 'kyoiku kohai', all stemmed from the educational policies developed by the government and the Ministry of Education. The union even viewed 'kyoiku kohai' as clear evidence of the failure of the government's policies. Therefore, the union's answer to the problem of 'kyoiku kohai' was simple: reforms and revisions of current educational policies and elimination of the government's 'improper control' over education. Nikkyoso also stated that it was not willing to take responsibility for the problem of 'kyoiku kohai' because the union did not have any voice in determining the educational policies which caused the problem.

In theory, Nikkyoso's argument is logical, but in reality, especially in the minds of parents and the general public, the argument seems to ignore the fact that it is the teacher who implements educational policy on the school grounds.

As the issue of 'kyoiku kohai' has become the top educational concern of the public and has been among the most significant and controversial social issues in contemporary Japan, Nikkyoso has come to realise the necessity of coping with the problem in some way. At the annual convention in 1983, then-chairman Makieda urged the members to see 'kyoiku kohai' as their own problem and to be prepared to work out a solution for themselves:

"[to overcome the problem of 'kyoiku kohai',] teachers have to strengthen co-operation with parents and the people and also have to make

a strong effort to forge a new vision of what schools and teachers ought to be."
(Asahi Shinbun, August 30, 1983).

Although Nikkyoso has not taken concrete measures to meet the problem of 'kyoiku kohai' to date, it has been under intense pressure to take steps to do so.

CONCLUSIONS

Nikkyoso and the Ministry of Education, the two major actors on the scene of post-war Japanese education, have been fighting each other for unilateral control of educational policy. It appears in retrospect that the consequences of their battles have been unfortunate for post-war Japanese education for two reasons.

In the first place, the end result is that a policy-making structure has been established which gives the Ministry of Education monopolistic power over every facet of education, leaving Nikkyoso, which respresents the majority of Japanese teachers, no direct access to the decision-making process.

Education is very much value-laden. This means that education can never be neutral and that a number of conflicts and confrontations are bound to take place over educational issues. It is also very difficult to reach a consensus about educational values. To take an example, some people emphasise equal educational treatment for all children, while others assert that children should be taught according to their abilities. Given the value-laden nature of education, it is not reasonable to expect decisions on educational policies to be made on the basis of substantive agreement. However it is important to have a decision-making process in which all concerned groups, each seeking to impose its own values, could participate.

In this sense, it is even tragic that educational policy in Japan has been formulated mainly by the Ministry of Education, which represents the Conservative government, without significant input from teachers, who are in charge of the education of children.

Secondly, in the course of the all-out battles between Nikkyoso and the Ministry of Education, little consideration has been given to the education of children; educational questions have been subordinated to the issue of control. Consequently, Japanese education has developed the testing system, under which high priority is put on the selective function of education rather than on the educational function itself. Today, children are suffering more than ever under the selection-oriented educational system. As one student put it:

> "Tests, tests, tests, . . . They have dominated our student days. They have kept us from taking the time to think about our society or the meaning of our own lives . . . Preparation for the college entrance exam has been a jealous mistress robbing us of the time to think about these problems. And even what we should have been able to regard as a haven from this robbery - our homeroom - was never a place where we could fully relate to each other as human beings. An education stressing competition and inculcating false falues, has, unawares, created a king of the person who thinks only of himself and is uninterested in others."
> (Cummings, 1980: 231).

It seems that Nikkyoso is now both at a crossroads and in a crisis. Nikkyoso could continue pursuing the path which it has travelled for the last three decades. It could still seek political unionism and continue asserting that only through changes in the existing political and educational order can the general problems of education be resolved. However, travelling this path would mean that Nikkyoso would remain an outside force, without any significant voice in the formal decision-making structure of Japanese education.

But there is another path available for Nikkyoso to take. Travelling this path would require Nikkyoso to carry dual goals: to aim for fundamental changes in the existing political and educational system as a long term and ultimate goal, while at the same time, as a short term goal, to attempt to improve the quality of education within the prevailing structure. This would necessitate, for example, that Nikkyoso be willing to accept the task of rescuing the children suffering under the current testing system. Pursuing this path would certainly demand greater social and educational responsibilities from Nikkyoso; however, it could possibly give Nikkyoso a greater chance to unite teachers once more, as the union did before under the slogan "Never send our students to the battlefield again".

NOTES

1. Perhaps the two best books yet written on Nikkyoso generally are Duke (1973) and Thurston (1973). My discussion of Nikkyoso in historical perspective is based on these two important works as well as Nikkyoso (1977).

2. To develop these models, I am indebted to Dunlop (1948) and Harris (1982), particularly Chapter 7.

3. See, for example, Etzioni (1969).

4. Despite the law which has forbidden Nikkyoso the right to enter into collective agreements, the union was able to meet occasionally with the Ministry of Education to discuss teacher salaries and working conditions. Such consultative meetings were ended in 1960 by the Minister Araki, who refused to meet Nikkyoso due to its political and ideological activities.

5. The purpose of Convention 87 is to guarantee workers freedom of association. The highlights of the Convention are as follows: (1) Workers shall have the right to establish and join organisations of their own choosing; (2) Workers organisations shall have the right to draw up their constitutions and rules, to organise their administration and activities and to formulate their programmes; (3) Workers organisations shall have the right to elect their representatives; (4) Workers organisations are not to be liable to be dissolved or suspended by administrative authority; and (5) Workers organisations have the right to establish and join federations and confederations, and to affiliate with international organisations of workers.

6. The Amendments generally did not liberalise the public employee unions' rights of representation, but, rather, restricted "the scope of membership, the scope of bargaining, the freedom of full-time union officers to take leave from public employment" (Cook, 1971: 29).

7. World Confederation of Organisations of the

Teaching Profession.
8. International Federation of Free Teachers Unions.
9. According to Nikkyoso, unlike the strike, the mass vacation is a lawful means of exerting pressure. In a mass vacation "a certain per cent of the teachers in the schools of a particular prefecture are asked by the prefectural union leaders to take time off on a specified day or days" (Thurston, 1973: 201).
10. Until 1963, salary increases for public employees were implemented in October, whereas those for employees in private industry were implemented in April.
11. The law, enacted in 1947, sets forth the aims and principles of education in accordance with the spirit of the Constitution. It reads in part: "Having established the Constitution of Japan, we have shown our resolution to contribute to the peace of the world and welfare of humanity by building a democratic and cultural state. The realisation of this ideal shall depend fundamentally on the power of education . . . Education shall not be subject to improper control, but it shall be directly responsible to the whole people."
12. According to the Ministry of Education's survey, as of October 1, 1982, Nikkyoso had 597,642 members.
13. Besides Nikkyoso, there are several unions for public school teachers. Among them is Nippon Kyoshokuin Renmei (Japan Teachers Federation), the second largest teacher union with about 40,000 members.
14. The biggest is Zen Hihon Jichi Dantai Rodo Kumiai (All-Japan Prefectural and Municipal Workers Union), Jichiro, with approximately 1,200,000 members. Both Nikkyoso and Jichiro are affiliated with Japan's biggest national labour centre, Sohyo (Japan General Council of Trade Unions).
15. The figure shown here is based on reports from individual schools, which are often reluctant to disclose such information. It is, therefore, reasonable to assume that only a small fraction of attacks is ever reported.

REFERENCES

Akioka, Nobukiko. (1974) "Nikkyoso: Gekika suru
    Sha-Kyo no Tairitsu" (The Japan Teachers'
    Union: An Intensifying Confrontation Between
    the Socialist and Communist Groups). Kikan
    Kyoiku Ho 14 (December) 160-166.
Arthur, Herman. (1983) "The Japan Gap: A Country
    Moves Ahead - But at What Price?" American
    Educator 7: 2 (Summer) 38-44.
Asahi Shinbun (Asahi Newspaper) (August 30,
    1983).
Beauchamp, Edward R. (1977) "Report from Japan"
    Educational Forum 56: 3 (March) 373-378.
- (1982) Education in Contemporary Japan Blooming-
    ton, Indiana: Phi Delta Kappa Educational
    Foundation.
Cook, Alice H. (1971) "Labour Relations in Local
    Government in Japan", in Public Employee
    Labour Relations in Japan: Three Aspects.
    Ann Arbor, Michigan: Institute of Labour and
    Industrial Relations, The University of
    Michigan, 29-37.
Cresswell, Anthony M. and Michael J. Murphy with
    Charles T. Kerchner. (1980) Teachers, Unions,
    and Collective Bargaining in Public Education
    Berkeley, California: McCuthan Publishing
    Corporation.
Cummings, William K. (1980) Education and Equality
    in Japan. Princeton, New Jersey: Princeton
    University Press.
Dore, Ronald P. (1970-1971) "Textbook Censorship
    in Japan: The Ienaga Case" Pacific Affairs
    43: 4 (Winter) 548-556.
- (1976) The Diploma Disease: Education, Qualifi-
    cation and Development Berkeley, California:
    University of California Press.
Duke, Benjamin C. (1972) "The Textbook
    Controversy" Japan Quarterly 19: 3 (July-
    September) 337-352.
- (1973) Japan's Militant Teachers: A History of
    the Left-Wing Teachers' Movement Honolulu:
    University Press of Hawaii.
Dunlop, John T. (1948) "The Development of Labour
    Organisations: A Theoretical Framework" in
    Richard A. Lester and Joseph Shister, eds.,
    Insights Into Labour Issues New York:
    Macmillan 163-193.
Egawa, Hiroshi (1977) Nikkyoso wa Ima (The Japan
    Teachers' Union Today). Tokyo: Rodo Kyoiku
    Senta.

Etzioni, Amitai (ed.) (1969) The Semi-Professions and their Organisation New York: Free Press.

Gendai Kyoikugaku 18: Kyoshi (Modern Pedagogy 18: Schoolteacher) (1961) Tokyo: Iwanami.

Handsaker, Morrison and Marjorie (1967) "The ILO and Japanese Public Employee Unions" Industrial Relations 7: 1 (October) 80-91.

Harris, Kevin (1982) Teachers and Classes: A Marxist Analysis London: Routledge and Kegan Paul.

Hiragaki, Miyoji (1976) "Dai-ni Kinpyo to shiteno Shunin-sei Mondai" (The Head Teacher Issue as Another Efficiency Rating System) Gekkan Rodo Mondai (June) 55-61.

Hoxie, Robert F. (1968) Trade Unions in the United States New York: Appleton-Century-Crofts, 1923; 2nd ed. reprinted.

Kaigo, Tokiomi (1963) "A Short History of Postwar Japanese Education" Journal of Social and Political Ideas in Japan 1:3 (December) 15-23.

Kerr, Steven et al. (1977) "Issues in the Study of 'Professionals' in Organisations: The Case of Scientists and Engineers" Organizational Behavior and Human Performance 18:2 (April) 329-345.

Kirst, Michael W. (1981) "Japanese Education: Its Implications for Economic Competition in the 1980s" Phi Delta Kappa 62:10 (June) 707-708.

Kobayashi, Tetsuya (1976) Society, Schools and Progress in Japan Oxford: Pergamon Press.

Kochan, Thomas A. (1980) Collective Bargaining and Industrial Relations: From Theory to Policy and Practice Homewood, Illinois: Richard D. Irwin, Inc.

Kusuyama, Mikao (1978) Kyoshokuin Dantai no Kisochishiki (Basic Information about Educational Personnel Organisations) Tokyo: Dai-ichi Hoki.

Levine, Solomon B. (1969) "Japan" In Albert A. Blum, ed. Teacher Unions and Associations: A Comparative Study Urbana, Illinois: University of Illinios Press. 141-199.

Liebermann, Myron (1956) Education as a Profession Englewood Cliffs, New Jersey: Prentice-Hall, Inc.

Makieda, Motofumi (1971) "Nikkyoso Undo no Ninaubeki Kadai" (Problems with which the Japan Teachers' Union is confronted) Gekkan Rodo Mondai 163 (October) 10-15.

- (1976) "Kyoiku no Jiyu o Mamore" (Protect the Freedom of Education) Gekkan Rodo Mondai 218 (February) 68-71.
- (1977) "Kibishii Jiko Tenken o" (Sincere Self-Inspection). Kyoiku Hyoron 346 (March) 16-17.
- (1977) "Chikara o Awasete Kyoiku no Tatenaoshi o" (Let's Restructure Education Together). Kyoiku Hyoron 347 (April) 26-28.
- (1977) "Kyoiku-teki Rikiryo no Toinaoshi o" (Let's re-examine our Teaching Skills) Kyoiku Hyoron 353 (September) 64-67.
- (1979) "Tomo-ni Kyoiku Kohai ni Tachimukaou" (Face up to the General Deterioration of Education) Kyoiku Hyoron 376 (April) 24-25.
- (1981) "Undo o Tsujite Soshiki no Kyoka Hatten o" (Let's Strengthen and Develop our Organisation through Activities) Kyoiku Hyoron 410 (September) 52-55.
- and Nishimura, Hidetoshi (1982) "Korekarano Nikkyoso Undo" (The Future of the Japan Teachers' Union) Kyoiku Hyoron 420 (June) 18-25.
McGrath, Ellie (1982) "The Test Must Go On: Japanese Students Are Driven by Shiken Jigoku" Time 119:11 (March 15) 80-81.
Ministry of Education, Science and Culture, Government of Japan. (1982) Education in Japan: A Graphic Presentation Tokyo: Gyosei Pub.
Mishima, Munehiko (1968) "Mukenri Jotai no Komuin Rodosha: Komuin no Roshi Kankei" (Public Employees without Rights: Labour Relations in the Public Sector) Gekkan Rodo Mondai 125 (August) 100-106.
Miyahara, Seiichi (1963) "The Japan Teachers' Union and Its Code of Ethics" Journal of Social and Political Ideas In Japan 1:3 (December) 102-105.
- et al., eds. (1974) Shiryo: Nihon Gendai Kyoikushi 1-3 (Data: The History of Modern Japanese Education 1-3) Tokyo: San Sei Do.
Mochida, Eiichi (1963) "The Reform of Boards of Education and Its Aftermath" Journal of Social and Political Ideas in Japan 1:3 (December) 43-47.
Mochizuki, Muneaki (1978) Tatakau Kyoshi-tachi (The Fighting Teachers) Tokyo: Rodo Kyoiku Senta.
Muramatsu, Takashi (1970) "Kyoiku Naiyo to Kyoshi no Sozosei" (The Content of Education and

Creativity of Teachers) Gekkan Rodo Mondai 150 (September) 23-29.

Nagai, Kenichi (1974) "Rodo Undo to Kyoiku Modai" (Labour Movement and Educational Issues) Gekkan Rodo Mondai 199 (August) 3-15.

Nakakoji, Kiyoo (1978) "Shunin-sei Toso no Genjyo to Tenbo" (Present and Future Struggles With the Head Teacher System) Kikan Kyoiku Ho 28 (June) 24-31

"Nikkyoso" (The Japan Teachers' Union) Japan Quarterly 21:4 (October-December 1974) 329-332.

Nikkyoso (1977) Nikkyoso Sanjunenshi (Thirty-Year History of the Japan Teachers' Union) Tokyo: Rodo Kyoiku Senta.

- (1979) "Shinki Saiyo Kyoshokuin Ishiki Chosa Hokokusho" (A Survey Report on the Attitude of new Educational Personnel) Gekkan Kyoiku no Mori 4:10 (October) 51-63.

Oshima, Yasumasa (1963) "Education in Japan: 1945-1963" Journal of Social and Political Ideas in Japan 1:3 (December) 2-10.

Ota, Takashi (1978) Sengo Nihon Kyoikushi (A History of Postwar Japanese Education) Tokyo: Iwanami.

Owen, John E. (1976) "The U.S. Labour Union Movement: Its History and Current Problems" Rivista Internazionale di Scienze Economiche e Commerciali 23:1 (January) 3-42.

Passin, Herbert (1965) Society and Education in Japan New York: Teachers College Press, Columbia University.

Royama, Masamichi (1963) "Politics and Education" Journal of Social and Political Ideas in Japan 1:3 (December) 37-39.

Saito, Masahiko (1980) "Nikkyoso no Soshiki-kiko Unei to Tatakai" (The Japan Teachers' Union: Its Organisation, Administration, and Movement) Kyoiku Hyoron 390 (April) 41-43.

Sato, Akio (1971) "Kanko Rodosha no Hoteki Chii" (The Legal Status of Public Employees) Gekkan Rodo Mondai 157 (April) 71-77.

Shinohara, Hajime (1978a) "Nikkyoso Undo ga Tomen tsuru Shokadai" (Major Problems Facing the Japan Teachers' Union) Gekkan Rodo Mondai 250 (July) 113-118.

- (1978b) "Sonogono Shunin Teate Kyoshutsu Undo: Kyoshutsu-ritsu no Teika ga Imisurumono" (The Movement to Donate Head Teacher Allowances: The Implications of Declining Donation Rates) Gekkan Rodo Mondai 254 (November) 66-71.

Suzuki, Shigenobu (1963) "A Critique on the Nature of the Japan Teachers' Union" Journal of Social and Political Ideas in Japan 1:3 (December) 112-116.

Takashima, Kazuo (1980) "Bunretsu no Kiki Fukamaru Nikkyoso" (The Growing Critical Split in the Japan Teachers' Union) Kikan Kyoiku Ho 37 (October) 186-190.

Tannenbaum, Arnold S. (1965) "Unions" in James S. March, ed. Handbook of Organisations Chicago: Rand McNally & Company 710-763.

The Textbook Sub-Committe of the Central Council for Education (1983) "Kyokasho no Arikata ni Kansuru Sho-Iinkai Hokoku" (A Sub-Committee Report on the Textbook System) Asahi Janaru 25:25 (June 17) 19-21.

Thurston, Donald R. (1973) Teachers and Politics in Japan Princeton, New Jersey: Princeton University Press.

Tsuji, Kiyoaki (1963) "Toward Understanding the Teachers' Efficiency Rating System" Journal of Social and Political Ideas in Japan 1:3 (December) 51-54.

United States Education Mission To Japan. (1946) Report Mimeographed. Tokyo.

Vogel, Ezra F. (1979) Japan as Number One: Lesson for America Cambridge, Massachusetts: Harvard University Press.

Wildman, Wesley A. and Charles R. Perry (1966) "Group Conflict and School Organisation" Phi Delta Kappa 47:5 (January) 244-251.

Yuasa, Mitsuru (1982) Sengo Kyoiku Rodo Undo no Rekishi (A History of the Educational Labour Movement in Postwar Japan) Tokyo: Shin Nihon Shuppansha.

Chapter Five

TEACHER UNIONS: SOME SWEDISH PERSPECTIVES

Leon Boucher

 With one full-time equivalent teacher for
every ten pupils in the public education system,
Sweden employs proportionately more teachers than
any other developed country. As a group, these
teachers enjoy conditions of work which their
colleagues in other countries might well envy.
Why this should be so has never been the subject
of any major study.[1]
 One explanation is no doubt to be found in
the respect which Sweden, in common with much of
continental Europe and at least the Celtic areas
of the British Isles, gives to academic
achievement. This may explain the status of the
academic subject specialist teacher relative to
the class teacher or the teacher of the more
obviously vocational subjects. It may also
explain why this group of teachers has been able
to retain differentials not simply in financial
but also in social terms. It does not, however,
explain the rise in influence of the other groups
of teachers.
 A possible explanation for the changed status
of class and vocational subject teachers no doubt
derives from the greater democratisation of the
country since the nineteenth century, and
especially since the middle of the twentieth
century. The men amongst these teachers have
tended to come from folket, the ordinary working
people, especially from the country areas of what
is still a relatively rural country or from the
ranks of the artisans and clerks of the towns.
The women teachers, however, tended to come from
slightly higher social backgrounds than the men.
For them, teaching, especially in the elementary
school, provided outlets for their talents and
aspirations which were denied them in other

socially prestigious occupations. But whether men
or women, such people tended to be in the
forefront of political and social reform
movements. They became members of parliament or
local councillors, or were active in social and
cultural pressure groups, and often became the
wives or husbands of such activists. Their voices
began increasingly to be heard.

One area in which the voices were raised was
trade unionism.   The origins of <u>Sveriges</u>
<u>Lärarförbundet</u>,[2] SL, reflects this. The first
documented teacher society dates from 1838 when
five elementary school teachers in the village of
Vekerum in Blekinge, a province in southern Sweden
met together in the belief that by sharing their
experiences they could collectively assist one
another. Further meetings were intended, but in
fact the five moved to other parts of the country.
Other local societies, however, rapidly emerged
and by 1879 there were 130 of them. As early as
1850, ideas were being put forward to set up a
national body, in particular to work for pensions
for teachers and their widows, and some large
regional meetings did take place. In 1880, the
Stockholm Society called for delegates from all
local societies to meet in August of that year in
the Hall of the Academy of Sciences. In all, 82
societies sent delegates, the largest number
coming from Skåne who sent twenty-two of the
ninety-six delegates who attended. The only
counties not to be represented were Gotland,
Jämtland, Västerbotten and Norrbotten; all
relatively isolated and sparsely populated areas.
A further 106 teachers of both sexes attended the
meeting as individuals.   The meeting set up
<u>Sveriges Allmänna Folkskollärarföreningen</u>, SAF,
open to all men and women teachers in elementary
and infant schools throughout the country. The
purpose of the society was "to work for the
increase of the Swedish elementary school and
public education provision, for unity and good
spirit among all teachers, and for the improvement
of the teacher's position in general". Members
had to pay a small subscription and they were
organised in local societies. This pattern of
work has remained the norm ever since, though the
subscription is now some 1% of a year's salary.

In 1906, the women broke away to form a
separate society, largely to fight for equal pay.
Similarly, in 1918 the teachers in the infant
schools also set up a separate society to promote

their own salary aspirations.   Between 1937 and 1940, recognised teacher associations achieved the right to negotiate their salaries with either the municipal or the central state authorities by whom they might be employed, and in 1944 these negotiations were co-ordinated through and conducted by the newly formed <u>Tjänstemannens Central Organisation</u>, TCO, the composite union of salaried employees analogous to <u>Lands-organisationen</u>, LO, which spoke collectively for manual workers.   These negotiations between employees and employers, on a national basis, were a characteristic feature of the <u>Saltsjöbad</u> agreement which gave Sweden its envied reputation for industrial democracy and a rational approach to wage settlements following the unrest of the 1930s.   By 1946, SAF became a federation of the separate class teacher unions and in 1963, all came together again to form SL, which now has a membership of some 70,000 active and retired teachers.

Parallel with these class teacher unions, there also developed professional associations for other categories of teachers.   The vocational subject teachers were in many cases originally members of craft unions, but also include those who have specialist qualifications in crafts, art, music or gymnastics.   They belong collectively to <u>Sveriges Facklärarförbundet</u>, SFL, and also number some 70,000 active and retired.   During the period of school reform since 1950, there have been various discussions and proposals for uniting SFL and SL, but separate interests have to date always prevailed.

The academic subject teachers found their first loyalties with their subject, as linguists, classicists, historians and so on.   Their point of reference for salaries and conditions of service has always been that accorded to persons with comparable levels of academic study employed in the public service.   As teachers they now belong to <u>Lärarnas Riksförbund</u>, LR, which in its turn is affiliated to <u>Sveriges Akademikers Centralorganisationen</u>, SACO, as its composite negotiating body.   They now number some 35,000.

These three major unions, together with very much smaller ones for Head Teachers, advisers and other specialist groups, enrol some 95% of all serving teachers to their ranks.   While not the largest occupational group - they are outnumbered by <u>Metall</u>, the composite union of manual workers

in industrial and engineering activities; and by
all in Kommunaltjänstemanneförbundet, the local
government employees - they form, nevertheless, a
very significant pressure group, especially when
'education' takes over 7% of the Gross National
Product and when teachers' salaries account for
some two-thirds of this expenditure. Numbers
alone, however, do not determine social or
economic power. Teachers have no industrial
'muscle', and indeed are limited by the agreements
and laws developed largely during the long period
of social democratic government which lasted for
forty-four years until 1976. Rights are
safeguarded to negotiate and achieve agreements,
avtal, on those matters which do not directly
affect the legal obligation of the public
authority in question. An employee cannot refuse
to carry out duties essential to the employer's
task, for example, to pay out grants of public
money under the law, make appointments, administer
the law, exercise control functions - those
activities known in Swedish as myndighetsutövning.
There exists a special main agreement,
särskilt huvudavtal, SHA, for public employees
whereby employer or employee can refer to a board
of thirteen persons to advise negotiators as to
what is or is not the lawful exercise of duty of a
public department. What is or is not a permanent
appointment, the order in which appointments may
be terminated, the length of appointment,
salaries, pensions, rights to leave of absence,
subsistence allowances, and for teachers questions
of the size of teaching groups, what constitutes
qualified status for a given post, and hours of
duty in the school, these and similar matters are
all subject to formal agreement, normally
renewable annually. Once such agreement has been
reached, employer and employee are required to
abide by its decisions until a revision is
introduced. If either party disagrees on the
interpretation of an agreement, the matter may be
referred to an employment tribunal,
arbetsdomstolen, AD. Public employees do have a
right to strike under the current law governing
public employment, LOA^3, but only over matters on
which agreements do not exist or when in sympathy
for strike action taken by other public employees,
whether by state employees in support of local
authority staff or vice-versa.
    The Public Employees law in 1976 was one half
of a major reform of employment law, designed to

consolidate and clarify a generation of
regulations concerning the democratisation of
working life. The other half was the law on joint
decision making, _Medbestämmande i arbetslivet_,
MBL[4]. This gave added rights to employees,
through their unions, to negotiate agreements; to
receive information on the general development of
the business or trade; to veto the employment of
'outsiders'; to negotiate agreements on how a
business is to be carried out; to give increased
rights to employees on the interpretation of
agreements. In sum, these laws gave increased
influence to employees, whether in private or
public employment. It might have appeared that a
new 'Saltsjöbad' agreement had been reached, that
the new democracy had arrived.

THE 1976 WATERSHED

     In significant respects, however, the late
1970s were a watershed in Swedish economic, social
and political life. As in many other western
countries, it was a period of rising costs,
related in part to the increased price of oil.
The notion of an ever-rising GNP, of full
employment, of financing public services from
greater productivity began seriously to be
questioned. A changing economic climate was met
by a changing social climate. There was an
uncertainty about the kind of society in which one
wanted to live. The debate on the use of nuclear
power, ultimately the subject of a referendum
which approved limited development of nuclear
reactors, reflected in part the desirablility of
sources of power to maintain production, and in
part the fear of a world killing itself either by
war or by ecological suicide. A whole generation
had grown up which did not share the hardships of
widespread unemployment and near revolution of the
1930s. They had experienced little but increasing
affluence, were the products of a national system
of education in which the differences between
schools and between regions had been massively
reduced. Such persons were beginning to replace
that generation of politicians, administrators,
managers and union leaders who had worked closely
together to bring about the almost arrogant self-
confidence which had characterised Swedish social
and political policies and which had given rise to
the notion of the Swedish model of social advance,
comparable in its own way to the German economic

miracle of the 1950s and 1960s. That generation
had learnt to know and understand each other even
when their political orientations or their social,
professional or academic backgrounds differed.
Their successors were less certain about the
future. The consensus of views, the feeling that
problems could be solved by involving as many as
possible in the dialogue of a social democracy
until government in the centre could pass a law or
issue a set of regulations which would enjoy
widespread support, was beginning to evaporate.
There was a feeling that there was too much
government, especially from the centre. Within a
general framework of 'fair shares for all' - there
was, and is, no real opposition, for example, to
the system of schools, common to all wherever one
may live - local democracy and individual choice
should have its place in the sun.
     The political effects of this shift of
consensus were at once apparent in the defeat of
the social democrat government in 1976, to be
followed by six years of uneasy centre-right
coalitions and a similarly uneasy return to power
of the social democrats in 1982. Consensus
politics, however, has not returned. The model of
trade union agreement with employers was broken in
1983 when the employers' federation, SAF,
announced that it would not have a general wage
agreement with LO in 1984. Even LO itself no
longer showed consensus when the mighty
<u>Metall</u>union, understandably fearful of job losses
in a changing industrial climate, also decided to
'go it alone'. Nor was it simply the centre-right
politicians who were anxious to cut public
expenditure and reduce taxes in a country where
the highest rates of tax reached 80%, where public
expenditure had doubled in real terms in a
generation, and where educational expenditure had
increased threefold as a proportion of GNP.
Social democrats also sought to curb public
expenditure. Notions of decentralised decision-
making, however, do not readily accord with
equally valid notions of central control over
total public expenditure, wherever it may occur.
     There has arisen, therefore, a massive
paradox.   On the one hand, the notion of
participatory social democracy encourages both the
development of laws and practices such as those
described above in the reform of employment
conditions, MBL and LOA, and the shift from
decision-making in remote central government

offices to close-at-hand municipal offices in each
kommun.   On the other hand, it has also to be
recognised that in a participatory democracy the
ultimate decision is essentially a political one -
even, in the Aristotelian sense, for it to be a
political decision to make no decision or to
permit decisions to be made by individuals.   In
educational contexts, the effect of this has been
to change the nature of the bodies which are
responsible for carrying out educational policies.
Centrally, the national Board of Education,
Skolöverstyrelsen, Sö, had until 1981 a board
which represented a wide spectrum of educational
interests;   along with MPs and officials, there
were representatives of teachers unions, parents,
employers and pupils.   Now, the board is a
political one.   The wider interests are
represented only through an advisory committee.
Similarly, at local level, the kommun, which is
responsible essentially for schools in its area
(albeit with certain oversight and co-ordination
from county boards), used to have a school board
on which teachers were represented.   Now, they are
wholly political, in proportion to the local
authority as a whole, and are served by a
professional Chief Education Officer, the
skolchef.
     In principle, these shifts of emphasis, from
centralised administration to decentralised, from
lay to political decision-making in public boards,
would have had little impact had the spirit of
consensus politics continued alongside increased
economic growth and employee rights to negotiate
agreements on conditions of work.
     In practice, the changed economic situation,
combined with the demographic fact of falling
rolls and the social consequences of polarised
expectations of the school system expressed by
political leaders, centrally and locally, have
required teacher unions to adapt to a changed
situation and to adopt new approaches.

POLITICAL ACTION AND UNION RESPONSE

     When the social democrats fell from power in
1976, it was immediately made apparent to the
leaders of the teacher unions, whether they tended
to be more left wing in the case of SL for the
class teachers or right wing in LR for the
academic subject teachers, that the new political
leadership tended to the view that "we are the

masters now"[5]. The moves to change the composition of the NBE were soon introduced, and since ceasing to be a member of that Board, the Chairman of SL in fact never even entered the NBE building for over two years[6]. In his view, the return of the social democrats in 1982 had done little to alter this situation. Opinions may be sought from the unions, but they remain both formally and informally divorced from the political decision-making processes. In May 1982, there was a unique demonstration outside Parliament in Stockholm when 4,000 members of the three main teacher associations, the two organisations representing pupils and the national home and school society, Hem och Skola, gathered to protest against the reduction of expenditure on schools which Parliament had just decided. Education was being required significantly to draw in its belts.

Not only were resources cut back rather more than in proportion to the declining size of the total school population. A major change was also introduced in the terms of teacher appointments, in two respects. First, and logically justified in terms of the legal responsibility of the local authorities to maintain the school system as established by Parliament, teachers were in future to be appointed by the kommun and not, as previously, by the county or, for the upper secondary school, by the central government. The terms of those appointments were still, however, to be governed by nationally valid agreements with the teacher unions. Secondly, the long established practice of providing for some 80% of all teaching appointments to be permanent, ordinarie, was abolished. For generations, it had been the normal career pattern to have initially a non-permanent post, extra-ordinarie, e.o., and over time to obtain a permanent position from which it was virtually impossible to be removed short of committing a major crime. There were, and still are, many persons who formally hold an ordinarie post in one school from which they have long-term leave of absence to serve in other posts elsewhere. Head teachers, rektorer, have until now been in this position. So, too, is the present editor of the SL journal, who has an ordinarie appointment as Lektor in Swedish in an upper secondary school, from which he has moved first as an adviser in the National Board, then as secretary of a major committee of enquiry into teacher education, and now to his present position. In future, all new teachers are appointed by and to the _kommun_ in which they are employed, and will be expected to give up that post on moving permanently elsewhere.

All teacher unions were united in opposing these changes. Their views, however, were disregarded. These were matters which, legitimately, belonged to the government to decide and which the NBE is required to administer. The unions are therefore left with the need to safeguard their members' interests by seeking to ensure that local authorities in fact employ teachers in accordance with the grant regulations approved by Parliament and the agreements, _avtal_, on conditions of work.

In order the better to exercise these functions, the unions have sought in recent years to strengthen the resources of their local representatives. SL, for example, has for some years run detailed courses on school administration, grant regulations, employment law and the like. Teachers, who have the right to remission of teaching duties and to leave of absence for union duties, have been given good travel and maintenance allowances by the union itself to enable them to attend these courses. They have also been encouraged to take part in local employment tribunals as lay members, in order the better to know and understand both the people and the processes involved. As governmental power has shifted from the centre, so the unions have strengthened their local knowledge. Indeed, it is probably true in most _kommun_ other than those in the major cities that the teacher union representatives know at least as much as, and sometimes more than, the handful of officials and elected members of the local school board about the rules and regulations of school administration.

The value of this approach was clear in 1982-3 when, through union vigilance, some 700 full and part-time posts were saved when various local authorities attempted to abolish them.   In one _kommun_, savings of 2% were sought by not providing short-term supply staff, and by appointing class teachers whose teaching duties are 29 periods a week rather than special education teachers whose duties are only 26 periods a week. At the same time, leave of absence without pay was made much less readily available. The first of these techniques of saving money was clearly illegal at that time: the then Minister for Schools made it clear in Parliament that it was contrary to the current Regulations.[7]

A year later, however, the government was proposing for 1984-5 that in future it should be the local school board, and not the Head of the school area, who should decide whether or not supply staff should be employed for the first two days of absence, a decision which could be made purely on economic rather than pedagogical grounds.   The proposal also said,

"if it is not possible to appoint teachers, the work may be covered some other way . . . There can be reasons to pay particular attention to certain groups of pupils, for example the youngest ones, and let them have a teacher or some other adult for all school days, while making lesser demands for other pupils whose need for supervision is not so great."[8]

So much for ideas of professionalism.

In most cases, local representation was enough to save posts.   The board members or the kommun finance officers often had not realised that their proposals were illegal, or that schools simply are not organised in such a way that the absence of one member of staff can be carried by the remaining teachers without making major changes in the composition of classes or the structure of the curriculum.   It is not that the union intervention was political: indeed, even in a very small town with only 150 teachers, all known to each other, an experienced Chief Education Officer who had himself taught in the town for many years at both Primary and Lower Secondary level, was genuinely unable to identify the political attitudes of the union representatives, nor was he able to distinguish in principle between the attitudes of the three main associations towards job saving.   He did, however, find it hard to negotiate with these associations separately over a matter of staff reductions in the very same school in which he had until recently been Head.[9]

In nine cases in 1983, however, the kommun was taken to the employment tribunal, arbetsdomstolen, In Ornsköldsvik, the right of the authority to terminate 14 class teacher posts was upheld.   In Sandviken and Kalix, the partners came to terms outside the court.   The remaining six will be decided in 1984.   In Umeå, 21 infant teachers' posts have been removed.   In Luleå, 23 infant and junior posts are involved: SL argues that some of these are qualified to take lower secondary posts which are being advertised.   In Gälve, 13 infant and junior posts are involved. In Mörbylånga, three teachers have been reinstated, but damages are being claimed.   In Säffle, five infant posts were removed even though the kommun know that other teachers had asked for leave of absence without pay.   In Göteborg, 23 infant and junior posts have been removed at the same time as the authority has advertised vacancies for special education teachers and there are also vacancies for basic school courses for adults.

The significance of these cases is essentially two-fold.   First, as the SL journal argued

> ". . . we can never accept that our members' security of tenure is to depend on the arbitrary use by local authorities of central government (specific) grant."[10]

Approximately half the expenditure on schools is met by central government grant;   and the regulations provide for some three quarters of the total resources of an authority to be devoted to statutory obligations in school provision.   A quarter of the resources may be devoted to the special needs of the authority, but it must all be used for proper purposes.

Secondly, the cases relate to the legitimate functions of different categories of teacher.   It has long been the practice in Sweden, as indeed is the case in most countries other than England, for the recognition of qualified status to be linked to specific educational and professional qualifications, to teaching specific age-ranges and specific curriculum areas, and to salary scales and conditions of service specific to the given qualification.   Thus the class teacher with 29 teaching periods differs from the academic subject teacher with 24 or 21 teaching periods, and so on.   There are, however, overlapping qualifications.   To give one specific instance.   A junior school teacher, qualified before the establishment of teacher high schools as an Elementary teacher (folkskolllärare) is qualified to teach children aged 7-14;   and if that teacher has subsequently taken subject academic qualifications to a given level he may also be

qualified to teach in the secondary school. If
that teacher holds an <u>ordinarie</u> post, an authority
would be required to find alternative duties if,
for example, falling rolls made it no longer
necessary to maintain the present junior school
post. Furthermore, if that teacher has been
teaching in the authority for many years, the
<u>kommunpoäng</u>, the 'points' earned for that service
count in preference to the qualifications of a
person from another authority who may seek a
vacancy elsewhere in the authority's service. At
a time of decentralisation of decision-making to
the <u>kommun</u>, questions of who is qualified to do
what and of what the <u>kommun</u> can require of those
whom it appoints become crucially important.

THE ÅSTORP AFFAIR

     This issue become something of a cause
célèbre in 1983 when Gösta Brodin, Chairman of the
school board in Åstorp, a small <u>kommun</u> in southern
Sweden, made public statements about teachers'
working conditions, and the apparent part-time
nature of their employment. Professionally a
carpenter, Brodin also moved a motion at the
woodworkers' annual congress that "the normal
working week for a teacher is effectively 30
hours" and he has in addition "a total period of
15 weeks holiday a year . . ." The resources of
the school can be better used: "In plain words,
that should mean 40 hours a week in the school",
and "holidays must be used for in-service training
together with local developmental and preparatory
work". The congress agreed on the need for a
commission to look at the way in which school
resources are used, and while agreeing that
teachers were employed full time, suggested that
the spread of work throughout the year might be
re-examined in new agreements on working
conditions. The impact of Brodin's comments on
teachers was inevitable, even if events in the
<u>kommun</u> became somewhat bizarre: some 30-40
teachers took sick leave, there were threatening
letters to Brodin's daughter, anonymous telephone
calls threatening reprisals against teacher union
representatives, and a 'mediating commission' set
up by the authority. Towards the end of the year,
the county school board stepped in to inspect the
schools, because 300 lessons had been cancelled
with teacher absences. The county concluded that
relationships "must be normalised as soon as

possible" and that "the school board has a common, heavy responsibility". Brodin remained in office, relatively unrepentant, and to widespread surprise supported by a majority of the local social democrat party.

The affair clearly demonstrated to all teacher unions the importance of formal agreements and the risks of local decisions adversely affecting conditions of work which should be the same all over the country.

WORKING HOURS

The question of teachers' working hours is far from new. In recent years, the three main teaching unions set up with government a major survey in 1964 on working conditions, known as ULA[11], which was to be used as the basis for negotiating agreements. In 1968, it was agreed that there should be a working year for teachers of 40 weeks instead of the then 39, with lessons of 40 minutes instead of 45. The unions also tried to reduce teacher class-contact time in conjunction with the introduction of the then new basic school curriculum, Lgr 69. The employers, who for the State are represented by an office called Arbetsgivarverk, SAV, were asked to suggest how the non-teaching time should be disposed, but no answer was then forthcoming. When ULA reported in 1971, after what was at that time the most expensive public enquiry that had ever been conducted, the teacher unions rejected it because it was based on the requirements of the 1962 curriculum and not that of Lgr 69. SL and SFL together were alarmed at the increased burdens imposed by Lgr 69 and together produced an agreed document, Lär Arb 73, as the basis for further discussions with the employers. The main stumbling blocks were on morning assemblies, travelling time and overtime, but the employers recognised only a common 'conference time', the so-called K-time, and the agreement of 1978 reduced class teaching contact time to 29 lessons with one hour for teachers' meetings, the need for which had grown with Lgr 69. In 1981, the Ministry of Education[12] invited the teacher unions to discussions on what part of the total working year should be at the disposal of the school. The unions saw this as an attempt to renegotiate the balance of teaching and non-teaching duties, and asked for a reduction of teaching time. The need

to confirm or amend the existing agreements made
SL wary of entering into formal discussions which
would have implied an acceptance of no sanctions
during that period. The Ministry did not reply to
the offer of less formal negotiation on the
specific issue.

The issue remains, however, very much alive.
In October 1983, SAV presented to the unions a
'sketch' of how it sees an agreement, as both
sides wanted, before July 1984. First, they want
a regulation covering a total working year of 1757
hours, as is required of all state salaried staff:
"in principle, an unchanged average volume of
teaching duties" but clarifying what that means.
SAV envisages a centrally negotiated agreement,
but one which delegates to the local authorities
the right to themselves to plan and share working
time for the individual teacher and/or teacher
groups.   Questions about the establishment of
posts and their content should not be the subject
of negotiated agreements, but as now should be
determined by statutory school regulations.
Finally, the sketch says

> "Of the total working time, a maximum of x
> per cent shall be carried out at the place of
> work and take place during the academic year
> (40 weeks) and in immediate contact with the
> academic year. Those days during term when
> classes are not held shall be free to the
> extent that the school requires the teacher's
> presence outside term-time."

In other words, days for sport or around Easter
other than the public holidays can be exchanged
for a certain (as yet unspecified) time during the
holidays. SAV also suggest that planning time
should be agreed locally; time in excess of the
agreed 'working time' would be regarded as
'overtime', and the present one hour a week
'conference time' would disappear.

The response to this from all unions has been
a series of local meetings which will ultimately
form for each of them their response to the
employer's suggestion.   There is some recognition
that the time when teachers are <u>visibly</u> at work
might be made more explicit. There is, at the
same time, abundant fear that in a period of
economic recession and limited public expenditure,
the proposals place too much power in the hands of
the local authorities. Swedish teachers do not
need to be reminded that traditionally the
academically qualified subject teacher was a high

status employee of the State;   or that the class
teachers had spent a hundred years seeking to
escape from the baleful influence of local
prejudice.   Under the 1882 elementary school
regulations, a teacher needed to show, in the
order given, "fear of God, honourable behaviour,
knowledge and ability to teach".   The degree of
objectivity by which the first two criteria might
be measured was always in question.   The phrase
"fear of God" remained until 1918, when it was
replaced by requiring membership of the Swedish
church (the local parish was responsible for
providing elementary education until 1958;   it was
the right of the local clergy to inspect schools
until 1930;   and the local vicar was ex-officio
chairman of the local school board.   As late as
1949, a teacher on first appointment had to give a
'trial lesson' before the local vicar.)   It was
only in 1963 that the specific requirements to
become a teacher were limited to knowledge as
measured by a prescribed course of study and
ability to teach as measured by the training
institution.   SL regard the SAV proposal with
undisguised scepticism.   LR bluntly regard it as
'unacceptable'.[13]

CONCLUSION

The contemporary economic and political
climate in Sweden is no longer as favourably
disposed to teacher unions as in the earlier days
of post 1950 school reform.   The extent of teacher
unrest in the late 1960s had been a major factor
leading to the extensive study of the ways in
which schools actually operate, SIA[14], which
seemed, along with participatory decision-making,
to herald a new era in which the social as well as
the instructional responsibilities of teachers
would achieve proper recognition.   Materially,
teachers are relatively well treated.   Their
duties, however, have tended to increase in an age
in which the working week has in general become
shorter.   Improved staffing ratios do not, in
themselves, compensate for this, nor for pressures
of what has increasingly become a parking place
for children and adolescents with the expectation
that its staff have total responsibility for both
behaviour and learning, but on terms decided by
the parents themselves.   The Swedish school is
subject to the same kind of criticism as schools
elsewhere[15].   Teachers as a group are expensive to

employ. Nationally and locally, they are increasingly seen as accountable, subject to the pressures of the society which employs them and which provides the schools themselves. How society controls these schools and teachers varies from time to time. Marklund, in a survey of the costs of schooling in relation to its development in an age of economy,[16] suggested that in the period 1946-62, there was strong control of resources, but weak control of regulations and goals; from 1962-76, resource control was weaker, but regulatory control was strong; since 1976, it is the control of goals which is strong relative to resources and regulations. He recognises that this is an over-simplified model: the periods of time are not exact, the categories of 'strong' and 'weak' are not absolute measures, and the three kinds of control overlap each other. Inasmuch as the model is useful, however, it would suggest that teacher unions, which are interest groups which influence and not political groups which determine the public's will, are likely to exercise greater influence in periods when resource allocations and regulations are the main means of control than they are in periods when determining goals is seen as the preferred control mechanism, as tends to be the case when resources are limited. It may well be, however, that the very demand to determine goals and to decentralise decision-making will itself be controlled by increasing need to allocate resources. If this were to happen, union influence may well rise again, and be all the stronger as a result of the knowledge and management skills developed in response to the attacks which goal-directed and finance-led policies are making on its members' interests. Time will tell.

NOTES

1. There is no study of teachers or teacher unions in Sweden. The most readily available in Swedish are Franzén, J. (1930) <u>Sveriges Allmänna Folkskollärarförening 1880-1930</u>, Stockholm; Sandberg, P. (1969) <u>Tjänstemanna-rörelsen, uppkomst och utveckling</u>, Stockholm, Tiden; Åberg, G. (1978) <u>Sveriges Smaskollä-rare och deras Förbund 1918-1966</u>, Stockholm, Sveriges Lärarförbund; in English, Boucher, L. (1982), <u>Tradition and Change in Swedish Education</u>, Oxford, Pergamon, Ch. 7

gives a brief descriptive summary.
2. Franzén (1930), op.cit.
3. Lagen 1976: 600 om offentlig anställning.
4. Lagen 1976: 580 om medbestämmande i arbetslivet.
5. Personal interview with Hans Hellers, Chairman, Sveriges Lärarförbund, September 1982.
6. Ibid.
7. Lärartidningen/Svensk Skoltidning, 12/1982.
8. Ibid. 29/1983.
9. Personal interview with Rune Åstrom, Skolchef, Tidaholm, September 1983.
10. Lärartidning/Svensk Skoltidning, 31/1983.
11. ULA (1971) Utredningen om Lärarnas Arbetsförhållanden, Stockholm.
12. Public administration in Sweden distinguishes between ministries, such as Utbildnings-ministeriet (Ministry of Education) which are responsible for the political decision-making of government, and 'boards' or 'offices' such as Skolöverstyrelsen (National Board of Education) or Statens Avtalsverket (Public Servants Employment Office) which carry out those political decisions. These boards are autonomous in that they have direct access to 'government' and to parliament, and are not responsible to any one minister.
13. Skolvärlden, 27/1983.
14. SOU 1974: 53, Skolans Inre Arbete, Stockholm. (The SIA report).
15. Husén, T. (1979) The School in Question, Oxford, University Press.
16. Marklund, S. (1982) Skolan och Svängremmen, Stockholm, Liber.

Chapter Six

MALTA'S TEACHERS AND SOCIAL CHANGE

Mary Darmanin

INTRODUCTION

        This article places organized teachers in
their historical and social context and examines
the ways in which teachers make and are made by
their history. It is premised on the theory that
the political alliances and antagonisms of
teachers colour and shadow their claims to
professional autonomy.
        In looking at the history of Maltese teachers
as an organized group, this article stresses the
interdependency of union activity with political
practice and concludes that such activity cannot
be divorced from political considerations. Policy
is politics. Nevertheless the article does not
make a priori assumptions about this dependency
but constructs, in a historical analysis, the
complexity of that relationship. Thus the first
section of the article serves to contextualize the
union activity of teachers in a colonized island.
Colonization created constraints that meant that
the Maltese teachers had to seek forms of pressure
that would be effective in the Home (sic) country.
Amongst these was the close link with the English
National Union of Teachers, which at the same time
that it afforded the Maltese union a direct line
to Parliamentary pressure in Westminster, also
meant alienation from other Maltese workers and
continued cultural imperialism by the British.
This is not to say that there were no alternatives
for the Malta Union of Teachers, but the history
of colonialism can be read in the unequal
relationship of the Maltese M.U.T. with the N.U.T.
        The second section, and a deliberate
chronological structure has been used so as to
stress the historical elements, shows the gradual

organization of the M.U.T. and its relationship
with a Maltese Department of Education as well as
with national governments. The British influence
is still strong for it is from the N.U.T. that the
Maltese union takes its line. At the same time
the union gains experience negotiating with
education department personnel and its success in
raising the status of the elementary school
teachers means a concomitant separation from other
workers. The political alliances made by the
union play a larger role than before and its
ideology of difference means that success in
gaining professional power is bought at the
expense of popular support.

The third section makes a case of the
relation between the M.U.T. and the Labour
Government of the seventies. With the election of
a popular workers' government alliances and
antagonisms dominate union activity and can be
read into such intimate details as the marking of
exam scripts. In such a climate debate on
educational policy and union rights is polarised
into political battles in which no one wins. The
confrontationism of the M.U.T. with the Labour
Government highlights the contradictions that
professional unions face when they claim that
interests arising out of their own welfare are
identical to national interest.

The political conflict that characterises the
Maltese case is not a unique experience. It is
not only typical of post-colonial societies but
what in capitalist societies are hidden structures
of power and conflict are, in such an arid and
bare scenario, stark reality. This case is
therefore only abnormal in the Freudian sense of
an exaggerated form of normality, and lends itself
more readily to a reading of conflict and
contradictions than the 'normal' concealed
structures of power in less unstable societies.

COLONIAL CONSCIOUSNESS

The Malta Union of Teachers (now The Movement
of United Teachers) began to organise in December
1919 following the Report of the Commission on the
Revision of Salaries of Government Employees which
proposed salary increases for all Government
employees except policemen and teachers.
Concerned with the anomalies between the grades
and salaries of Government employees, the union
strategy was two-fold. Firstly, it used its

affiliation to the N.U.T. in England and Wales to represent its claims at Westminster and secondly, it differentiated itself from sections of Government employees which were not working for professional status. When the Government passed the Malta Trade Union Council Constitution Act, in 1924, which excluded trade unions affiliated to foreign associations from membership the M.U.T. chose to continue its close affiliation to the N.U.T., and this was to colour its relations with Maltese organized labour. Injustices suffered under colonisation and aggravated by the Second World War were not enough to induce teachers to join the new union for all workers, The General Workers Union (1946). Its strategy seemed to be that which Poulantzas (1979, p.20) aptly described as 'petty bourgeois',

> "[not wanting] to break the ladders by which it imagines it can climb."

The growing willingness of the M.U.T. to participate on national negotiating bodies was founded on its ability to push for separate representation and bargaining when that form of pressure was most suited to its needs.

The twenty years of union activity between the wars was marked by its isolationist and corporatist form of struggle that was premised on an ideology of differentiation between mental and manual labour. The professionalisation of teachers' work was to be met by raising the standard of education in the elementary schools and in the training of their teachers.

Educational Expertise and Professional Power

Despite the disbanding and requisitioning of most of the schools and the dispersal of teachers all over the islands, the inter-war years saw a renaissance in teacher consciousness and union activity. The 1942 Ellis Report which describes teachers as 'a depressed class' and which made several important recommendations[1], amongst them that the method of appointing staff, the system of classifying staff into categories and the salaries they receive be revised, gave the teachers new hope and impetus. Equally important was its stress on secondary education which would mean an increase in staff and which gave substance to the union's calls for higher standards of teacher training. In 1942 only three male teachers were employed in the elementary schools and the history of the M.U.T. is in part the history of these men entering the profession, and their struggle to give teaching the same status as other professions. In this they were somewhat aided by a marriage bar which prevented married women from keeping their jobs after marriage. It is to the credit of the M.U.T. that at the same time that it acknowledged the prestige gained from an increase in the male complement it also consistently defended the right of its women members to keep their jobs after marriage. Though the question of gender differentials has been neglected here for reasons of space, it is relevant to note that questions of certification and pay increases for teachers in training dominated union policy in periods of increased male intake. This operated on two levels, firstly that in representing men the union had a larger chance of success especially in question of pay and scale issues for the dominant ideology acknowledged the right of men to a just and decent wage, and secondly that most of the men had had more chances of higher education and gave the M.U.T. scope to represent higher grades of the teaching staff. The affiliation of the University academic staff in 1979 was the zenith of M.U.T. success in trapping high status male members.

The Union was almost exclusively dominated by elementary school teachers, with Grammar and other Secondary school teachers registered in the Lyceum and Secondary School Teacher Association. The extension of secondary education and the introducation (by the newly elected Labour Government) of the 1946 Compulsory Education Act, gave the union the possibility of increasing its membership and vindicated its own war cry that the part-time system should be abolished[2]. There was a renewed thrust of professional expertise pushed through union recommendations to Government on items such as the size of classes, school buildings, the design of desks, entry requirements for the Lyceum and Technical schools, compulsory education, as well as on promotions, the filling of vacancies and the revision of salaries and grades. The union combined its professional interest in the quality of educational provision with a narrower interest in the returns that teachers would expect for the services they could and would provide. Manzer, (1970, p.82) shows how the National Union of Teachers also used this emphasis on technical power "to communicate to higher levels information about the provision of education in the schools which is indispensable to decision-making".

The expansion of the education sector meant that the Department had to maintain a level of co-operation with the union. The first step was the formal recognition and registration of the union in 1943 (<u>The Teachers' Magazine</u>, December 1944), followed by the representation on the Joint Committee and more significantly, the inclusion of Mr. A. Buhagiar, General Secretary of the M.U.T. in the Committee on Primary Schools (1948). The Committee's terms of reference "to make suggestions regarding the qualifications and training of teachers for such classes" as well as more specialised details of curriculum planning in the primary schools[3] showed, in the inclusion of the M.U.T. representative, the union's recognised competence as a professional organization.

It was precisely at this time of growing professional influence that the union made fundamental changes in its code of rules and laid out the procedure by which it was to operate for the next forty years. The Code of Rules not only incorporates the ideology by which the union stands[4] but also details the hierarchical structure of the union and its complex voting procedure[5]. Koziara (1975) claims that the M.U.T. has a "maximum amount of democratic participation within a minimum amount of hierarchy", but notwithstanding the democratic organization at school level, the Rules allow council members a wide margin of initiative. In many respects they are not bound by the decisions of the general meetings and the general secretary as a full-time employee and council member has a strong executive position. It is he who deals with every-day problems, he who negotiates with the Department on individual grievances, who calls for special meetings, issues press releases, participates in international conferences, prepares the agenda for council meetings, has access to officials in the Education Department and in toto represents the real power of the union. The structural position of Secretary carries with it power and prestige and the incumbent can use this ex officio power to his own[6] and the union's advantage. In the debate surrounding comprehensivization of the secondary schools there is a clear split between the leadership of the M.U.T. and the school teachers who support streaming and selection[7].

In 1946, however, the objective of the union

was to organise in line with the renewed emphasis on educational provision. The revised Code of Rules and the opening of a Teachers' Institute were the first steps along that road. The second strategy to acquire public recognition of professional status was to strengthen international credentials. Thus, the years leading up to the 1955 elections saw increased union involvement in international meetings. The struggle between the M.U.T. and the Lyceum and Secondary School Teachers' Association was fought as bitterly in the World Congress of the Teaching Professions as it was in Maltese newspapers (The Times of Malta, 24 September, 1954). The L.S.S.T.A. accused the M.U.T. of asking the W.C.O.T.P. to exclude it from participation in its meetings. The L.S.S.T.A. was a member of F.I.P.E.S.O.[8]. The M.U.T. had not associated itself with the secondary school teachers' association so as not to divide its members between F.I.P.E.S.O. and I.F.T.A. the primary teachers' international section. The M.U.T. had stressed its role as the representative of all teachers, regardless of grade or sector. It was important therefore that it received international recognition of this representation. As a founder member of W.C.T.O.P. it had always participated in meetings in its capacity of representative of all Maltese teachers and it was here that the L.S.S.T.A. contested the M.U.T. seat (The Teacher, October 1954).

The association with W.C.O.T.P. was exploited time and again. A report to the Congress on the status of the Maltese teacher who also used to negotiate with the Labour Government of 1954 for increased salaries, increments and a teacher training (The Teacher, July 1955). Similarly, a questionnaire for the same Congress (1957) revealed that the number of teachers employed with less than minimum qualifications was forty-five per cent in the secondary sector, whilst of the 701 temporary and emergency teachers in the primary sector, 478 possessed the necessary qualifications for college training, and the remaining 223 were not qualified enough to enter the training colleges. Such publicity gave the union more negotiating power than it could otherwise depend on. In the increasing friction between the Union and the Ministry, international backing enhanced the Union's standing in the eyes of its members and of the public. When the union's right to consultation on transfers and seniority was questioned by the Ministry, the M.U.T. responded by quoting from its correspondence with the Director General of the I.L.O. and cited as evidence Resolution No. 28 on the conditions of employment of teaching staff[9]. The exchanges between the M.U.T. and the Ministry were published in <u>The Teacher</u> (October 1955, p.6) and following this publicity, the Ministry ceded the right to consultation. Subsequently, M.U.T. protestation against the employment of emergency teachers (for the primary schools) who lacked even the minimum entry requirements for training college, led to a quick response from the Ministry and a promise to give these teachers training in as short a time as possible gave the M.U.T. further kudos.

EXPANSION AND ECONOMIC CONSTRAINTS

The M.U.T. continued to press for a basic scale and for comparability with appropriate grades in the public sector. A memorandum submitted to the Civil Service Commission (1956) was taken seriously by the Labour Government, though at this stage of national development and educational expansion, it was utopian to hope for any major changes in salary structure. The 1957 <u>Crichton-Miller Report</u> in reviewing the progress made during the past twenty-one months, recommended capital investment in teacher training and in new school buildings. The report saw the extension of secondary education <u>for all</u> as a natural corollary to the Compulsory Education Act. In Labour Government's efforts to live the letter of this report, it needed to expand the teaching complement to an unprecedented degree, hence the employment of 700 emergency teachers (<u>The Teacher</u>, August 1957). The request for salary increases at this stage were bound to cause consternation, not only because such an exercise would necessarily involve a revaluation of salary scales for the entire public sector, but also because of the uneven structure of the teaching complement. A shift in policy that requires a change in the size of the school population and increases the scale of recruitment, renders impossible the introduction of new restrictions upon entry in the interest of raising the qualifications of teachers. It also renders impossible substantial salary rises, especially in a centralized national system (as Malta inherited from British colonialism) since even a small increment granted to such a large number put greater demands on the budget than the claims of any other professional group (Jackson, 1970; Coates, 1972). In Malta the problem was multiplied by the need for rapid industrialisation, and though education was high on the list of priorities, the main thrust of investment went into capital expenditure such as the building of schools and technical institutes and residential training colleges and not on salary increases for special groups.

The Labour Government expressed its commitment to educational expansion by following the programme outlined in the Crichton-Miller report and by increasing staff in order to abolish the half-time system in the primary schools. Nevertheless the petitions of the M.U.T. regarding salaries and scales were taken seriously by the follow-up Miles Davies Report (1961). The terms of reference of the report[10] were to consider and make recommendations on the introduction of a system of additions and allowances on Burnham lines to teachers holding special qualification or occupying posts of special responsibility. Other specifications included: (a) the manner in which the proposed scheme is to fit within the framework of the new Government salary structure, and (b) the question of dealing with serving teachers not possessing the minimum qualifications for entry into the new pay structure. The report demonstrates the M.U.T.'s success in turning its international affiliations to its advantage. The M.U.T. had followed closely the N.U.T.'s negotiations with the Burnham Committee in England and Wales and had used it as a model for its own case. The M.U.T. used pressure in the House of Commons through N.U.T. affiliates there and it is significant that the Miles Davies Report was submitted in the troubled years of a suspended Constitution when Maltese internal policy was directly under British rule.

The internal contradictions that the union was experiencing through the new recruitment of teachers were evident to a large degree and in the same contradictory manner in the Miles Davies Report. Amongst them we find pressure to raise status through qualifications, and at the same time to keep the new membership that the unqualified emergency teachers provided; to represent the interests of the primary teachers who had been seconded to the secondary schools without the appropriate allowances; to keep differentials (graduate/non-graduate) without losing any members from the largely non-graduate primary teachers and at the same time to demand the introduction of a basic scale for all teachers with 'minimum qualifications'.

In the report, however, the M.U.T.'s insistence on the basic scale was ignored and additions were recommended for those who had approved college training, or who had graduated from the University. By the time an elected Government took office in 1962 the M.U.T. with help from Mr. J. Wickham Murray, O.B.E., M.A., their salary consultant (and former president of the N.U.T.) had made even stronger submissions which covered the interests of the non-graduate teachers in secondary schools, seconded teachers and unqualified emergency teachers. The insistence was on adequate remuneration for secondary school teachers and illustrates the union's long term plans to unionise the teachers of the, as yet, unopened secondary schools. The two leading parties (Labour and Nationalist) were talking in terms of secondary education <u>for all</u>, and the M.U.T. was making ready to extend its power base.

The M.U.T. shifted its pressure from the Department of Education and policy issues to the Ministry and corporate interests. The M.U.T. demands were at this stage out of proportion to the development of the education sector. Compulsory education for children up to the age of fourteen was a relatively recent phenomenon, secondary education was limited to a small group that entered a highly differentiated, tripartite system. Moves were being made to extend secondary education to all children regardless of performance at 11-plus. These changes needed support from teachers. Entry into the profession had to be flexible and capable of expansion and not subject to the restrictions that M.U.T. control of entry proposed. Just as Crosland could not agree to professional self-government at a time of teacher shortage (Coates, 1972, p.54), neither could under-developed Malta let its teachers determine its future. Controlled recruitment and a new system of allowances would have repercussions throughout the entire public sector (Hall, 1981). In retrospect the sixties seem to be marked by union participation in

Government planning reports and also in formulating its own policy objectives, such activity however to be limited in influence to the paper on which it was printed. M.U.T. recommendations were gladly received by the Colonial government of 1958-62 and the Nationalist Government of 1962-72, but sadly ignored by them, partly because of the impossiblity of fulfilling some of the more radical proposals and partly because of a lack of commitment to any real change.

The Malta case suggests that a union cannot hope to secure a place in formulating national policies and at the same time place its own corporate interests above all other considerations. A closer look at these interests, as expressed in the <u>Submissions to the Education Committee</u> (1962), <u>Redundancies in the Education Department</u> (1973) and in the negotiations with the Salaries (Anomalies) Commission shows that not only could the M.U.T. not resolve contradictions within the union itself but also that those interests clashed with national objectives and that to follow M.U.T. proposals in one area would be to create problems in others. The contradictions such as the proposals to control entry at a time of expansion, to accentuate differences between graduates and non-graduates through allowances and additions and at the same time propagate the ideology of a basic scale and a united profession, to call for a comprehensive secondary school for all and yet to resist the necessary redeployment and central planning that such a system would require, all point to one conclusion: that the early aims and alliances of the union prevented it from directing its attention to the real needs of a developing country. The parallel path (though with Malta lagging slightly behind) that the M.U.T. shared with the N.U.T. on issues such as Burnham Scales, control of entry and later, strike action, and refusal to provide services outside normal teaching activities, shows that Malta's teachers were responding more strongly to outside influence[11] than to internal realities. Often, the leadership of the M.U.T. in what can only be seen as an attempt to keep up with international practice, put forward as union policy documents so out of sync with the Malta situation as to make the real intentions of the union highly disputable[12]. It is with this history that we can

167

understand the obstructionist and often
provocative role that the union and its leadership
were to play in the crucial years of Malta's
transformation from colonized dependence to
republican development.

POLICY AND POLITICS

        In concentrating on specific historic moments
this article has so far treated as unproblematic
the relationship between organized teachers and
the State. It is important, therefore, before
going on to a more detailed case study on
relations between the M.U.T. and the Labour
Government, elected in 1972 and still in office[13],
to discuss briefly some of the theoretical
premises of this paper. Althusser's (1977, p.128)
concept of the relative autonomy of the state as
well as his distinction between state power and
state apparatus lends itself most obviously to the
type of argument I am making. That is, in the
political class struggle the state apparatuses may
survive in the ruling ideology even after
political state power has been acquired by the
rising class. The state is a site for political
struggle, a struggle in which one has to
distinguish between state apparatuses as supports
of the dominant mode of production, state power
that has to be acquired through hegemony or
coercion and class power whereby a class tries to
hegemonise different elements under its 'umbrella'
ideology[14]. Gramsci's distinction between
hegemony and coercion (p.57) indicates that a
rising class needs to hegemonise as many diverse
groups as possible before it can sustain itself as
the legitimate representative of the 'people'.
Laclau (1979, p.161) demonstrates that rarely is
class struggle found in its pure form, for to be
hegemonic a class must be able to articulate
different visions of the world in such a way that
their potential antagonism is neutralized. He
calls this 'popular-democratic' struggle[15]. These
theoretical distinctions bewcome meaningful when
one looks at the events surrounding the suspension
of the Constitution (and self-government) in 1958.
        The newly elected Labour Government of 1955,
with its young and radical leader Dom Mintoff,
inherited a series of structural problems.
Amongst them a heavily war damaged island, an
imbalance in labour power and no industrial sector
(apart from the naval dockyard) where productive

labour could create surplus (Kay, 1975). In the period between World War II and the mid-fifties net emigration amounted to 45,000 persons. Out of these, male emigrants over the age of fourteen numbered 26,085, of which 53% were considered to be skilled workers. According to the Balogh and Seers Report (1955) the islands lost about half of its skilled labour, mainly in construction and engineering. At the same time that the potential productive labour force was being depleted the unproductive labour of the state sector had grown to a disproportionate size. Gauci (1981, p.32) shows that this is typical of colonies where state employees tend to form part of a social stratum which acts as a stabilising force by helping to maintain a balance of power favourable to the metropolitan country. More than 45% of the work force was engaged in work oriented towards the needs of the British Government and when an independent Malta would not be capable of maintaining (Gauci, 1981, p.34). A general strike in protest against the proposed transfer of the Naval Dockyard to a British civilian firm (and with the threat of job loss associated both with this transfer and also with the rundown of the British Forces) led to civil strife. The strikers were attacked and arrested by the Maltese police, who acted on the orders of the British Governor rather than on the orders of their Minister and Prime Minister, Dom Mintoff. Mintoff, elected representative of the working class had not consolidated enough state power to control the state apparatuses. The British were constitutionally responsible for foreign affairs and defence so that the Army was controlled by them. The police, the other arm of the repressive state apparatuses, were nominally under Maltese national control but in reality they showed allegiance to the Governor and his allies.

The middle-class and their representatives were well served in the state apparatuses, and it was the industrial workers (and Mintoff supporters) who participated in the general strike. With the suspension of the constitution, the Nationalist Party and the Catholic Church exercised their own coercive power in a campaign against the Labour Party and its supporters. In this campaign, religion was the main ideological weapon, the Church condemned the leaders of the Labour Party and interdicted them. It articulated a discourse of catholicism and nationalism that excluded any elements that participated in the 'anti-clerical' Labour Party (Darmanin, 1978). The Church managed to hegemonise many groups in its attacks against the Labour Party (Boissevain, 1976) but Labour supporters were equally committed to their party and staunchly withheld these attacks, including physical assaults. The shift from hegemonic ideology to coercive impositions such as the withholding of the sacraments from Labour activists, the penalty of mortal sin on those who read or circulated Labour newspapers, or who voted for the Labour Party served to intensify the struggle and widen the already existing social divisions[16]. In 1958 with a state apparatus loyal to the British, a ruling class that had the open support of the Catholic Church[17], the elected representatives of the working class, occupants of state power, as they supposedly were, had to resign from office and let Malta fall completely under British rule.

Relations between this short-lived Labour Government and the M.U.T. had been good. Labour was attentive to the teachers' needs and demands and committed to educational expansion. The stress on technical education was consonant with M.U.T.'s reports and memoranda, as was the move towards extended secondary education. Nevertheless at the political level and outside government, teachers were well known supporters of the Church and Nationalist sympathisers. The open alliance of teachers with the Church is illustrated in symbolic and symptomatic episodes such as the opening of Education Week (1959) with a religious rally and a mass said by the same Archbishop who had condemned the Labour Party. Meanwhile local newspapers contained editorials and letters that praised the loyalty of the teachers to the Church[18]. The training colleges opened in 1954 were both run by religious orders though St. Michael's training college was not Church property. The whole tone of the training was religious rather than secular and it is important to add that apart from ensuring that qualified teachers were Catholics loyal to their Church, the colleges served to eliminate 'undesirable' elements from the schools. Apart from this insurance against secularisation of the teaching profession the other form of Catholic hegemony was in the number of teaching staff who were themselves members of a religious order. In 1957 out of a total teaching personnel of 3,051 in

Government and private schools, five hundred and thirty-one were religious.

The militant activity of the M.U.T. in the late 1960s was not simply a question of growing strength and sophistication but also a preparation for confrontation with a new Labour Government. The Nationalists had twice been elected on a 'mortal sin' ticket (1962 and 1966), the Labour Party had to accept some form of concordat with the Church so as to lift the damaging ban. In such closely run and won elections the dropping of the mortal sin proviso made it likely that 1971 would see a Labour victory.[20]

Stability and Status Quo

The nine years under a Nationalist Administration provided a period of relative stability for teachers. They did not have to emigrate because of the rundown of British troops; on the contrary, the state sector was a rapidly expanding arena of employment. The Nationalists, secure in their control of state power and unburdened by commitments to economic development and social change, adopted a laissez-faire programme.

The M.U.T. used this time to consolidate its technical bargaining power. The training colleges (residential since 1954) had produced a few generations of specially trained teachers. The plans to provide secondary education for all children gave the union the opportunity to influence the future of secondary education not only in terms of ensuring that its own expertise provided the backbone of policy-making but also that its members would carry out that policy in a context favourable to the M.U.T. A plethora of M.U.T. reports[21] argued clearly and constructively against the introduction of secondary education based on the tripartism already existing in Malta. The reports pointed out not only to the flagrant inequalities aggravated by the existing structure but also drew on human capital theory to show the damaging effect selection has on social structure and transformation.

Much of the argument was in line with that popularized by Sir Ronald Gould in his many visits to Malta[22] and the union continued to draw on international links for support. The General Secretary's report to the M.U.T. general meeting (23rd June 1970) articulated these elements of union narrative:

"the system being established in October 1970

is an outdated one which has been discarded
by all educationally advanced countries. The
M.U.T. has made it clear that it does not
agree with the tripartite system which the
government is adopting but the union promised
its full co-operation to make the best out of
a bad system. This co-operation, however,
will only be forthcoming as long as the
interests of teachers are to be safeguarded."
(The Teacher, October-
December 1970)

The M.U.T. blueprint for a new Education Act
envisaged reform of the primary as well as the
secondary schools and was as far-sighted as it was
premature. Far-sighted in that, apart from the
moral question of equal opportunity, it also laid
out the investment potential[23] of a comprehensive
system, and showed that the strict central
planning[24] of the Department was decreasing the
productivity of the schools. The linking of
selection at secondary level with a weak primary
school that only serves to train the few
candidates for the grammar and technical schools
constituted a major, and still relevant critique.
The reports showed careful planning by the union
in attempts to maximise both the opportunities for
working class children as well as opportunities
for professional enrichment of their teachers[25].
The prematurity of these plans was revealed at two
levels; first, in the expectations the union had
of its members as a radical and flexible group,
and secondly, in the expectations the union had of
the Nationalist Government as a source of social
change. In the first case, though the leadership
of the M.U.T. were conversant with[26] and probably
committed to comprehensivization, the majority of
their members, especially in the primary schools,
were not. The union had not taken it on itself to
instruct its members and except for speeches by
leadership at seminars, there was no real effort
to explain what a shift from tripartism to
comprehensives would involve. The majority of
teachers were not prepared for such radical
changes. In the secondary schools there was more
interest in these plans[27] but a report submitted
by the Graduate Teachers' Association (1970)
revealed a basic difference of opinion between
those who supported the M.U.T.'s official position
on selection at secondary level and those who,
like the majority of the M.U.T. members, wanted to
retain a selective system. The Graduates

Association (and among the authors of their report
are persons who now occupy top planning posts in
the Education Department) proposed two
alternatives; the first, identical to the
M.U.T.'s plan[28] for a two-tier system where
selection for <u>subjects</u> takes place at 13-plus, and
the second based on a comprehensive model of mixed
ability classes but with a curriculum aimed at
G.C.E. examinations. This second proposal
constituted a retention of the status quo, with
graduate teachers following the same curriculum
they had taught in the grammar schools[29].

The M.U.T. was politically naive to expect
that a Nationalist Government, having only
prepared for increased entry in secondary schools
by accelerating capital investment in school
buildings, rather than in expanding the teaching
staff, would be in a position to consider the
complex organisational redistribution of children
and their teachers that comprehensization
necessarily entails. It was equally naive to
expect a Government premised on social differences
to consider the abolition of a selective system in
the schools which in Hall's (1981, p.16) words

> "(were) seen as playing a function of
> maintaining and transmitting the unequal
> distribution of opportunities and rewards;
> generally, as performing the role of helping
> to fix, for each generation the general
> structure of social class . . ."

The slogan of 'secondary education for all' has
been described as a political gesture[30] on behalf
of the Nationalists, and it is significant that
these schools were opened on the eve of 1971
'free' (from mortal sin) elections[31].

Once the new secondary schools were opened in
1970, the already existing inequalities were
exacerbated by the acute difference in resources
in the established grammar and technical schools
and the new secondary moderns. In this scenario
it fell upon parents to put pressure on the
Government and thereby safeguard the interests of
their children. A group of mothers, co-opted from
parents in towns and villages, organized under the
name <u>Ommijiet Maltin Maqghuda</u> (United Maltese
Mothers)[32] and successfully exploited public
disquietude through media coverage to put forward
a strong case against the new schools. They
emphasized resource inequalities such as the lack
of textbooks, under-qualified teachers, shortage
of teaching staff (and many free lesson periods),

lack of school transport, and finally they contrasted the 5-year grammar school course with the 4-year course their children received in preparation for the G.C.E. 'O' level exams. The stress on concrete realities rather than ideological debates characterized O.M.M.'s parental sincerity. The M.U.T., approached by the women in O.M.M. made no effort to support these women who had to withstand personal vilification in Parliament[33] and who campaigned so strongly for their children's future. The M.U.T. was more concerned with fighting the battle for itself and since the selectivity of tripartism was firmly ensconced in the new schools as it had been in the established schools, the union turned the increased intake of pupils in the secondary schools to its advantage.

In the build-up to the 1971 general elections, the Nationalists had arranged a reorganization of salaries and grades in the public sector. The main thrust of the exercise was a percentage increase in salaries of public sector employees, to maintain differentials between grades and benefit the higher echelons of the civil service. Lower grades protested and made recommendations that were subsequently taken into consideration by the Salaries (Anomalies) Commission (1969). The M.U.T. in its turn also made individual claims, claims that were based on its ideology of difference (Johnson, 1977: Ginsburg, Meyenn and Miller, 1980). The M.U.T. general secretary's annual report (June 1970) is a useful indicator of the articulation of M.U.T. ideology.

"Under the various guises of regrading and reorganization salaries assessed by the Commission at a lower level than teachers' salaries were increased considerably by the extension of scales and through change of designations. When the Council saw that the relativities established by the Commission were being disrupted to the detriment of the teaching grades, it immediately made a formal request to the Minister of Education, Culture and Tourism for a regrading exercise in the Education Department. The M.U.T.'s view is that while the union is not against improved salaries for other government workers — indeed such improvements are welcome — teachers should not be discriminated against."[34]

The M.U.T. exerted pressure on the Salaries (Anomalies) Commission by refusing to co-operate with the Department's proposals for the recruitment of teachers for the secondary schools. The Department's call for applicants from amongst primary school staff was boycotted by the union, which insisted that those appointed as secondary school teachers be appointed unconditionally and not subject to performance in in-service courses and exams. It demanded their immediate appointment as full-time masters and mistresses. The union also refused to participate and be signatory to the Department's plan to change policy regarding eligibility for the appointment of heads of secondary schools and in the opening of the inspectorate (which had been the perogative of primary school headteachers to promotion to that grade) to secondary school staff. The M.U.T. finally turned to the first militant action in its history and called a strike, the object of which was to draw attention to the need of a reorganization of grades within the Education Department.

The strike of all teaching grades on Wednesday, 10th June 1970, was a massive success for the union[35]. It was the first real test of its strength and managed to unite its members on issues close to their immediate welfare. The Government's desire to keep the peace with teachers and carry out the much publicised opening of the secondary schools before the elections meant that prompt negotiations resolved most of the impediments to M.U.T. co-operation. The union continued to use militant tactics such as instructing members not to apply for posts in the new secondary schools until all differences had been resolved[36]. The action was well timed[37], the union could flex its muscles without expecting any backlash from a Nationalist Government on the eve of elections.

Premature Labour

The election of a Labour Government in 1971, with a narrow majority[38] and with a legacy of structural problems was to prove the main challenge to independent Malta. Political independence had come in 1964 but economic independence had to be constructed through hard work. In the educational arena despite the turbulent history of the Labour Party as a political force, and the uneven response of teachers to that history, there appeared grounds for consensus on objectives and practices. Both the Labour Government and the M.U.T. wanted an end to strict selectivity, both were committed to raising educational standards, to raising the standard of living of all Maltese and to balancing "the needs of a mass clientele with the requirements of qualified person power"[39]. The new Government granted an across-the-board cost of living increase of 15/- a week (in contrast to the percentage increases of the previous Government). The M.U.T. was invited to a four-hour meeting with the Minister of Education and Culture (who had held the same post in 1955-58 and who was arrested and imprisoned in the troubles of 1958) during which the M.U.T. were assured of their representational standing and where problems such as timetabling, appointments of emergency teachers and transfers were discussed. Arrangements were made to hold regular meetings between the Director of Education and the M.U.T. every first Tuesday of the month (M.U.T. Circular 9/72).

Labour had a tight schedule in trying to bring the provision in the new secondary schools in line with the established schools. Often this over-zealousness to push through new measures was experienced by the teachers and the public as political immaturity, not based on the proper planning that was expected of a serious government. Such was the case when the secondary schools were changed (by Department Circular 46-72) into comprehensives, exams were abolished both at 11-plus and in the other years of secondary schooling, the primary schools were no longer streamed. The union had not been consulted in this sudden change and the movement of teachers from one section to another as well as a change in pedagogical and curriculum practices was its legitimate concern. On the other hand, the union had for many years been advocating this system and the consternation of both leadership and members served to highlight the insincerity of their commitment to comprehensives. Lawn and Ozga (1981, p.117) say of British teachers

"If, by professionalism, we mean a concern for the quality of education, the resources of education and access to it by the working class, then this was the general view of the elementary school teachers, expressed in a number of (possibly contradictory) policies."

The professionalism of Maltese teachers was articulated in a discourse of self-interest, when it came to the crunch they refused to collaborate with the elected representatives of the working class.

The M.U.T. did not reject the policy change on ideological grounds for to do so would be to go back on their own words. They registered their consternation in a campaign of obstructionism and confrontation. Every move by government to organise the secondary schools was resisted by the union. The proposed in-service course and exam for emergency teachers was not accepted by the M.U.T. despite its declared policy of professionalisation through certification (M.U.T. Circular 25/71). Similarly, just as the number of children in schools increased to full capacity, the union directed members not to undertake midday and other supervision duties till they had negotiated a revised rate for these duties (M.U.T. Circular 24/72). Directives to the teachers of the first class in the secondary schools to teach only their subject specialisation created an acute shortage and undermined attempts to timetable an increased and mixed intake (M.U.T. Circular 7/73). Refusal to participate in in-service courses outside school hours (M.U.T. Circular 19-73), to correct annual exams (2/74) and similar incidents were common practice. In many cases the union was justifiably pushing for a larger say in department decision-making and planning, but the frequency and rigour of the obstructionism was construed as political manoeuvring rather than legitimate trade union practice.[40]

In this context, and considering the vehement and somewhat unfounded public criticism that the Minister of Education directed at teachers[41], it was to be expected that the rift between teachers and government would extend outside the educational arena and take on a more overtly political angle. Thus, though the teachers were subverting government plans to ameliorate educational provision and falling back on their historical allies in doing so, it is also true to say that the Labour Government in its attention to the rival General Workers Union, in its exaggerated personalized attacks on teachers[42], in its exclusion of the M.U.T. from planning stages, failed to hegemonise those teachers who would have been willing to co-operate in the transition to a non-selective system. The M.U.T.'s gradual political polarisation alienated some of its membership, and as with government, the loss of

177

consensus did not bring a reconsideration of tactics. A ban on dual membership (M.U.T. Circular 16/70) was followed by appeals to members "not to look at the union with dark glasses, because the day will come when those (critics M.D.) will realise that all that the union has done in these last years was only in the interests of teachers and of the profession in general."[43]

The Labour Government's 'marriage' to the General Workers Union ensured a period of industrial peace in the productive sector. In turn, these workers were assured of all the benefits of a welfare state, with cost of living increases, bonuses, and a more even distribution of power and wealth. The G.W.U. was to be party to all major policy formulations at Cabinet level (Koziara, 1975). The public sector, aware of the special attention given to productive workers[44] and fearful of losing their own privileges, called a one-day strike[45] in which different public employees' unions collected under the umbrella Civil Service Staff Organization[46]. The strike was not centred round any specific dispute but raised a series of issues for government consideration[47]. A memorandum to the Prime Minister (10th April 1972) articulated the main concern of C.S.S.O. that "Government employees will not be made to shoulder burdens not imposed on the rest of the community."

The M.U.T.'s participation in this strike (according to union sources 92% of all teachers followed the directive) marked the union's first industrial action on issues not directly connected or negotiable with the Education Department. It also marked the beginning of a move away from isolationist 'non-political' activity to direct confrontation with the Labour Government. Having taken that stand, the M.U.T. complied with C.S.S.O. follow-up directives (the work to rule, 17th November 1973) with withdrawal of midday supervision duties and sporadic strikes (24th November 1973).

M.U.T. circular 28/72 boasted that "the pandemonium in the schools effected, especially in the larger schools, is unbelievable and conditions will get worse as the action intensifies". A measure of agreement was eventually reached between C.S.S.O. and Government, with M.U.T. continuing unilaterally with its ban on midday supervision. Similarly, when the newly organized

Confederation of Malta Trade Unions (an umbrella union incorporating C.S.S.O. and virtually all unions not amalgamated in the General Workers Union, the C.M.T.U. is a predominantly white collar union representing amongst others professionals such as doctors and architects) met the Prime Minister to discuss recruitment and vacancies, the M.U.T., though an active member of C.M.T.U. made separate negotiations on salary arrears[48]. Thus, whilst on the one hand the union preserved its autonomy in order to forward the immediate interests of its members, on the other hand it became heavily involved in industrial action and alliances, the shape of which often jeopardised its claim to impartiality. A fly-sheet[49] circulated at the time of the first C.S.S.O. strike, raised, inter alia, the following questions:

Teachers
- Since when have civil servants been so close to you?
- Do you really know who the C.S.S.O. are?
- Why are you letting them use you?
- When the period of economic change of our country is over, will you be better off by this strike?
- Is this negative attitude going to help you as teachers?
- Is it true that you were happy under a Nationalist administration as Mr. Giglio alleged?
- In who's interest are you taking industrial action, for clerks, for drivers, or for...?

The sheet ended with a call to teachers not to let themselves be used for political motives and despite its anonymity it expressed the feelings of a substantial section of public opinion.

Within the union itself there was a growing reluctance on the part of some of the members to follow union policy and the Council "decided to exclude from all activities of the M.U.T. and to deprive from the privileges of membership all those members who are disregarding the Union's directive regarding the stoppage of midday supervision duties". Consensus was not forthcoming and 1974 saw more punitive measures; equally significant was the 'botched' election for M.U.T. Council (with discrepancies between the number of votes cast and counted) in the middle of troubled 1973.

Alliances and Antagonisms

The readiness of public sector employees to take militant action against the Government revealed the precarious balance of power. The working class had enough class power to elect its own representatives but this power did not incorporate state power and the state apparatuses both politically and ideologically remained the support of the still dominant middle-class and Nationalist Party. The antagonisms that followed were not articulated as class struggle, though I would argue that that is what the tensions expressed. The state employees did not identify themselves in class terms but as 'the other' the counterpose to the apparently dominant power bloc, the Labour Government. Their control of the state apparatuses and the relative weakness of the Government in the face of these antagonisms[51] was underplayed. In the strikes that were to follow, and leading to the 1977 Medical Association and Telecommunications employees strike, the main ideological articulation of antagonism was the ability of these sectors to present themselves as 'the people' or 'the workers'[52]. This discourse originated in October 1974 when the Malta Government Professional Officers Association, on the grounds that arbitration machinery promised to public servants in the 1971 Labour manifesto was not forthcoming, directed its members not to start work at the same time as industrial workers. Architects followed the directive, were suspended and later reinstated (Koziara, 1975, p.33). A mass rally for government employees was called "to defend fundamental trade union rights". The M.U.T.'s response was to follow attendance at the rally by another meeting in the Teachers' Institute, during which teachers were directed to participate in a half-hour strike on October 24, 1974. This half-hour was a token of the support that teachers were ready to give to the civil servants and professional unions and a telling warning to Government of their readiness to disrupt school life for political unionist activity.

In the intensification of clashes following Labour's re-election in 1976, the M.U.T. was at the forefront not only in promising backing to affiliated unions in the Confederation of Malta Trade Unions, but also in 'lending' its leaders to the so-called 'free trade unions'[53]. In the 1978 C.M.T.U. Congress the M.U.T. was represented by 28 delegates, with M.U.T. president elected vice-president of C.M.T.U. and the assistant general secretary of C.M.T.U., a well-known M.U.T. activist[54].

It is not possible, given the scope of this paper, to detail the capacity of trade unionism to neutralize or conceal class conflict, nor to show how the workers' movement in assuming its class identity and creating class barriers was unable to hegemonise popular struggles and fuse popular democratic ideology with its socialist class objectives into a coherent political and ideological practice (Laclau, 1977). But it is possible to indicate some of the obstacles that the Labour Government faced, and still faces, in transforming the islands. Despite the goodwill and sheer hard work that the majority of teachers show, their union, as an organized body, has often placed them as a stumbling block to quick and efficient change. In the years of heightened antagonisms, the Government tried to achieve some form of compromise with the M.U.T. For example, after the unfortunate rush-job on comprehensives, Labour reverted to a selective system. The M.U.T. kept its line of anti-selection and was strongly critical of the reversion[55] yet had shown no co-operation when Government implemented official M.U.T. policy. Bitter personal clashes between the Minister of Education and Culture and the M.U.T. were followed by a Cabinet reshuffle and a new Minister who negotiated the 1975 Reorganisation Agreement, wherein was detailed the new grade and salary scale for teachers. It was premised on a basic scale model and gave teachers the comparability with higher levels in the civil service they sought. With the re-election of Labour in 1976 both signatories went back on that spirit of negotiation. The Ministry often resorted to petty public attacks, to unexplained transfers of teachers from one school to another and other forms of disruption. The M.U.T. on its part continued its confrontationist tactics as with the strike on the removal of what had been two Carnival (Public) holidays (M.U.T. Circular 8/78). The response from the workers' movement is evidenced by the harsh criticisms that appeared in the press[56]. Amongst them an article 'Too many privileges' (Malta News, 15.5.78) drew unfavourable comparisons between the teachers and other workers[57].

Less serious obstructions, such as the

refusal "to fill in marks and calculate percentages in connection with the annual exams in Maltese" because "teachers are reminded that this is purely clerical work and should not be undertaken by them" (M.U.T. Circular 10/79), the directive to teachers in the new middle schools not to teach more than two subjects (M.U.T. Circular 14/80) and the perennial problem over midday supervision, contributed as strongly as did political clashes, to a breakdown of relations with the education Ministry. Meetings between union and Ministry personnel had ceased for over four years and were resumed in November 1980 with little chance of success.

In preparing for the 1981 election, the Labour Government made no attempt to placate teachers or involve the union more constructively in department planning. Given the union's history there seemed little scope for rapproachment and the M.U.T.'s Memorandum to Political Parties (1981) was an indictment of Labour policy. The memorandum did contain some constructive criticism that a new government could incorporate and develop into effective educational practice[58]. Unfortunately, the anomalous results of the election[59] meant a prolongation of conflict and instability. In this scenario the Nationalist Party felt secure enough to call an overtly political strike or stoppage of work as it was euphemistically put, the pretext was the celebration of the feast of St. Peter and St. Paul (June 29, 1982). The large number of public employees who followed the party's directive found themselves suspended and though they had their unions' backing (as with M.U.T.) the unions could not defend their case because it was ultra vires. Prior to that date confrontation between Government and the unions in C.M.T.U. had taken place over industrial disputes or agenda, and political manoeuvring had been concealed in popular-democratic or corporatist ideology[60]. The failure of the June 29 incident saw a retreat from this form of pressure. The M.U.T. in particular reverted to its role as a traditional pressure group in pushing its technical expertise (Coates, 1972, p.32).

CONCLUSION

The importance of the union as technical adviser and partner in education planning cannot be understated, but the history of the M.U.T.'s relationship with the Labour Government has made it difficult for genuine co-operation to take place. It will take more than intelligent proposals and memoranda for Government and the workers' movement to trust the M.U.T. and it will take more than reorganization agreements for teachers to invest total commitment in state education for the masses. The hard lessons of the last ten years have finally led to awareness of the need to compromise on both sides, and without being too optimistic I would venture that a renewed sense of tolerance will lead to consensus, and with it, new vigour in our schools. The issue of The Teacher (Winter, 1983) shares the same hopes:

"The appointment in September of Dr. C. Mifsud Bonnici, Senior Deputy Prime Minister, to the Ministry of Education immediately brought about a complete change of attitude and a lowering of temperature. So far the Movement's (M.U.T.) officials have had seven meetings with the new Minister (more than throughout the seven years tenure of Dr. Muscat) and friendly relations with the M.U.T. have been restored. It is only in such a climate of healthy industrial relations that teachers can perform their onerous duties efficiently and effectively for the good of their students and their country."

The main argument of this paper has been to stress the necessity of a political reading and placing of teachers and their work. In such an analysis neither class place (in a reductionist sense) nor teachers' self-concept as professionals, nor either a placing of teachers as reproducers of relations of production (and I would argue that the same transmitting of skills can also transform relations of production [Hogan, 1981]) are, in themselves, adequate to the task. Teachers operate as organized teachers in other moments of social life, those moments have implications not only in determining their place in the state apparatus but also in the teacher/client relation in the school. This emphasis on political alliances and practices is to register a concern with that type of research that isolates the world of the school (the teacher's domain) from the outside world of political antagonisms. In my view (and though, for reasons of space I have neglected to show how these 'extra-mural' practices impinge on the life of the school), there seems to be little theoretical, and still less social relevance to research that does not declare its politics in political assessments.

ACKNOWLEDGMENTS

I would like to thank Mr. A. Farrugia, General Secretary of the M.U.T. for generously making available all back numbers of The Teacher as well as M.U.T. Circulars and documents, and for giving me two extremely useful interviews.
I would also like to thank Mr. V. Magri, librarian in the Melitensia section of the University of Malta library, not only for fishing out obscure references but also for keeping the fan on in the long, hot summer of 1983, The Association of Commonwealth Universities for financial support and the University of Malta for giving me study leave, without which I would not have been able to write this paper.

NOTES

1. Ellis Report, 1942 recommended the opening of schools for the mentally retarded, the expansion of school medical services, the setting up of school Advisory Committees, adult education centres and a draft for the setting up of training colleges.
2. The Teacher's Magazine, September 1944, p.233, and the M.U.T. General Meeting of December 1944.
3. The Primary Schools (1948) Report of the Committee appointed by the Hon. Minister of Education (Malta Government Printing Office, 1949).
4. M.U.T. Code of Rules, op.cit.
5. Koziara, E.C. (1975) The Labour Market and Wage Determination in Malta, The Union Press, Valletta, p.31.
6. Manzer, R.A. (1970) Teachers and Politics, London.
7. Interviews I held with Maltese primary school teachers in 1982 referred back to the short period of no streaming. Not only were the majority of teachers in favour of streaming in the primary schools but amongst them were some who told me of strategies they had

adopted in their schools so as to avoid having mixed ability classes. Usually two or more teachers would agree to stream their classes by ability and to keep a classroom register of their classes as they now were. However, they also kept what amounted to a fictitious register of the mixed ability classes so that in the event of a visit from an executive officer they could quickly reshuffle their classes and pretend they had kept to official policy.

8. Federation Internationale des Professeurs de l'Enseignement Secondaire Official.

9. The Teacher, 1955, July Note on the Proceeding of theThird Session (Geneva, May 1954) of the Advisory Committee on Salaried Employees and Professional Workers.

10. Miles Davies Report (1961) On the introduction of a System of Allowances on the lines of the Burnham Committee for Teachers of the Education Department of the Government of Malta.

11. Especially the close contact with Sir Ronald Gould.

12. As late as 1983 (L. Orizont, 4 July and 7 July 1983) letters and articles in the press harping back to M.U.T. policy contradictions:
   L:M.U.T. qatt mhi kuntenta - The M.U.T. is never satisfied.
   L:M.U.T. anomalija fis-socjeta Maltija - The M.U.T. an anomaly in Maltese Society.

13. Last elections held in December 1981.

14. See Gramsci (1976), p.25 and Millband (1973).

15. Laciau, E. (1977) Politics and Ideology in Marxist Theory London: New Left Books for a more detailed discussion of State theory.

16. The Curia's Second Circular 'Directives to Confessors', May 1961, quoted in Mintoff, Dom. (1963 Priests and Politics in Malta, Malta: Freedom Press, p.37:
   "'Therefore His Grace and Archbishop condemns The Voice of Malta, il Helsien and the Whip as a dependant of the Executive of the M.L.P. author of this 'invitation'. This means that no one without committing a mortal sin (my emphasis M.D.) can print, write, sell, buy, distribute or read these newspapers . . . It is to be remembered that in the Church, all power resides with Her leaders, chosen by God and not by the people and that therefore when the Church, within her province, issues any

directives, no son of hers has the right to criticise, still less as has been said on occasions, to condemn her.'"

17. Mintoff, D. (1963) op.cit. p.29
"The Commissio Diocesena decided that no member of any Catholic organization may at the same time be a member of the Malta Labour Party under the present leadership nor in any way give it support or vote for it: because it is a great contradiction to claim to be a soldier of the Church whilst simultaneously giving support to those who are defying her."

18. Lehen is-Sewwa, 20 May 1959, in an editorial Maltese Teachers
"The respect and devotion of Maltese teachers towards the Ecclesiastical authorities is a very comforting and encouraging sign in the difficulties Malta is facing."
See also an article 'Red Menace' in The Times of Malta, 6 May 1959.

20. Mr. G. Borg's letter to The Sunday Times, Malta (20 November 1983) on voting patterns in Maltese elections, also Boissevain, J. (1974) 'Conflict and Change' in Davies, J. ed. (1974) Choice and Change, Essays in Honour of Lucy Mair.

21. Report on Education in Malta, Malta Union of Teachers, 1967 Lux Press, "Supporting Statement" ghar-Rapport dwar l'Edukazzjoni f'Malta M.U.T., 1969, Lux Press.

22. In 1969 to address an M.U.T. seminar on Education and Change, his speech dealt with the transition from a selective to a comprehensive system. (The Teacher, April-September 1969). During another seminar Education in the 70s, Sir Ronald stressed the political power of teachers as well as attacking selectivity (The Teacher, May 1970).

23. 'Supporting Statement' (1969) op.cit. p.3.

24. Report on Education in Malta (1976), op.cit. p.20 on the importance of flexibility and diversity.

25. Report ibid.
"We are, hereunder, including the widely acknowledged principal advantages of the comprehensive system; a) the abolition of the unreliable entrance examination; b) the breaking down of social barriers, erected by the segregated system and the promotion of social unity; c) children of different

interests and levels of attainment mix freely together." (p.9).

26. Through participation in international meetings.

27. M.U.T. Report on Education in Malta, 1967.

28. The M.U.T.'s plan was to have a three year post-primary comprehensive school after which children would transfer to specialised centres, largely corresponding to grammar, technical and trade/vocational model.

29. The Graduate Teachers Association included 'safeguard' clauses in their second proposal that, possibly, there should be no streaming. If any streaming has to be done, it should be based by aptitude. (g) that these secondary schools are to provide a 5-year course of general education, leading to a G.C.E. with school leaving classes in the year previous to compulsory school leaving age.

30. Letter by Benny Camilleri, 19 April 1973, The Times of Malta, for one example.

31. October 1970. Elections were held in June 1971.

32. O.M.M. is the Maltese for mother. L-Orizzont, 17 February 1971, also the Memorandum sent to the Minister, 29 September 1970, a report on a meeting of O.M.M. with the Director of Education (L-Orizzont, 17 February 1971).

33. In an interview I held with Mr. Farrugia, General Secretary of M.U.T. (22 Autust 1983) I was told that the M.U.T. had been contacted by the Committee of O.M.M. but that this contact had not been followed up by M.U.T.

34. The Teacher, January-March 1971, p.5.

35. M.U.T. Circular 11/70. In the primary schools nearly all the teachers participated, in secondary schools out of 700 members, 500 were on strike. In Gozo only 13 teachers went to work.

36. The Teacher, October-December 1970, p.5.

37. Compare this with the sanctions campaign and salary disputes of the N.U.T. in 1967-70, the build up to strike tactics reinforced by obstructionism. Coates, R.D. (1972) Teachers' Unions and Interest Group Politics, Cambridge University Press, pp. 67-75.

38. A one seat majority.

39. In the words of the M.U.T. General Secretary The Teacher, 1971.

40. See note 12 supra.

41. One such attack was when the Minister, addressing the Cottonera boys secondary school "told members of a students' council to watch out for teachers who are often absent from their duty and report them to the Headmaster, or the Director of Education, or even, if necessary, to her personally, so that the Department of Education would investigate whether these absentees cases were genuine." The Sunday Times of Malta, 19 May 1973.

42. Apart from public attacks such as the Minister's Prize Day Speech at the former Lyceum, 22 June 1973, where he accused teachers of using school electricity for their personal use, there was also an increase in transfers even of the whole M.U.T. school committee (M.U.T. Circular 27/72).

43. President's call on members to rejoin the union (M.U.T. Circular 10/76).

44. Used here in the narrow sense of productive, i.e. creating surplus value, see Kay G. (1975) Development and Underdevelopment: A Marxist Analysis, London: Macmillan (for similar usage).

45. Koziara, E.C. (1975) op.cit. 17 unions represented government employees who numbered approximately 20,000.

46. M.U.T. Circular 27/72 and The Teacher, December 1972.

47. Amongst them (a) cost of living increase; (b) recruitment and promotions; (c) arrears and salaries; (d) negotiating machinery.

48. M.U.T. Circular 17/73.

49. Which I found in an M.U.T. box file in August 1983.

50. M.U.T. Circular 7/73.

51. Following Miliband R. (1975) The State in Capitalist Society, London, for distinction between State and Government.

52. Laclau (1977) op.cit. p.114 argues that "the struggle for the articulation of popular-democratic ideology in class ideological discourses is the basic ideological struggle in the capitalist social formations"; also Poulantzas, N. (1978) Political Power and Social Classes, London: Verso; and Poulantzas, N. (1979) Classes in Contemporary Capitalism, London: N.L.B., p.290.

53. M.U.T. Circular 12/78 and 14/81 calling on

M.U.T. members to contribute 25 cents to the C.M.T.U. "The Confederation and its affiliates have during the last decade been engaged in a relentless struggle to preserve democratic trade unionism in Malta. The battle is by no means over, and attempts to smash the free trade unions are likely to be intensified in the coming months."

54. M.U.T. Circular 22/78, December 1978.
55. M.T.U. Circular 10/83, Memorandum to Political Parties 1976, 1981.
56. L-Orizzont, 13 May 1978 'L-Karnival u l-Qaddisin' Carnival and Saints, and 17 May 1978 'Toninu ma jmurx skola' Toninu skips school (plays truant).
57. An article 'Too Many Privileges' Malta News, 15 May, 1978:
   "Monday and Tuesday have been removed as Carnival days for all workers in Malta and these include members of the Confederation of Trade Unions of which the M.U.T is also a member. The majority of the members of the C.M.T.U. also enjoyed halfday leave on these days, yet none of the C.M.T.U. members has struck.
   We cannot see why, therefore, the M.U.T. is making all the fuss. Primary and secondary school teachers already enjoy two and a half months holidays in summer on top of other breaks during the scholastic year. All told they have 60 days off during the year compared to 20 days of all other workers in Malta. If there is discrimination, this is not against the teachers who still enjoy enormous privileges which the Labour Government has allowed to go on for too long, in spite of its efforts to stabilise social justice in Malta."
58. Especially the emphasis on resources and the plan for a two-tier secondary school.
59. With Labour winning a majority of seats in Parliament but the Nationalists gaining the majority of votes, approx. 1% more than Labour.
60. For example the C.M.T.U. rally supporting Solidarnosc in January 1982.

REFERENCES

Althusser, L. (1977) Lenin and Philosophy and other Essays, London: New Left Books.

Darmanin, M. (1978) 'Ideology: Religion and Nationalism in Malta 1955-64' unpublished Master's thesis, University of Essex.

Gauci, P. (1981) Planning for development in a post-colonial small island economy: the Maltese experience, (M.A. Regional Planning and Resource Development, University of Waterloo, Waterloo, Ontario, 1981).

Ginsburg, M., Meyenn, R. and Miller, H. (1980) 'Teachers' Conceptions of Professionalism and Trade Unionism; an ideological analysis' in Woods, P. (ed.) Teacher Strategies Explorations in the Sociology of School, London: Croom Helm.

Gramsci, A. (1976) The Prison Notebooks ed. Hoare, Q. and Howell Smith, G., London: Lawrence and Wishart.

Hall, S. (1981) 'Schooling, State and Society' in Dale, R., Esland, G., Fergusson, R. and Macdonald, M. Schooling and the National Interest, Sussex: The Falmer Press.

Hogan, D. (1981) 'Capitalism, Liberalism and Schooling' in Dale, R., Esland, G., Fergusson, R. and Macdonald, M. Schooling and the National Interest, Sussex: The Falmer Press.

Jackson, J.A. (1970) ed. Professions and Professionalization, London: Cambridge University Press.

Johnson, T.J. (1977) Professions and Power, London: Macmillan Press.

Leggatt, T. (1970) 'Teaching as a Profession' in Jackson, J.A. ed. Professions and Professionalization, ibid.

Miliband, R. (1973) 'Poulantzas and the Capitalist State' New Left Review, No. 82.

Ozga, J.T. and Lawn, M.A. (1981) Teachers, Professionalism and Class, London: The Falmer Press.

PART II

PROBLEMS IN THE LABOUR PROCESS

Chapter Seven

MERIT PAY AND ORGANIZED TEACHERS IN THE U.S.A.

Wayne J. Urban

The subject of merit pay for teachers has
recently come to the fore in the public
discussions of American education. The spark for
this movement was provided by President Reagan's
National Commission on Excellence in Education and
its report, <u>A Nation At Risk</u>[1]. In that report,
after substantial critical discussion of American
schooling, the Commission makes a number of
recommendations grouped into categories such as
Content of Schooling, Standards and Expectations,
the Time to be devoted to various subjects,
Teaching, and Leadership and Fiscal Support.
    Under the Teaching category, we find seven
recommendations, including the following
stipulations relating to merit pay:
        "Salaries for the teaching profession should
        be increased and should be professionally
        competitive, market-sensitive, and
        performance-based. Salary, promotion,
        tenure, and retention decisions should be
        tied to an effective evaluation system that
        includes peer review so that superior
        teachers can be rewarded, average ones
        encouraged, and poor ones either improved or
        terminated."[2]
This suggestion has provoked a number of
initiatives and reactions at the local state and
national levels. The topic that interests us here
is the reaction of teacher organizations to merit
pay proposals from the National Excellence
Commission and other national, state, and local
bodies. This reaction, which has not been
uniformly negative, is surprising to anyone
familiar with the history of teacher organizations
and their position on the merit pay issue. Before
accounting for the contemporary reaction, and its

difference from the past, a look at merit pay proposals and organized teacher reaction to them in the past is in order.

Merit pay plans have been a controversial part of the American educational picture at least from the earliest part of the twentieth century. An integral part of the controversy, when teacher organizations have existed in places where merit pay has been proposed, is the implacable opposition of the organizations to the merit pay plans.

As early as in 1903, Chicago's organized elementary teachers, through their Chicago Teachers Federation, fought the imposition of a merit pay plan which involved examinations and supervisors' ratings of experienced teachers. This merit plan was introduced shortly after teachers had been granted a salary scale with regular increments for each year of service. The fact that the scale had yet to be fully funded indicated to teachers that merit ratings would provide a rationale for not funding the salary scale. In 1915, Atlanta's organized teachers fought an attempt by the school board to substitute a merit system of pay for the existing salary scale. Though the Atlanta Public School Teachers Association was initially unsuccessful in opposing merit pay, the results of the first year under the merit system, a net reduction in the total system payroll of $15,000, confirmed the organization's worst fears about the intention of the board, namely to punish some teachers and reduce the total payroll, and sparked the teachers to renewed agitation against the merit system which soon proved to be successful. The early twentieth century experience of merit rating and salaries based on the ratings was not limited to Atlanta and Chicago. Minneapolis, St. Paul, Cleveland, and several other American cities saw battles between superintendents and teachers over merit rating plans and other administrative reforms which served to consolidate the super-intendents' executive powers and bureaucratic control over the schools.[3]

These early battles over the merit rating and merit pay issues found teacher organizations, which had just recently won or were currently engaging in battles to establish regular salary scales, bitterly fighting the merit pay principle as a throwback to the earlier system of teachers being rewarded on the basis of the local board's opinion of their worth. Merit pay proposals continued to spring up from time to time in the 1920s in various localities, as did organized teacher opposition to them. By and large, teacher organizations successfully fended off merit pay, though they often did not eliminate the actual rating of teachers by superiors. The rating process proved to be one of a number of steps which provoked a tension between teachers and principals that had not been present previously. Teachers and their organizations were not happy with this situation but consoled themselves with the understanding that the defeat of merit pay plans preserved the seniority principle and the salary scale which institutionalized it. Teacher organizations, like most occupational organizations, have been vigorous protectors of seniority rights since that time.

In the 1930s, the schools in almost every American locality were beset by a financial crisis precipitated by the Great Depression. In this climate, merit pay receded from the forefront as an issue, replaced by the struggle by all teachers and administrators to maintain existing levels of school support, or at least minimize the budget cuts which were often proposed and implemented. World War II brought still another set of circumstances to the schools which forced the merit pay issues into the background. The schools concentrated on helping to wage the war effort and struggled to find faculty to staff the classrooms abandoned by men called to serve in the armed forces and women who left the schools for the higher paying factory jobs which often opened up to them because of the shortage of able bodied men to do this kind of work. Shortly after the war's end, however, the merit pay principle once again surfaced as an issue of controversy.

Several factors contributed to the rise of merit pay as a topic of controversy in the post-World War II period. A great deal of mobility out of teaching during the war meant a concern for stability in teaching once the war was over. This stability was thought likely to be accomplished through higher salaries. The realization that the war and post-war years were producing a baby boom which would soon ovetake the elementary schools also was cause for concern about salaries high enough to attract the number of teachers which would be needed to staff the schools. Merit pay was a way to raise some salaries without having to raise all salaries. Neither of these factors, however, was the primary reason behind the movement for merit pay. Merit pay was proposed, it seems, mainly because teachers in most American big cities and many smaller cities and rural areas were being paid on the basis of a 'single salary scale'. What the single salary scale provided was equal pay for equal work for all teachers. Prior to enactment of the single salary scale, men teachers were often paid on a different scale and received more than women, elementary teachers were often paid less than secondary teachers, and black teachers were sometimes paid less than white teachers. With the enactment of the single salary scale, however, all teachers, whatever their sex, level taught, or race, were paid according to their place on the salary scale. One's place was determined on the basis of number of years taught and amount of higher education (college and university study) completed. Teacher organizations had worked hard in the early 1940s and immediate post-war years to institutionalize the single salary scale and, like the teachers three and four decades earlier who fought merit pay as an attack on the principle of a salary scale, teachers and their organizations now saw merit pay as an attack on the recently won single salary scale.

One of the first of the post-war attempts at merit pay was undertaken in the state of New York in 1947. In that year, in response to a push from the New York State Teachers' Association and groups of New York's school administrators, the legislature adopted a new set of state salary minimums for teachers as well as specified yearly increments. These increases were substantial, raising the state minimum from $1000 per year to $2000 per year, but they were not uniformly felt in localities throughout the state, since many communities already paid well above the minimum by supplementing the state moneys with locally appropriated funds. Nevertheless, the legislature felt that it was making a significant increase in its financial commitment to the schools and, wanting not to make a simple across the board commitment, specified that some of the proposed increments would be granted on the basis of the merit principle, rather than on the basis of seniority. The legislature empowered the State Commissioner of Education to set up a committee to decide how merit would be determined. The committee recommended that merit be based on evaluation of performance by superiors as well as other factors such as service in outside of school organizations like the Boy Scouts, Girl Scouts, Rotary and Kiwanis. Its recommendations proved to be quite controversial, particularly among the state's organized teachers.[4]

At the National Education Association convention in June of 1947, New York's teachers were instrumental in getting a report on teachers' salaries approved that reflected the point of view of most of the organized teachers. Among the provisions of the salary resolution was one that spoke specifically to the subject of merit pay.

"Second, early in our discussion the group considered and rejected so-called merit-rating schemes as related to salary schedules. These rating schemes, now commonly advocated by tax fighting groups, and others with special interests, are recognized throughout our profession as being incomplete and inadequate measures of teaching performance. Yet such schemes are being urged in many states, even to the point of state legislative enactments. We, in the profession know how destructive to morale so-called merit ratings can be and how easily these devices lead to favoritism and violation of professional ethics."[5]

In 1948, New York's teachers were again active at the NEA convention in spearheading opposition to merit pay. One New York teacher proposed a resolution on merit pay that after a number of preliminary clauses stated: "Be it resolved: That salary differentials be based only on objective evidence of professional preparation and successful experience; and that subjective merit rating for salary purposes be rejected as invalid, unreliable, and detrimental to professional morale"[6]. In subsequent discussion of that resolution, another New York teacher who had been called in to serve on the state committee to determine criteria for merit described meetings of teachers, held by the committee throughout the state, where "at every one ... the opinion of the teachers was unanimous against this law ..."[7]. He went on to say that the law was used to avoid paying the top salaries on the scale to all teachers who qualified, since only a certain per cent of teachers were to be paid the increment at the top step of the scale, and that it used irrelevant criteria to determine merit such as participation in the Boy Scouts. Other teachers from Ohio, Indiana, Michigan, Washington, and Massachusetts added their voices to those of their New York colleagues against the merit system.

The merit issue continued to be discussed at NEA conventions for the next several years and, in 1951, the organization went on record reaffirming its traditional support of the single salary scale and opposition to merit pay.[8] By this time, New York's teachers had successfully opposed merit pay to the point that the governor and legislature amended the merit pay provision, removing the percentage limits for those who could receive merit pay and applying the merit principle to salary increments only in the last year of a non-tenured teacher's probationary period and in the twelfth year of service. These provisions signalled the effective end of the merit pay fight in New York state. However, the issue would continue to be debated in the educational literature throughout the 1950s and into the 1960s.

In 1952, for example, the Harvard Educational Review devoted an entire issue to the teachers' salary problem. In this issue, the NEA had a chance to air at length its views on the topic. In an article on teachers' salary schedules, two members of the Research Division of the NEA began with a reiteration of the Association's commitment to the principle of equal pay for equal work and its implementation in the single salary scale. With regard to the single salary scale, the authors commented that it represented "the best thinking of the profession" to that point in time, that it gave credit "for experience under the assumptions that quality of work increases with professional maturity", and that it allowed teaching to stand as "a career, with the higher rewards for those who devote their lives to the profession"[9]. Moving on to discuss the 'merit principle', the authors noted that merit rating was borrowed from the business world and was usually advocated by businessmen, most of whom erroneously assume "that teaching has many of the same characteristics as the mass production lines of industry", and believe "in the objectivity and reliability of current rating techniques". Not all business advocates of merit pay were misguided, however, according to the authors.

Some "are motivated by a general conviction that through merit rating linked with salary schedules the total cost of schools can be reduced"[10].

The authors concluded that most "teachers object to the application of existing merit rating schedules to salary schedules" and that the NEA had long been on record against merit rating. Reflecting the fact that the NEA had administrator as well as teacher members, the article did defend the practice of evaluating teachers, but again pointed out that any teacher evaluated as competent should make normal progress on the salary schedule. After discussing a number of other aspects of teachers' salaries, the authors ended their discussion with a lengthy quotation from an official NEA document on 'Professional Salaries' which contained the following explicit repudiation of merit pay: in salary matters, "Equity of treatment to classroom teachers of like qualifications and experience" is a must.[11]

Despite the success of teachers in stopping merit pay in New York state and in several other places, merit pay schemes continued to pop up in several states and local school districts throughout the 1950s and 1960s. The educational journals also continued to run articles debating the merits of the issue and keeping track of the latest places to implement and give up their merit pay schemes. Few, if any, authors doubted the fact that most teachers opposed merit pay plans. For example, the Journal of Teacher Education devoted its June, 1957 issue to the topic of Merit Salary Schedules for Teachers. In this issue, again the NEA Research Division was responsible for an article on the topic, but this time the opposition of teachers to merit pay, though mentioned, was not referred to as favourably. The tack of this article was to describe the various attempts to implement merit pay, to define carefully what did and did not constitute genuine merit pay proposals, and to indicate the great difficulty in arriving at a fair merit pay plan[12]. Despite this apparent softening in the NEA Research Division's position, none of the other articles, though some favoured merit pay, argued that teachers supported merit pay plans.

The minutes of the NEA convention for that same year, 1957, indicate that though some association staff might seek a more moderate position on the merit pay issue than flatfooted opposition, the Department of Classroom Teachers, the sub-unit of the association most attuned to the concerns of working teachers, was not interested in moderation on this issue. In a discussion of a resolution on merit pay, a former president of the Department of Classroom Teachers noted that the Department, in its 1956 and 1957 meetings as well as in a special conference called on the topic during the previous year, had consistently opposed merit pay plans because teachers considered the merit principle to be "an objectionable thing" which has "invariably resulted in failure" wherever it has been tried, and has "harmed the students and the schools and teachers". This entire debate on the issue of merit pay during that year revealed that some elements of the NEA no longer felt that simple opposition to merit pay was a sufficient position for the association. Speaking of the NEA's public relations image and efforts, these elements tried to make sure that the association not appear as simply an opponent of merit pay. Thus, the resolution which was passed contained two paragraphs, one of which opposed merit rating or what the resolution called "subjective rating" and a second which called for continued efforts to "discover means of objective evaluation of teaching performance". Thus, one could have concluded that the NEA position was in opposition to existing merit pay plans, all of which involved 'subjective' rating of teachers by their principals and other administrators, but that the NEA might not be in opposition to a merit plan that would use some kind of 'objective' rating scheme to arrive at salary recommendations.[13]

The NEA's major rival for the organizational allegiance of teachers was the American Federation of Teachers. A part of the larger labor movement through its affiliation with the American Fereration of Labor, the AFT did not have to make as many turns and twists on merit pay and any other issues as did the NEA which strived to maintain its administrator members. The AFT was limited to classroom teachers only as its members and thus was freer to advocate a strictly pro-teacher position on merit pay and other issues. Of course, because of its single minded advocacy of teacher interests and its affiliation with the labor movement, the AFT did not have as ready access to educational journals for its opinions and positions as did its less militant rival. In 1961, however, the AFT did break into the professional discussion of the merit pay issue.

As part of a five article series on merit pay which appeared in the educational journal the <u>Phi Delta Kappan</u>, Carl Megel, president of the AFT discussed the AFT position in an article entitled 'Merit Rating is Unsound'. Megel noted that merit rating tended to appear in times of high living costs and to be used as a way to pay high salaries to some but not all teachers who deserved them. He stressed that the AFT had been opposed to merit rating for over thirty years and that it had seen merit pay plans fail in city after city. While merit pay had some allure in an ideal world, Megel contended that "it is the impossibility of fairly judging and rating one teacher above another on a dollar and cents basis which makes the merit system unworkable". He contended that the only way to pay teachers fairly was "by the use of an adequate single salary schedule based upon training and experience". He then proceeded to list the foibles of merit rating including the following points: merit rating rewards conformity, puts a premium on acquiescence in teachers, fosters competition rather than co-operation among teachers, strikes at the job security of teachers, cannot improve the quality of education, will not relieve the teacher shortage, and does not reward superior work. The AFT alternative, according to Megel, was "a sound, satisfactory salary schedule" which will both "interest competent, capable young men and women in choosing teaching" and "permit the experienced teachers to perform their services in an atmosphere of dignity and personal satisfaction".[14]

The 1960s were a decade punctuated by a good deal of controversy in various aspects of American life, and education proved to be no exception. the most notable activity among organized teachers in this decade was their frequent recourse to strikes to win various concessions from local education authorities. Most of these strikes were undertaken by AFT local organizations in the largest cities of the country, particularly New York City. Merit pay was not a key issue in these strikes or in much of the educational literature in this decade. Given that in strike situations and in the early collective bargaining situations that often followed strikes teachers took the initiative in making proposals to school boards, this is hardly surprising. By the end of the decade, however, the controversies surrounding merit pay or merit rating were to be resurrected, though this time under a new name, differentiated staffing.

Differentiated staffing proposed to separate teachers into several roles and/or positions, and pay the inhabitants of the different positions at different rates. An early article in favour of differentiated staffing attempted to distinguish it from merit pay plans which had failed, but the authors tellingly noted that what differentiated staffing shared with merit pay was the repudiation of the single salary scale. "So long as we have the single salary scale", argued the authors, no one will get the highest amounts which should go to the highly specialized teachers who would advance to the highest ranks of the profession[15]. While differentiated staffing plans varied considerably from district to district, they usually involved some expansion of steps in a teaching career on a ladder similar to that found in the university faculty rankings of Assistant, Associate, and full Professor. For example, one California school district differentiated its teaching staff into the positions of Associate Teacher, Staff Teacher, Senior Teacher, and Master Teacher. Of course, since teachers advanced through the ranks, not automatically through seniority and education, but rather through some process by which their work was judged as satisfactory and worthy of promotion, many teachers and teacher organizations were suspicious of these plans as merit pay in disguise. The arguments of advocates did little to allay this suspicion. The article illustrating the four tier plan discussed above, for example, noted that it was but one of several plans and remarked that what all plans had in common were the elements of "job responsibilities, functions, and rewards (typically monetary)"[16].

Differentiated staffing was advocated by administrators and other educators because it did offer a way to pay some teachers handsome salaries. But, since these salaries were not to be granted on a seniority basis in terms of one's place on a single salary scale, advocates pointed out that differentiated staffing need not result in greatly inflated total salary costs for school systems.[17] Since differentiated staffing hit at the single salary scale and was often advocated in journals such as that of the then male educational honorary, <u>Phi Delta Kappa</u>, women teachers had serious reasons to question whether or not differentiated staffing was simply a way to re-establish sexual differences in pay among the teaching force which had been bridged by the single salary scale.

Teacher organizations, as already indicated, were not persuaded by the new attack on the single salary scale. The NEA first considered a resolution on differentiated staffing in 1969. The resolution came from a part of the NEA which was concerned with teacher education and personnel standards. It carefully avoided taking a firm position for or against differentiated staffing, preferring instead to prescribe the criteria which should be followed if a plan were to be acceptable, the most notable of which was that "any design for differentiating staffing . . . must meaningfully involve classroom teachers and the local associations from the initial stages of development through implementation and evaluation". One teacher opponent of the resolution argued that it was too generous to the concept of differentiated staffing which was, in reality, "just a code name for merit salary pay". By 1972, the association had come a way toward the position of the delegate who flatly opposed differentiated staffing in 1969. The 1972 resolution, while not specifically opposing differentiated staffing, made clear that any plan needed to adhere "to the Association's principles for professional salaries", namely the single salary scale, and that the NEA "strongly opposes adoption of unilaterally imposed differentiated staffing plans and will assist any local affiliate in its opposition to the same".[18]

In the late 1970s and early 1980s, the merit principle would resurface in American educational discourse, this time in a version which reflected some of the changing conditions in which American schools and teachers now found themselves. Because of a decline in the number of school age children, combined with a general funding crisis that affected all public institutions because of a decline in the American economy, American schools found themselves in the 1970s and early 1980s in a position for which they were ill prepared, a situation where they had to contemplate how to 'lay off' or remove teachers for whom there was no longer sufficient work or funds to pay them. In this context, teacher organizations again resorted to their time honoured principle of seniority and argued that teachers should be laid off, if there were to be any layoffs, on a last hired, first fired basis.

One illustration of this phenomenon was provided in the city schools of Atlanta, Georgia in the early 1980s. In May of 1981, the city school board passed a Reduction in Force or RIF policy which called for teachers to be laid off on the basis of a complicated point system which purported to be based in large part on an evaluation of their performance. Both of the city's teachers' associations, one affiliated with the American Federation of Teachers and the other with the National Education Association, reacted vigorously to this attack on seniority as a basis for layoffs. The president of the AFT local addressed the board while it was contemplating the proposed performance based RIF policy and spoke on behalf of a seniority based RIF.

"AFT contracts elsewhere traditionally provide for layoff by seniority. You have proven the quality and dedication of your most senior employees. The use of seniority as a means of determining who will be RIFed . . . protects the employee from abuses often advocated by school systems which would prefer to replace a $20,000 employee with a less senior $12,000 one."[19]

Despite the organized teacher opposition, the board passed the performance based RIF procedure and the teacher groups responded with an even more vigorous attack on performance and defense of seniority. In August, 1981, the local AFT president paraphrased comments by Albert Shanker, national president of the American Federation of Teachers, which attacked performance based alternatives to the seniority principle. After noting several weaknesses in performance, the Atlanta Federation of Teachers president quoted her national leader "Seniority, like democracy, is certainly not a perfect system. But also, like democracy, it's better than any other yet invented"[20].

Through continual lobbying and political action, Atlanta's teachers were finally able to get the performance based layoff system lifted in favour of a return to the existing seniority system. One of the sources that both Atlanta's unionists and Albert Shanker relied on was the work of an economist of education at Yale University, Richard Murnane. In several studies of educational productivity, Murnane concluded that given a number of factors currently operative in American public schools, including the existing technological characteristics of education and evaluation and the commitment of the schools to education for all children, "seniority-based employment contracts may be more effective in promoting public education than performance-based contracts"[21].

Another researcher who studied performance or merit based layoff procedures in four suburban Massachusetts school systems, Susan Moore Johnson, failed to endorse ringingly these procedures, even though she indicated that she entered into the study as an advocate of performance reductions over seniority reductions. Johnson found that, while all four school systems claimed to have some combination of performance and seniority as the criterion for layoffs, in two of the systems the procedure for laying off in practice followed strict seniority. In the two which did utilize performance evaluations as part of the layoff procedure, the results were not uniformly positive. In fact, in the one district which most strictly followed standard evaluation and rating procedures in layoffs, the results included, in the words of one school principal that "he had never seen morale as bad" as it was, because of the ill will created by the performance evaluations and layoff procedures. According to Johnson, the system wide evaluation procedures which were required to implement a merit based layoff procedure were shown to "alter the role of the principal, undermine staff morale, and threaten the autonomy of the teacher, principal, and local school". She discussed the assumptions which underlie the performance based evaluation, namely that "teacher effectiveness can be defined, observed and measured" as unwarranted by the existing research literature on the topic. She concluded her article by noting that the effect of performance based layoffs on the total school climate, teacher-principal, and teacher-student interactions was likely negative: "In an institution that, at its best, promotes acceptance and inclusion, performance-based layoffs introduce competition and exclusion"[22]. A fair reading of this article, not authored by a friend of teacher organizations and their opposition to merit based procedures, indicates that there is significant agreement between the views of the author and the arguments that teacher organizations have made against merit based personnel policies throughout this century.

Having looked at merit pay plans in the early twentieth century and in the 1940s, at differentiated staffing which utilized some performance evaluations in the 1950s and 1960s, and at merit related layoffs in the 1970s and early 1980s, it seems clear that teacher organizations, as well as many of the teachers whom they represent, have consistently opposed these measures. Also, the research evidence introduced in the discussion of the latest merit based measures, performance based layoff procedures, indicates that there is ample reason to sympathize with the suspicions of organized teachers about the implementation of the merit principle in personnel procedures. Of course, our purpose here has not been to judge the adequacy of the procedures, but to get a perspective on the organized teacher opposition to them and the reasons for this opposition. Still, it seems in order at least to suggest that organized teacher suspicions of the merit principle reflect legitimate suspicions of the enterprise. What remains in this essay now is to discuss the very latest invocation of the merit pay idea in American education, that of President Reagan's National Commission on Excellence in Education and the organized teacher reaction to it which, at first glance, may reflect a softening of organized teacher opposition to merit.

Before getting to the specifics of the two main teacher organizations' reactions to the President's educational initiative, it must be noted that the discussions of merit pay are almost all taking place at the central or national level of American educational discourse while the actions and plans for implementing merit pay or any other educational proposals will take place at the state and or local district level. This situation reminds us of a fundamental anomaly in American education in the late twentieth century; while policies are made at the state and local levels, public opinion on education and most other issues, under the influence of the centralizing power of the national media, is shaped at the national level. Thus we have a conservative,

Republican President, committed to a diminution of the national effort in educational funding and control, also successfully setting a rhetorical agenda for educational reform at the national level and making merit pay a prime item on that agenda. It is this situation that accounts, at least in part, for the changes in tone of the organized teacher opposition to merit pay that may be taking place.

Both national organizations, the NEA and the AFT, considered and passed lengthy resolutions on educational reform at their respective national conventions which took place in July of 1983. The two organizations are now more alike in their orientation and policies than they have been at any time previously. In the early 1970s, the NEA cast off its open stance to all educators and became an increasingly teacher oriented union, alike in most ways to the AFT. Yet, the two organizations are now, more than ever, locked in combat with each other for the dues money of prospective members and local affiliates. Thus, it is not surprising that they may attempt to differentiate themselves from each other on merit pay or any other issue, in an attempt to appeal to unaffiliated teachers and teachers who belong to the other organization.

The NEA, meeting a few days before the AFT, passed a statement on educational excellence, drawing the title of the statement from the title of the President's commission's report title. This statement, according to newspaper reports, includes a position on merit pay that is quite similar to the statements and reactions that have characterized organized teacher opinion throughout most of the twentieth century. It notes that the NEA "is categorically opposed to any plan, whether designated a merit pay plan, a master teacher plan, or by some other name, that bases compensation of teachers on favoritism, subjective evaluation . . . or other arbitrary standards". The new Executive Director of the NEA, Don Cameron, was quoted as attributing the motivation behind the President's advocacy of merit pay to the fact that "Ronald Reagan is attempting to distract the nation's attention from his abominally poor education record by pulling a merit pay rabbit out of his hat"[23].

At its own convention, the AFT also passed a lengthy statement on educational reform which was a bit more ambiguous on the issue of merit pay.

According to the union's newspaper, "The statement did not express support for any merit pay proposals, saying that most of those proposed in the past have not worked". However, "since the public is discussing merit pay and wants a response from teachers, the AFT offered one". The paper goes on to indicate that the AFT, while recognizing that merit pay is not union policy, understands that certain conditions may make appropriate the negotiation of merit pay clauses or policies by state or local affiliates. It then went on to list seven qualifications before any merit pay should be approved, including higher pay for all teachers, evaluation procedures that prevent subjectivity and local school political pressure from being applied, all teachers being eligible to be considered for extra pay, no sanctions against teachers who do not receive merit increases, and teacher approval of the plans through the collective bargaining or some other suitable process.[24]

The difference in emphasis in these two statements caused some newspaper reporters, and President Reagan (who was invited to and did address the AFT convention), to contrast the AFT's position with the more rigid opposition to merit pay from the NEA. Fueling the notion of difference between the two organizations on the issue was the opposition of the NEA's state affiliate, the Tennessee Education Association, to a master teacher (differentiated staffing) plan proposed by that state's governor. The AFT, in its own publications, also stressed the flexibility of its own views and contrasted them with the rigid NEA position.[25] Close scrutiny of the situation, however, leads one to conclude that the differences in the positions of the two organizations are not as large as one would think. The reasons that the NEA's Tennessee affiliate opposed the governor's master teacher plan, according to NEA reports, include the facts that the plan contained a limitation on the number of teachers who could receive the promotion to the higher paid ranks and that the governor proposed the plan without consulting with the state education association.[26] Both of these seem to be violations of the AFT's conditions under which merit pay can be endorsed. It therefore seems likely that if the state organization were an AFT affiliate, that national union would also have opposed the governor's plans.

At a panel on merit pay and master teacher plans at the August 1983 meeting of the Education Commission of the States, Tennessee's governor discussed the issues with AFT President Albert Shanker and NEA Executive Director Don Cameron. According to reports of this discussion, the NEA leader softened his group's opposition to master teacher plans, stating that it was the Tennessee plan his group's affiliates opposed, not the concept of master teacher itself. A reading of one set of excerpts from this panel discussion leads to the conclusion that the differences between the two union leaders on the issue are minimal. Both seemed to court the governor by indicating the conditions under which they would be inclined to accept a master teacher plan.[27] In another apparent softening of its flatfooted opposition to current master teacher plans, the NEA's president participated in a coalition of national education organizations which drafted a report favouring many current reforms proposed for American education, including a master teacher like plan for "Establishment of a career ladder with different roles for beginning teachers, experienced teachers, and master teachers". The NEA president pointed out, however, that the group did not endorse merit pay, that history shows that merit pay does not work, and that it did endorse the career ladder plans because they are more palatable to teachers because they allow all teachers who meet the criteria to advance.[28]

Thus it seems that the differences between the two organizations on the issues are overdrawn. The commonalities of the two groups' stances on the issue of merit pay-master teacher are that thay both realize that, rhetorically, a conservative national administration has managed to focus attention on the merit pay issue and to distract attention from many other real educational issues. The groups must, in their own minds, meet the rhetorical advantage of the President and other conservatives by not simply restating their traditional opposition to merit pay in whatever is its current version. They thus must state conditions under which they might endorse merit pay or master teacher schemes. None of these sets of conditions has yet to be met and it seems likely that they will not be met. If a plan contains enough guarantees and protections for the rank and file members of the teachers' unions that the organizations serve, it is unlikely to serve the purposes that caused it to be offered in the first place.

To believe that a teachers' union whose first job is to protect the interests of its members would participate in a pay plan which would give some of its members a considerable financial advantage over most of its other members seems to me to contradict the very reason for being of the union. The bulk of this essay has been devoted to showing how opposition to merit pay in many versions has characterized teacher organizations in this century. It is political disadvantage that now pushes these organizations to avoid flatfooted opposition to current master teacher plans. To expect them to go further and support the plans, thereby reversing their traditional orientation to protection of their members is unrealistic. It violates the purposes for which the organizations were established. Further, much evidence and argument, only a small portion of which has been cited in this essay, indicates that merit pay in the versions we have known it in America in this century is a flawed concept that does not and will not work. Why should we expect teacher organizations to abandon their members for an idea whose 'merit' has yet to be proven?

NOTES

1. The National Commission on Excellence in Education, A Nation at Risk (Washington: U.S. Government Printing Office, 1983).
2. Ibid, p.30.
3. Wayne J. Urban, Why Teachers Organized (Detroit: Wayne State University Press).
4. J. Cayce Morrison, 'History of New York State's Approach to the Problem of Relating Teachers' Salaries to the Quality of Teaching Service', Harvard Educational Review, Vol. 22 (Spring, 1952), pp. 124–31.
5. Journal of Addresses and Proceedings of the National Education Association, Vol. 85, 1947, p.61; hereafter cited as NEA Proceedings.
6. NEA Proceedings, Vol. 86, 1948, p.195.
7. Ibid, p.197.
8. NEA Proceedings, Vol. 89, 1951, p.160.
9. Frank W. Hubbard and Hazel Davis, 'The Constructions of Salary Schedules for Teachers', Harvard Educational Review, Vol. 22 (Spring, 1952), pp. 83–96; see quotations

on p.86.
10. Ibid, p.86
11. Ibid, pp. 87, 95.
12. Hazel Davis, 'Facts and Issues in Merit Salary Schedules', Journal of Teacher Education, Vol. 8 (June, 1957), pp. 127-35.
13. NEA Proceedings, Vol. 95, 1957, pp. 216, 214.
14. Carl J. Megel, 'Merit Rating is Unsound', Phi Delta Kappan, Vol. 42 (January, 1961), pp. 154-56.
15. M. John Rand and Ferwick English, 'Towards a Differentiated Teaching Staff', Phi Delta Kappan, Vol. 49 (January, 1968), pp. 264-68; quotations from p. 264.
16. James L. Oleveio, 'The Meaning and Application of Differentiated Staffing in Teaching', Phi Delta Kappan, Vol. 52 (September, 1970), pp. 36-40; quotation from p.36.
17. Carl W. Swanson, 'The Costs of Differentiated Staffing', Phi Delta Kappan, Vol. 54 (January, 1973), pp. 344-48.
18. NEA Proceedings, Vol. 107 (1969), pp. 280, 580 and Vol. 110 (1972), p.694.
19. Remarks of Mary Lou Romaine, President, Atlanta Federation of Teachers, to the Atlanta Board of Education, May 4, 1981, (Document in possession of author).
20. Romaine to the Atlanta Board, August 3, 1981, (Document in possession of author).
21. Richard J. Murnane, 'Seniority Rules and Educational Productivity: Understanding the Consequences of a Mandate for Equality', American Journal of Education, Vol. 90, November 1981, pp. 14-30; quotation on p.14.
22. Susan Moore Johnson, 'Performance-Based Staff Layoffs in the Public Schools: Implementation and Outcomes', Harvard Educational Review, Vol. 50.
23. 'Merit Pay Stiffly Opposed by NEA Convention', Atlanta Journal-Constitution (July 4, 1983).
24. The American Teacher, Vol. 68 (September, 1983).
25. Ibid. and Atlanta Teachers' Federation Voice of the Union (August, 1983) both have headlines indicating AFT 'leads the way' on education reform.
26. 'Interview with Don Cameron', Education Week (June 8, 1983) and Tennessee Education Association TEA News (July 15, 1983).

27. Education Week (August 17, 1983).
28. Education Week (October 26, 1983).

Chapter Eight

AUSTRALIAN TEACHERS
AND THE IMPACT OF COMPUTERIZATION

R.D. White

State school teachers in Australia have
experienced a dramatic decline in salary and work
conditions and in the 'occupational worth' of
teaching in the last few years. As indicated by
the analyses presented in other articles in this
volume, this occurrence is by no means unique to
Australia. Although the specific form of
educational change may vary depending on the
country, educational debates in the advanced
capitalist countries have been characterized by
systemic attacks on state educational institutions
and the personnel within these institutions.

In Australia, attempts to de-legitimate state
schooling have gone hand in hand with increasing
government cutbacks in the educational sector and
the re-orientation of schooling towards more
narrow and immediate economic goals. As
elsewhere, the contemporary transitions in
Australian education have been ideologically
legitimated through reference to calls for
'educational efficiency', 'accountability' and
'back to basics'.

The issues facing state school teachers in
these circumstances span a range of occupational
and educational concerns. Generally these include
problems associated with such things as
unemployment, class sizes, staffing arrangements,
salary levels, funding and curriculum development.
One trend in particular, however, is rapidly and
radically changing the educational landscape in
this country. Namely, the introduction and
expanded use of computers in Australian schools.

This paper provides an exploration of the
social and economic significance of computer-use
in the educational sphere in relation to the work
activities of teachers. The aim of the paper is

to outline existing trends in the schools and to raise or put on the agenda a series of issues which teachers and teacher organizations should be aware of and making efforts to come to terms with. Included in the discussions are consideration of state efforts to reduce costs, the changing skill content and task orientation of teaching, and the significance of computer-use with respect to the form, content, and direction of education. The paper concludes with a critical look at teacher responses to technological innovation and briefly charts out a series of concerns surrounding the development of appropriate strategies.

COMPUTERS IN THE SCHOOL

The General Context

The trend to computerization in the educational sphere results from a combination of forces linked to both private and public sector responses to the crisis. We find, for example, a convergence of measures adopted by capital to bolster its profit margins, and state measures designed to accommodate the deterioration of economic and social conditions in general.

In the former instance, the restructuring of capital worldwide – that is, a new international division of labour and accelerated technological development – has a number of implications for the nature and direction of schooling in advanced capitalist societies. From the point of view of the economic priorities of capital, the school is important for three inter-related reasons: as a site for the teaching of 'smart' and 'compliant' labour capacities (Wexler et al., 1981), so that students entering high technology fields are flexible in their approaches to complicated and rapidly changing work tasks; as a source of corporate investment (for example, computers, videos, technical devices) which translates accumulated capital holdings into profitable earnings; and as a field for the development of new consumption patterns related to the use of new technological hard- and software (see White, 1983 for elaboration). The mainspring of these concerns is the use and expansion of technological equipment in the schools.

Such a phenomenon is by no means 'neutral' when it comes to the labour of teachers. For instance, the introduction and expanded use of technology can have the consequence of reducing the number of teachers needed for particular tasks and/or changing the skill content of particular tasks. Furthermore, as Braverman (1974: 193) points out: "machinery also has in the capitalist system the function of divesting the mass of workers of their control over their own labour". We shall explore these ideas a little further on.

In the case of state responses to the capitalist crisis, there are several trends apparent which have a direct bearing on the labour of teachers. The fiscal priorities of the state, for example, means that not only a re-direction of expenditure is necessary (that is, away from the social services), but that the salary levels of state workers in general need to be reduced. Simultaneously, the social and economic consequences of the crisis has meant considerable pressure being placed upon the state to make education as closely geared as possible to the needs of the labour market; to use the school as a holding tank for the unemployed; and to see the schools as performing a major social welfare/control role in order to enable the young to better 'cope' with the crisis.

The consequences of these trends for teachers are that teacher labour is subject to intensification as well as shifts in task orientation. In addition, the economic constraints on state finances means that labour costs have to be reduced. This can be accomplished via the introduction of technology, using employment pressures to make teachers perform even more unpaid work, and so on.

The Australian Case

Roger Dale (1982: 145) has commented that:
"Currently, we are witnessing strenuous efforts to impose greater central control on the education system, to impose some kind of bureaucratic/technology form(s) on teachers as state employees. Exactly what form(s) are put forward will be dependent on the outcome of the struggles between 'the bureaucrats' and 'the technocrats' within the state apparatus . . ., and of the nature and effectiveness of the teaching profession's resistance to them."

In Australia both of these forms of control are gaining ever more sway. With respect to the specific case of technology, it is notable that in the March 1983 Federal election both the Liberal Party and the Labor Party offered to spend considerable amounts of money to equip schools with computers as part of their policy platforms. Support for greater computerization has similarly been expressed by the Commonwealth Schools Commission, State education administrators, the media in general, and of course computer companies themselves. In more concrete terms, the Minister for Education and Youth Affairs announced in July 1983 that $18 million would be made available to the Schools Commission during the 1984-86 Triennium for a Computer Education Programme.

It was reported in 1983 that in the State of New South Wales alone there were approximately 2,200 microcomputers in government primary and secondary schools (Commonwealth Schools Commission, 1983: 8). The rate at which schools are acquiring microcomputers makes precise figures at the State and national level somewhat difficult to pin down. For example, as of February 1981, 160 schools in Queensland were using a total of 310 computers. By February 1983, the figures had risen to 420 schools, and 1550 computers in use (Commonwealth Schools Commission, 1983: 11). Insofar as it is State governments which have the primary responsibility for non-tertiary schooling and technical and further education (TAFE), the extent of computerization varies considerably from State to State. The pace of computerization, however, is extremely rapid and given the increasingly widespread financial and ideological support for the use of educational computers it will not be long before they are a common feature in virtually every school across the nation.

States which have tended to lag behind in this process have nevertheless at least made large investments in hardware purchased by schools themselves. Moreover, in the push for computerization government administrators have made it clear that computers are to be high on the priority list in terms of budget allocations. This re-ordering of priorities means that "State education departments now face a difficult situation in that growth in any one area is ultimately at the expense of cutbacks in other parts of that area or in some other areas" (Hoffman, 1983: 88). The 'difficult situation' for education administrators, however, does not relate so much to whether or not one should increase funds to the technology area, but to the means whereby one can determine which areas of funding can be reduced or dropped altogether as a result of computerization.

The Use of Computers

The development of computerization at the school level takes several forms. We can make an initial distinction here between 'teaching computer use' and 'using computers to teach'. In the first case, the primary purpose of classroom computers is seen in terms of providing students with 'computer education'. This would include, for example, lessons on the history of computers, basic familiarity with the technical aspects of the equipment, and initial training in computer programming.

In the latter case, computers are viewed less as objects of study than as devices to aid in the teaching-learning process. Caelli (1979: 101) informs us that:

"Basically, the use of a computer in a teaching or learning situation is described as computer-based curriculum (CBE). CBE, however is not only a system of hardware (equipment), software (computer programs), courseware (educational materials); rather, CBE is an educational environment characterized by specific applications of educational and computer technologies to aid the learning process."

The 'specific applications' alluded to in this passage are of particular concern if one is to understand how the form in which computerization takes place can affect the activities of teachers.

The shift from the more specific training function of 'teaching computer use' to a generalized reliance on computers as teaching aids in the school has a number of implications for the kinds of tasks teachers will have to perform. It is this aspect of computerization with which the following discussions will be concerned.

TECHNOLOGY AND THE WORK OF TEACHERS

Labour Costs and Technology

As we are acutely aware, the fiscal crises of the state in the advanced capitalist countries has meant a severe cutting back in needed funding in the social services in general and in education in particular.

Conservative groups in Australia have been adamant in their demands that the notion of a 'user-pays' principle in education be adopted, in the process comparing the private and public education sectors on the basis of standards, outcomes, accountability, and 'choice and diversity'. This has been accompanied by concerted moves on the part of the State and Commonwealth governments to encourage pupil transfers to the non-government school sector through direct and indirect financial support (Marginson, 1982). The ideological climate surrounding the education debate has served to pave the way for the further stepping up of government efforts to reduce expenditures on public schooling.

With respect to the teaching force, computers constitute one means whereby the state can reduce labour costs through capital-labour substitution. Computers are not only cheaper than 'living labour' but they can store more information and in some cases enable children to progress more quickly in certain areas (for example, reading and mathematics).

It is important then to recognize that the introduction of computers gives the state considerable advantage in allocating labour tasks in the most 'cost-effective' manner. The use of new 'teaching aids', for example, is generally seen to have the technical function of increasing the productivity of the labour of educational workers.

This view of what technology can do is widely held, regardless of that fact that empirical studies reveal that the data on the benefits of computer assisted education appear to be mixed (Lawton and Gerschner, 1982; Senter, 1981). Students have reacted variably to the use of computers, and while some studies claim a 20 to 50 per cent reduction in the time required for a subject while still resulting in the same end performance, others show that students in individually paced computer assisted courses are less likely to complete course material than students placed in the traditional format (Senter, 1981).

Insofar as productive capacities are brought to the foreground in discussions of the use of computers in the schools, however, a proportion of teachers could possibly be seen as expendable – for with greater efficiency through the utilization of technological devices, presumably less human personnel would be required. This in fact has been foreshadowed by Fenton Sharpe, Director of Studies for the New South Wales

Education Department who has been quoted as stating that "Any teacher who can be replaced by a computer deserves to be" (Daily Telegraph, 1983).

Considering that the drop in hardware and software costs will continue while 'conventional' instructional costs (for example, teacher salaries) will grow, if only at a slow pace, then it can be expected that teaching jobs will be under considerable threat. Not only may the new technology be seen as doing a 'better' job than teachers at transmitting information, but microprocessor technology has the further advantage (from the point of view of the employer) of being able to handle large quantities of simple information. This could serve to accelerate the substitution of machines for labourers in the educational institution. Such a situation would also entail the increased ability of the state to use technology-induced growth in teacher unemployment as a lever to push the salaries of employed personnel even further downwards.

However, there are limits to how far the state could actually reduce the overall number of teachers as a result of computerization. This is because of the crucial role teachers have to play in non-technical (that is, not based strictly on 'factual' information transmission) tasks in the classroom in a period of heightened social unrest and high levels of unemployment.

Even granting that a considerable number of teaching personnel would still be required regardless of the growth in the use of technological devices - for reasons relating to the legitimation (social welfare/control) role of the school - such innovations are nevertheless likely to have a major social impact. As Hill (1980: 69) comments: "The tool of machine intelligence will, as with other major changes in basic techniques of a society, transform the user . . ." We have to wonder then what the social consequences of technology are with respect to the nature of the context in which teachers perform their tasks.

Teacher Skills

Let us consider for instance the broader significance of educational innovations such as the machine known as 'Speak and Spell'. Venning (1980: 154) explains how the device works:

"The machine, the size of a large book, randomly pronounces a word . . . The child then tries to spell the word by typing the spelling on to the screen (limited at the moment to eight-letter words). Right answers earn verbal and visual praise. A wrong answer and the child is encouraged to try again. A Speak and Spell student progresses through four levels of more than fifty words each, working at his own pace."

Recent developments on the market offer even greater possibilities for 'educational' instruction. IBM, for example, has developed a software programme that "provides a computer-assisted instructional system in reading and language arts for elementary and junior high school students. Each student receives individualized practice and testing, and the teacher is informed which students need additional instruction in particular skills" (PC Magazine, 1983).

Clearly in both of these instances the task of education has been reduced to a technical problem which ignores fundamental philosophical, social and political questions relating to the form and content of the learning process. Seeing technology as a neutral aid in the educational context also has severe repercussions as to how the educational process is to be organized. Plater (1980: 24) observes for example that:

"To adapt the job to the needs of a computer, there has to be a sequencing programme with well defined hierarchical modules. Information becomes more important than the process and the information, as opposed to knowledge, is broken down into smaller and smaller pieces and defined by arbitrarily chosen subject areas."

If this feature of computer programming is linked to the efforts of educational administrators and state bureaucrats to make the educational system more efficient while turning out quality products, then a clear picture of the 'banking' conception of education emerges (Freire, 1970). In pedagogical terms, the standardization of the schooling process implies that students are to be treated as 'receptacles' to be 'filled' by teachers with the use of their pre-packaged curriculum materials and computer programmes, as opposed to both teachers and students taking a more active part in the learning process.

(i)   Deskilling

In terms of the position of teachers within the educational process, the introduction and expanded use of technology may erode many of the 'technical' teaching skills needed by teachers to perform in the classroom.

The technical tasks of teaching are informed by what Harris (1982) calls 'teaching process knowledge' and 'content knowledge'. The former refers to learning theories, teaching techniques, and principles and practises of motivation with which teachers have been trained and familiarized in preparation for the carrying out of tasks at the classroom level. The latter makes reference to knowledge of particular subject matter which teachers are employed to teach. The expansion of computer-based education threatens the basis of the technical tasks of teachers insofar as firstly, the computer undercuts their specialized knowledge base (that is, information storage and processing), and secondly, computerization involves a uniform method of information transmission (for example, behaviour modification techniques). With the extension of computer assisted instruction, then, the individual skill and craft of classroom teachers will be increasingly subordinated to standardized methods, content and objectives.

Furthermore, it has even been suggested that teachers should strive to distance themselves from the educational process where technology is being used. For instance, a teacher in New South Wales has argued that:

> "Computers in primary classrooms is about getting pupils' hands on the keyboards, learning that they control the technology and not the reverse. We, as teachers, must get off 'centre stage' so that our pupils can be confident masters of the 'little boxes'. They have no fear of the little boxes and neither should we."
>
> (Manfield, 1983: 12)

The teachers' reliance on expert intervention and computer technology is fostered by the ever increasing responsibilities of teachers within the classroom. Computerization effectively allows for the release of the teacher from many of the 'routine' tasks which have to be carried out. However, this involves a re-definition of 'education' from the development of creative and critical thinking to the more technical concentration on the production of measurable skills in the student (Ryan, 1982).

But it also means that teachers would be able

to devote more time and energy in performing 'non-teacher' tasks which have been foisted upon the school as a whole - that is, the social welfare role. Thus, the deskilling of the teacher in relation to technical teacher tasks also creates the conditions whereby the social control function of the school can be brought to the foreground.

(ii)   Polarization of skills

On the other hand, it could be argued that the 'average' skill content of teacher training has in fact been growing in recent years. This trend has been supported by the recommendations of both National (Auchmuty, 1980) and State (Correy, 1980) reports on teacher training which call for a minimum initial training period for teachers of four years as well as endorsing in-service training programmes. The increased education of teacher trainees in particular is seen as a necessary pre-requisite for entering the teaching service. While education as a property of the worker has increased in significance as a job credential, the actual work undertaken in the schools, however, does not necessarily reflect the knowledge and expertise gained outside of the teachers' work setting.

In fact, there is a fragmentation and polarization of skill tasks in the school reflecting on-the-job technical divisions of labour. Thus we find a tendency to 'specialization' in the educational system which is partly due to the heavy workload experienced by teachers in the classroom. The result is increasing reliance on the part of classroom teachers for expert advice in specialist areas such as curriculum development and school/community liaison.

As well, there is a routinization of 'technical' teaching tasks insofar as technological aids can be utilized to transmit information more efficiently than traditional 'chalk and talk' methods.

Nevertheless, a certain degree of reskilling on the part of classroom teachers is necessary in that the use of computer technology requires a basic familiarity with the appropriate procedures and devices. As an indication of how teachers are being reskilled, Apple (1982: 256) points out that in the United States:

> "We can see signs of this at both teacher training institutions, in in-service work-shops and courses, in the journals devoted to

teachers, in funding and enrolment patterns, and not the least in the actual curricular materials themselves. While the deskilling involves the loss of craft, the ongoing atrophication of educational skills, the reskilling involves the substitution of the skills and ideological visions of management."

Although administrative expectations are growing vis-à-vis the technological capabilities of classroom teachers, few teachers are in a position with respect to funds or time however to acquire high level skills, except perhaps outside of paid working hours. This is tending to create divisions between those teachers who have the relevant computer skills and knowledge of computer programming and those who simply use the new technology. Institutions such as the Centre for Continuing Education of Teachers (CCET) in Tasmania do provide an avenue where significant numbers of teachers can receive in-service training in information technology. The tendency, however, is for educational administrators to view such personnel as a specialist category. As the Director of Education Services in Western Australia puts it: "I believe that a major policy responsibility at the systems level involves the establishment and support of a cohort of full-time officers who can provide a combination of expertise, qualifications and experience in both education and information technology" (Hoffman, 1983: 87). Hence, while technology is reducing the overall skill content of tasks for the majority of teachers, a new category of teachers is emerging in response to the skill demands associated with the handling and development of micro-electronic education equipment.

The traditional role of the teacher in imparting information via a range of pedagogical methods may be subject then to change as a result of chronic work overload and the expanded use of technology. The increasing division of labour within the educational sphere means that educational work is thus susceptible to even greater bureaucratic modes of organization and practical distinctions being drawn between 'simple' labour and that which requires specialized knowledge and training.

Teacher Tasks and Control

The social significance of computerization also has to be situated in relation to the issues of control in and over education. A useful summary of the implications of the expanded role of technology in the school is provided in the following passage:

> "The material presented to students: the curriculum is designed, compiled and controlled outside of the school. Teachers, parents, students and administrators are unable to intervene, to alter or modify what is being presented. The vital component of human interaction is missing, and instruction is often highly individualised in the case of computer based programmes. They also tend to employ Behaviour Modification Techniques. The curriculum and the way in which it is presented will reflect the values and interests of those who control the technology."
>
> (Australian Teachers Federation, 1981: 68)

Indeed, there is a strong indication that the educational needs of the community will increasingly be determined according to (national and transnational) corporate definitions of what 'education' should be like. For example, in the May 1983 issue of The Australian Teacher (a national journal for teachers), there appeared a glossy four-page lift-out advertisement for a company calling itself the 'biggest name in classroom computing'. As part of one of the deals offered, the company included a series of "complete secondary and post-secondary classroom package[s] consisting of overhead transparencies for 10 lessons, teacher's manual with instructions and answers, 25 student workbooks . . ."

For teachers, the expanded use of computers and pre-packaged materials may appear at first as a God-send (as one company put it - "no need for constant teacher supervision!"). The use of classroom computers may be seen as offsetting features of their work related to the intensification of their tasks (which itself is in part a consequence of state cutbacks in funding).

On the other hand, with increasing corporate interest in the 'knowledge industry', there is a tendency for even less input from teachers and other education workers into the production of educational materials. Even so-called 'curriculum specialists' will be hard pressed to do little more than choose between 'alternative' packages when it comes to the use of technological aids in the school. In this regard, it is significant that an advertisement placed in The Australian Teacher in its September 1982 issue by the same electronics firm mentioned above was to boast that "We're not just a hardware company. Our education division has produced more courseware than any other microcomputer manufacturer, even more than most major education publishers!".

With the development of expert knowledge and technology related to the school situation, the teacher's tasks are not only simplified, but teachers will experience a decline in the relative power they have in the educational process. In addition to the narrowing in scope of technical teaching tasks and less input into the content of educational materials, teachers will have to perform "a new type of work concerned less with direct instruction and more with direct administration and control, itself subject to more administration and control from above" (Harris, 1982: 137). For example, computers facilitate administrative duties such as record-keeping, attendance and course details. They also allow for an easy method of standardizing testing. Assessment exercises can be drawn from computer banks, and the results marked and analyzed by computer (Sale, 1983). This also means, however, that a possibility exists for teachers themselves to be evaluated on the basis of how well their pupils perform on 'objective' tests in comparison to State averages for those tests.

The erosion of the ability of teachers to secure 'professional' privileges, both in terms of occupational salary remuneration and individual on-the-job autonomy, can be explained by the undercutting of their specialised knowledge base through organizational and technical innovations. The greater the degree of rationalization of their tasks, the less control teachers will have in decision-making and actively participating in the pedagogical process. This does not just refer to higher level decision-making as to what tasks are to be performed, but to control over the execution of tasks as well. Thus, the labour of teachers will be subject to processes which will lead to increasing technical and political alienation from decision-making about what and how the educational system should be teaching.

Task Re-orientation

Meanwhile, the pedagogical tasks of teachers will become less important than social welfare concerns. This is to say that at the same time as a deskilling of certain categories of teacher labour is occurring, the duties of classroom teachers are expanding with respect to custodial functions. The technical features of teaching (for example, the knowledge base of pedagogy and management of this base in the classroom) are being superseded by a greater emphasis on developing social skills geared to social welfare concerns and (implicitly if not explicitly) taking more responsibility in the social control of children.

The technical and social functions of the teacher are apt to come into conflict in this situation in that classroom control and welfare considerations are no longer immediately related to the pedagogical tasks of teachers. The tendency, (and one suspects this to be particularly the case in working class schools), is for the primary role of the teacher to be shifted to non-technical teacher tasks - that is, for the teacher to in effect perform the function of 'social worker' as opposed to information transmitter.

But even in the new emphasis on teaching children how to 'cope' in uncertain times, technology has a major role to play. At the general level of the relationship between human beings and technology, for example, considerations of computer education often beg the question of the effects of this relationship on children. Not only does computer assisted education bring to mind dangers associated with the artificial separation of values, 'facts' and interpretation, and the processes associated with this (for example, who produces the facts), but it raises the spectre of isolated passive human beings who have no skills, need or desire for extended social contact.

Because of the nature of technological developments to displace workers, and of the new international division of labour, unemployment on a large scale is going to remain as a major feature in the advanced capitalist countries. At the time of writing, the idea has been mooted by politicians in Australia of raising the school leaving age to eighteen. This would only exacerbate tensions within an over-loaded state school system where enrolments in the upper forms have already increased due to the lack of job prospects for young people. Youth unemployment poses a great challenge to the powerful to ensure that social unrest does not engender social revolution. And the school will have a major task in trying to teach children of the working class how to survive, but not change, their social environment.

To be a teacher in such circumstances is undoubtedly a very difficult task indeed. The 'advantage' of computers in this kind of situation is that they can be used for the purpose of social control in the classroom. Thus, for example, one can envisage the use of computer games as a means of reward and recreation in administrative efforts to maintain order and pacify the bored and angry. The fascination for technological devices on the part of students can lead to cases where students who are not going to 'make it' in the world outside of the school will find solace in their technological games and devices. This certainly has a number of implications with respect to the ability of students to locate themselves in the social world, to comprehend their situation, and to act in concert with others to adopt strategies to improve their immediate and long-term living conditions and life-style.

RESPONSES TO TECHNOLOGICAL INNOVATION

To this point the paper has provided but a brief exploration of some of the issues relating to the expansion of computer use in the educational sphere as this affects teachers. While further discussion and debate is needed on the questions and problems which have been identified, this must not preclude the development of practical responses to the issues raised.

It appears that a common response of teachers and educators is simply to draw up lists charting out the negative and positive aspects of technology (see, for example, Laver, 1980). The problem with this kind of approach is that it often ignores social and political aspects of technological innovation and development by focusing on technology per se as the issue (Thompson, 1980). In talking about the uses of 'programmed learning', evaluations are made on the basis of what the technology itself can or cannot do, rather than on the power relations and sectional group interests which condition the ways in which technological application occurs. Related to this, there may be a tendency among some writers to highlight the negative and positive possibilities of computer use in the schools at the expense of an adequate analysis of what is actually happening at this very moment.

Choices and Obstacles for Teacher Unions

Teacher unions have a major role to play in coming to grips with the differentiated uses of technology in that they have the organisational, research and financial strength to exert considerable pressure on the path of educational change. How they act, however, is conditioned by a number of political and occupational factors.

At a general level, teachers appear to have three choices regarding the use of technology in the schools: to adopt a Luddite kind of stance and reject technological innovation outright; to view technological development as inevitable (which, by implication, means that nothing can be done); or to accept new technology with the proviso that decisions concerning the use of such devices must reside with teachers, teacher organizations, students and parents.

In practice, the Luddite response has not carried much sway. On the other hand, the response of teachers has not mirrored the other choices available in clear-cut fashion either. While not viewing technology as inevitable and as somehow detached from the wider social context, teacher unions have nevertheless been hard pressed to influence the way in which technology is used in the educational sphere. Hence, at a concrete level, it may well appear to many classroom teachers that the existing form in which computerization is taking place is 'natural' or inevitable.

This is not to suggest of course that teacher unions have no recognition of the issues involved. The Australian Teachers Federation (1981: 75), for example, is very conscious of the fact that:

> "As control over information and ideas come under more centralised control, as the controlling classes develop more efficient mechanisms for promoting their own views, working people will need to maintain democratic schools as a basis for preparing their own values and for educating their children to understand the forces operating on them."

Furthermore, the 1983 ATF Research Programme (a co-operative structure of investigations contributed to by the ATF's teacher union affiliates) includes research into the area of 'technology and education'.

But the formulation of relevant and appropriate strategies, and more importantly, the translation of these strategies into practice, is proving to be a slow process and is conditioned by other developments in the educational sphere.

First of all, the pace of computerization has increased markedly in the last year. Even with increased government funding for computer systems, separate institutions have been active in their own fund-raising efforts. For example, it is not uncommon now to encounter schoolchildren selling raffle tickets for the purpose of 'helping us buy a computer for our school'. At the schools level, the use of computers has been fomented by an extensive media hype and company advertisements extolling the virtues and necessity of computer systems, as well as by pressures to keep up with what the other schools are doing. With the ideological groundwork laid, and a substantial number of computer systems already in place, teacher unions will have a major task ahead educating members about the immediate problems associated with computer use, and establishing controls over programme developments which more and more appear as routine and unproblematic.

Secondly, since the issue of control in and over education is the biggest problem to tackle it will require a considerable amount of support from the rank-and-file members of a teachers' union. However, as Kate Nash of the Victorian Teachers' Union points out, mobilising the membership will require a sustained campaign against certain attitudes and perspectives. In the course of her involvement in developing policy on computers at the federal level with the Australian Teachers Federation and the Commonwealth Schools Commission, she has observed that:

> "The prevailing view amongst teachers is that engagement with new technology requires a high level of technical expertise and sophistication. This view is encouraged by those teachers who have developed themselves as 'experts' . . . It is an 'enthusiast-led' revolution in schools, and this is having the effect of immobilising the majority of teachers."
>
> (Nash, 1983)

Aside from teachers who are blindly committed to 'high tech' whatever the form, or those who are

simply indifferent to the issue, the teachers that
unions will have the hardest time to convince of
the importance of the issues are those who are
suffering from chronic work overload. State
schools are becoming ever more notorious in this
regard as needed government financial assistance
is not available and out-of-work adolescents go
back to school for want of anywhere else to turn.
In this type of situation, many classroom teachers
would understandably be reluctant to sit upon
('yet another!') school committee, or more
generally, have pressures placed upon them not to
use technological devices as a means to keep the
students busy and therefore manageable.

Thirdly, it can be noted that the evaluation
of teacher performances in terms of narrow
technical goals and broader welfare objectives is
carried out on a teacher-by-teacher basis, as
opposed to consideration of the occupation as a
whole. In the framework of increased calls to be
accountable, this has the consequence of
fragmenting teacher efforts for collective
responses. As Ryan (1982: 32) points out:

"Accountabilitist strategies deflect attention from common problems and discourage the
co-operative pursuit of improved educational
conditions. Instead, they sanction the
technocratic imperative that teachers be
competitive with each other for a dwindling
number of jobs and promotion positions,
supposedly according to unambiguous and
measurable criteria of teaching success."

We might also add here that those teachers who
occupy the new specialist categories arising from
the use of educational computers may not support
union policies which appear to undermine their
position in the division of labour.

Fourthly, union resources and personnel are
currently stretched over a number of areas, each
of which demands a degree of immediate attention.
In New South Wales, for example, the Teachers
Federation has had to mobilise its members over a
series of issues (for example, state aid to non-
government schools) in recent months. Within the
union, major debates are currently being waged
over changes to the teaching service promotional
scheme and the State Government's plans to change
secondary school curriculum. In this context,
even if policy on technology is agreed upon,
actions to implement the policy recommendations
are often given a low priority in the overall

scheme of things. Simply put, the prevalence of other issues in the educational sphere may effectively deflect teacher attention and activities away from the possible consequences of computers on their labour and for education in general.

Fifthly, the scope of the teachers' undertakings on the issue of technology and education may be limited solely to educational innovations. This is to say, the main area of concern may centre on classroom computers, at the expense of critically evaluating and understanding the social significance of technology in society as a whole. If we recognize the linkage between the economy, schooling and technology, then an adequate response by teachers must be situated within the context of the wider labour movement.

Related to this, teacher unions also have to consider the impact of new technology with respect to their own staff. A word processor, for example, may be purchased as a means to increase administrative efficiency but it nonetheless will have an impact on the nature of the work to be carried out and on the employees of the teacher union who have to perform the relevant tasks. Hence, teacher unions will at some time have to develop industrial policies which reflect the employer-employee relationship within their own organizational setting.

Developing Teacher Responses

It is essential that when tackling the problems associated with computerization teachers and their unions formulate responses which centre on their location in the educational milieu. State school teachers are public servants and thereby subject to state controls over their working conditions and wages, and the kinds of tasks to be performed as part of the job description. As workers, teachers have an immediate interest in computerization as this relates to state efforts to roll back labour costs in the education sector. This could prove to be a major battleground for the unions, especially given the high levels of unemployed teachers at the moment and recent state efforts (for example, as with casual and primary school teachers in New South Wales) to reduce the overall number of teachers in the teaching service.

At the same time, teachers have to step up their efforts to defend the degree of control they have in the educational institution. As it stands at the moment:

> "General cuts in school funding, and
> particularly reduction in funds allocated for
> teacher professional development, are
> seriously inhibiting the capacity of teachers
> to learn to take control of new technology."
>
> (Nash, 1983)

This means that they must fight for the resources
necessary to allow them to train members in
computer use and in the production of computer
courseware. Administrators will naturally be keen
to buy materials produced elsewhere because of the
costs involved. Similarly, this would allow for
standardization and therefore easier and cheaper
methods of pupil (and teacher) assessment.
Teachers must not allow this to happen if they are
to have a say in the schooling process.

As educators, it is imperative that teachers
be conscious of the negative consequences of
computer use by children and adopt 'corrective'
policies accordingly. For instance, they should
have a role in determining such things as which
courses are to be computer assisted and how this
is to take place. And they must be sensitive to
the needs and requirements of specific educational
groupings - migrant children, Aboriginal children,
the handicapped, female students, working class
children - and plan courses of action which
recognise specific problems confronting these
people.

There is a need as well to determine how many
hours per day or week a student (and teacher)
should spend in front of a computer console.
This has significant health, psychological and
social ramifications. So too, it may be necessary
to organize a series of group activities for
teachers and students as a means to offset the
social and political isolation engendered by
extended computer use, that is, to encourage
students and teachers to take an interest in the
world beyond the audio-visual screen.

If technology is to be developed and applied
in a manner which is geared to meeting social
needs (and not simply for profit or purposes of
social control), then teachers must be militant in
their demands for control over the distribution,
use and production of computer hardware, software
and courseware. It may be the case that, for
example, the Australian Teachers Federation is
represented on the Schools Commission National
Advisory Committee on Computers in Schools.

Similarly, teacher unions in most States have some input into policy bodies, and are making serious efforts to raise the issue amongst their members. The crucial question, however, is whether or not Australian teachers will be able to politicise the issue in a way which directly addresses the power relations governing the manner in which the process of computerization is occurring in this country.

REFERENCES

Apple, M. (1982) 'Curricular form and the logic of technical control: Building the possessive individual', in Apple, M. (Ed.) Cultural and Economic Reproduction in Education, London, Routledge and Kegan Paul.

Auchmuty Report (1980) National Inquiry into Teacher Education, Canberra, Australian Government Publishing Service.

Australian Teachers Federation (1981) 'Paper submitted by Australian Teachers Federation', in Report of the ACTU Federal Unions Conference on Technological Change, Melbourne, Australian Council of Trade Unions.

Braverman, H. (1974) Labour and Monopoly Capital, New York, Monthly Review Press.

Caelli, W. (1979) The Microcomputer Revolution, Crows Nest, The Australian Computer Society.

Commonwealth Schools Commission (1983), Teaching, Learning and Computers. Report of the National Advisory Committee on Computers in Schools (November pre-release copy), Canberra, Schools Commission.

Correy Report (1980) Teachers for Tomorrow. Report of the Committee to Examine Teacher Education in New South Wales, Sydney, New South Wales Government Printer.

Daily Telegraph (1983) 'Schools Move into Fast Lane', 3 February.

Dale, R. (1982) 'Education and the capitalist State: contributions and contradictions', in Apple, M. (Ed.) Cultural and Economic Reproduction in Education, London, Routledge and Kegan Paul.

Freire, P. (1970) Pedagogy of the Oppressed, New York, Seabury Press.

Harris, K. (1982) Teachers and Classes: A Marxist Analysis, London, Routledge and Kegan Paul.

Hill, S. (1980) 'Economic and Industrial Transformation: The Waves of Social Consequence from Technological Change', in Boreham and Dow (Eds.) Work and Inequality (Vol. 1): Workers, Economic Crisis and the State, South Melbourne, Macmillan Company of Australia.

Hoffman, N. (1983) 'Information Technology Education Policy at the Systems Level', in Goldsworthy, A. (Ed.) Technological Change: Impact of Information Technology, Canberra, Australian Government Publishing Service.

Laver, M. (1980) Computers and Social Change, New York, Cambridge University Press.

Lawton, J. and V. Gerschner (1982) 'A Review of the Literature on Attitudes towards Computers and Computerized Instruction', in Journal of Research and Development in Education, 16, 1, pp.50-55.

Manefield, B. (1983) 'Hands on Computers!', in Education: Journal of the New South Wales Teachers Federation, 1 August, pp.12-13.

Marginson, S. (1982) 'The Privatisation of Schooling in Australia', A Preliminary Position Paper, Canberra, Australian Teachers Federation.

Nash, K. (1983) Personal Communication, 2 December.

PC:The Independent Guide to IBM Personal Computers (1983) 'New On The Market' section, 1, 11.

Plater, G. (1980) The Social Impact of Microprocessor Technology - Its Impact on Schools and Unions, 1980 Eric Pearson Memorial Travel Grant Report, Sydney, New South Wales Teachers Federation.

Ryan, B. (1982) 'Accountability in Australian Education', in Discourse: The Australian Journal of Educational Studies, 2, 2, pp.21-40.

Sale, A. (1983) 'Information Technology and Education', in Goldsworthy, A. (Ed.) Technological Change: Impact of Information Technology, Canberra, Australian Government Publishing Service.

Senter, J. (1981) 'Computer Technology and Education' in The Educational Forum, XLVI, 1, pp.55-64.

Thompson, H. (1980) 'The Social Significance of Technical Change', in Journal of Australian Political Economy, 8, pp.57-68.

Venning, P. (1980) 'Microcomputers in the Classroom', in Forester, T. (Ed.) The Micro-computer Revolution, Oxford, Basil Blackwell.

Wexler, P., T. Whitson and E. Moskowitz (1981) 'Schooling by Default: The Changing Social Functions of Public Schooling', in Interchange, 12, 2-3, pp.133-150.

White, R. (1983) 'Education and Technology: Exploring the issue of computers in the classroom' Paper presented at the Eighth National Political Economy Conference, Canberra, 2-4 September.

Chapter Nine

TEACHER CONTRACTS AND TEACHER 'PROFESSIONALISM':
THE EDUCATIONAL INSTITUTE OF SCOTLAND

J.T. Ozga

INTRODUCTION

This chapter is about the EIS, the Educational Institute of Scotland, which is Scotland's largest teacher union. However, it is not a description of EIS organization and policies, being much more concerned to discuss the implications of the Teachers' Contract which applies in Scotland largely as a consequence of EIS action. After a period of considerable militancy over salaries and qualified teacher status, the EIS concentrated on achieving a teachers' contract, and this has undoubtedly been effective in protecting teachers during the current economic crisis. Would such a contract be of use to teachers elsewhere in the UK? This question raises a number of problems, indeed the operation of the contract is problematic, particularly when it is contrasted with ideas of teacher 'professionalism'. Does such a contract undercut teacher union claims to professional status? Does a contract make the teachers into 'employees' rather than 'partners', and does this weaken rather than strengthen their position?

PROFESSIONALISM AND PARTNERSHIP

One of the most hackneyed descriptions of British education consists of characterising central government, the local authorities and the teachers as 'partners', a description intended to convey unity of purpose and equality of status. A refinement is to accord 'chairmanship' or 'senior partner' status to central government, and to admit to conflicts among the partners which create a 'triangle of tension': tension which both holds

236

the partners together and maintains the distance between them. This 'dispersed' control has often been lauded as the distinguishing characteristic of the British system, apparently preventing direct political control of education and protecting local and professional interests.[1]

The idea of partnership is interesting as a product of its time: of educational reconstruction, expansionism, extension of opportunity - but even more interesting in terms of its ideological content and uses. In relation to teachers, partnership status has been allied with 'professional' behaviour and the adoption by organized teachers of certain forms of communication with their partners: consultation, formal deputation, joint membership of various advisory committees, 'gentlemen's agreements' etc. - and the eschewing of less harmonious forms of relationship, which might have damaged the partnership, and led to withdrawal of that status, which was, it seems, granted to teachers "less by legal status than by convention".[2]

The price of partnership - from the teachers - was good 'professional' behaviour. Certain factors in the 1960s made such good behaviour relatively easy to obtain - in particular, the availability of resources for education and a joint commitment to educational expansion. The rhetoric of partnership was an extremely significant device in fostering a limited and limiting view of professionalism which concentrated on classroom autonomy and harmony of interests between teachers and their employers.

The idea of partnership was generally applied to British education, despite significant differences within the UK, especially apparent in Northern Ireland. Partnership did not transfer entirely successfully as an explanatory concept to education in Scotland either. The different histories of educational provision in the two countries made the rhetoric of partnership less immediately applicable there, where there was less of a tradition of autonomous local provision linked to local government, but rather of parish-based provision given strong central direction, first by the Kirk, and then by the SED. Thus the period of educational expansion, marked in England by the proliferation of consultative mechanisms aimed at incorporating the teachers, was marked in Scotland by central directives aimed at promoting change, by teacher militancy and by the setting up of the General Teaching Council, of which more below.

Was it the lack of incorporation through 'partnership' which encouraged Scottish teachers to pursue strategies which culminated in the teachers' contract? Or are there other factors to be taken into account?

ORGANIZED SCOTTISH TEACHERS — SOME BACKGROUND

One immediately apparent advantage possessed by organized Scottish teachers is that nearly all of them are organized: some 95% belong to a teachers' union. Furthermore approximately 85% of them belong to the EIS, the Educational Institute of Scotland, which can therefore claim to be the representative body. There are other sectional unions, e.g. the Scottish Secondary Teachers Association, and the National Association of Schoolmasters/Union of Women Teachers also recruits in Scotland. None of the smaller unions can compete effectively with the EIS, not only because of its size, but because it draws its membership from all sectors of provision.

How have organized teachers in Scotland succeeded in avoiding the divisions which have so weakened their English colleagues? This is a far from easy question. It seems that, despite its prestigious-sounding choice of names when it was founded in 1847, which suggests parallels with the College of Preceptors, the EIS has had a consistent commitment to achieving and maintaining solidarity among teachers. Its then president, William Brunton, speaking in 1858 against those who criticized the EIS for being "too democratic in its constitution", asserted:

> "Why, this is the finest feature of the Institute, its all-embracing arms open wide to the Teacher of the Ragged School as well as to the Rector of the first-class Academy. Are not teachers all brethren engaged in the same great work; and the Teacher of the lowest class is as necessary and as useful as the Instructor of the highest, and needs fully more encouragement. And was not the condition, the benefit of all classes, the great, the main, the paramount object of this Association?"[3]

There have been breaks in the unity, however. Both the secondary teachers and the class teachers formed separate associations between 1895 and

1917, but were reunited with the Institute at the end of that period. There were further problems in the 1940s when the Scottish Secondary Teachers' Association (SSTA) broke away from the EIS, principally over the issue of protecting and advancing the interests of male secondary school teachers, following a decision of the 1945 Annual General Meeting of the EIS to pursue a policy of seeking a common scale for primary and secondary teachers. The SSTA had an initial success, but has not maintained its early numbers.

Although some of the pressures which caused disunity to break out among teachers' organizations in England existed in Scotland – particularly equal pay and the feminization of teaching – they did not lead to the loss of EIS predominance. Perhaps this was because other factors were largely absent or not so apparent. At this point mythology clouds our interpretation of events – it is always tempting – at least for a product of the Scottish system – to subscribe to the idea of the democratic tradition in Scottish education, so eloquently invoked by Brunton in the earlier passage. The myth, of course, conceals the narrowness of that tradition, its concentration on the academic excellence of the few at the expense of the many, its contradictory, democratic elitism[4]. All these caveats have to be kept in mind when any explanation of the Scottish educational scene invokes the democratic tradition. However, that said, there probably was less social class division among teachers in Scotland than in England – and that may well remain the case. Rural schools in Scotland were, to a large extent, comprehensive in organization and intake if not in content and teaching method well before 10/65 was issued in England. School teaching was looked upon as a good career for working class men as well as women – in the Secondary sector, at least, the normal route to teaching was through university. The lack of 'public schools' – except in Glasgow, and, to a greater extent in Edinburgh – meant that the Scottish teachers were not overshadowed by headmasters, nor were they so obsessed with improving their status. Their status was, it could be argued, already high, in a society which applauded self-improvement regardless of social origin, and accorded a somewhat unthinking respect to education. Even if this discussion veers dangerously towards acceptance of the myth, and underplays the divisions in Scottish society, it remains a valuable aid to explanation in that people, then and since, believed the picture it presents to be broadly true.

A further factor which may have helped hold teachers together - then and since - is the Scottish political context. English teachers are politically divided - at least in terms of the way they vote - but the majority of them seem to vote Conservative. Scottish teachers who vote Conservative are in the minority, the majority are Labour voters[5]. This partly reflects a difference in social class origin of teachers in Scotland, and partly also suggests the continuing identification of the Labour party with Socialist educational ideals which have strong, if romantic, Scottish associations - especially in Glasgow.

All this, it must be admitted, is very tentative, in the absence of any study of organized teachers in Scotland. Other factors which may contribute to unity are the small scale of the country - the EIS having about 49,000 members compared to the National Union of Teachers' 270,000, and its tradition of direction by the SED, of change initiated from the top, rather than initiated by the teachers. Acceptance of central direction by Scottish teachers has, it is suggested, reduced opportunities for dissension among them.

What remains to be looked at is the role that the EIS itself plays in maintaining its members' allegiance despite sectional pressures. To explore this we need to look at EIS policies and EIS structure and organization.

STRUCTURE AND ORGANIZATION[6]

The structure and organization of the EIS is very similar to that of the NUT, (with which it has both formal and informal links - e.g. NUT members taking up permanent posts in Scotland are entitled to EIS membership).

The EIS has an elected President and Vice-President, as well as full-time (appointed) officials - General Secretary, Treasurer, etc. - who do not have voting rights. The business of the Institute is conducted by the Council and its Committees, the Executive Committee, Finance Committee, Education Committee, etc. The Council is elected by the local associations, each of which is represented by at least one Council member, more being allocated depending on the size of the membership in that area. Further members are elected to represent sectional interests - Catholic teachers, Nursery and F.E. teachers, etc. The Council meets at established times on four occasions throughout the year and during the Annual General Meeting. The Executive Committee of the Council consists of 24 elected members, plus the officers. The Education Committee consists of 22 elected members, with the stipulation that eleven shall be secondary teachers and eleven primary teachers. Its responsibilities include curricula and topics concerned with educational establishments (including universities) as well as with research in education and the training and qualification of teachers. The Salaries Committee is similarly divided in its membership - there being six primary and six secondary members. The local structure of the EIS is also similar to that of the NUT, allowing, as it does, for a degree of local autonomy, and the consequent risks of confusion or division between the local organization and the executive. There are however, in the bye-laws of the EIS, indications of rather more stringent limits on local autonomy than the NUT's executive has, so far, been able to achieve. Indeed the description of EIS local association responsibilities is, to a large extent, a list of what the local association - or the divisional body, which groups together local associations - may <u>not</u> do. Local associations and divisional bodies, may, subject to the control ofthe Council, negotiate with their education authorities, and regulate and transact the business of the Institute in their area, but they:

> "Shall not communicate with national bodies, that is to say bodies operating at Scottish or English or Welsh or United Kingdom levels or International bodies without reference to the Council or the Executive Committee of the Council."

Each local association elects its own executive committee and office bearers, and Institute representatives are appointed in each school or college in the local authority's area.

This structure obviously allows for a degree of local autonomy, and for union democracy, though the extent of both will depend very largely on the degree of participation of the membership as a whole. It appears that on most issues, except for salaries and conditions of service, the union membership is apathetic, accepting or at least not resisting, policies advocated by their leaders "who are generally articulate, committed, and to the left politically".[7]

The issue of union structure is a very important one in the context of the government's attack on educational provision. The NUT has been wrestling with its unwieldy local structure for some time now, attempting to find a compromise which allows a degree of branch autonomy without loss of efficiency, and attempting to exert closer control over individual local members, while not stifling local activism. The neglect of the local structure during the days of supposed national influence has resulted in a gradual accretion of policy-making powers to headquarters, conflict between local associations and divisions at the local level, and a demoralization of local activists. The pressures for greater centralization in pursuit of efficiency and tighter control of a membership assumed to be apathetic are many, as the service is attacked at national and local level - the need to co-ordinate strategies for resistance, or at least attempt equality of treatment in negotiated agreements is obvious. The pressure is increased by the success of the NAS/UWT in projecting an image of itself as a highly centralized, efficient protector of its members' interests.

Yet the breakdown of the national partnership throws the NUT back on to its local structure, and makes the role of local activists an important one. In Scotland, the EIS leaders operated a centrally-controlled union which reflected the centre's control of the education system by the SED, but did not attempt - or did not achieve - the degree of influence over educational policy claimed by the NUT before the recession. It is interesting to note, however, that the EIS structure is currently under revision. That revision may tend towards decentralization. This is reflected in both the establishment of Regional Executives and in the establishment of Regional Organisers. This may reflect the consequences of Scottish local government reorganization in 1973 which established a Regional Structure (nine regions, plus three Islands authorities) and which abolished many small scale authorities. The size of some of the Regions encouraged their development as agencies of local government, despite the unfavourable timing of their appearance. The emergence of regional executives seems to indicate a degree of independence in policy formulation. However this may be exaggerated - regional officials are appointed by the National Executive and are responsible to the General Secretary. The development of a regional structure could, in fact, be interpreted as a mechanism for the more effective implementation of national policy throughout the country.

A further factor has been the decline in SED influence since 1979, in the face of determination of policy by the Treasury. The EIS has responded to the growth of Regional influence by strengthening its regional organization, and may be able to exploit the position of achieving agreement with the Regions which the SED finds hard to circumvent without friction between it and them. The English local government scene presents an instructive contrast, since the demise of the AEC there has been no one representative group with whom the teachers could make an effective partnership, and their ability to make common cause at local level has been subsequently weakened.

In parallel to the EIS's creation of a Regional sub-structure, there appears to be a move to encourage greater workplace involvement in the union, through an expansion of the activities of the school representative. This fits in with a more consciously trade-union style of organization, in itself a consequence of increased activity in issues relating to conditions of work and definition of duties. It is also hoped that by developing school-based activity members may be encouraged to play a more active part in the union, generally. The problem of devolution to school representatives is the problem of devolution to local associations in microcosm, too much freedom may lead to conflict with national policy, too little to apathy and withering of the grassroots. The expansion of workplace activity may be easier for the EIS because of the policy on working conditions, of which more below. In England, the NUT, like the EIS, has introduced training for school representatives, but there remain enormous variations in how individual school representatives see their functions. The NAS/UWT has attempted to expand its school representative-role in the direction of the industrial shop steward, but there are indications that this has met with some resistance.[8]

UNION POLICIES

The question of structure cannot be looked at in isolation from the question of union policy. The movement of the EIS towards a structure more akin to that of industrial trade unionism has taken place in parallel with its increased involvement in trade union issues, especially salaries and working conditions. In the field of salary negotiation, the EIS departed from the accepted norm of teacher union activity by organizing widespread strike activity, in the area of working conditions the union has, following a campaign of industrial action, achieved a set of conditions of service which effectively constitutes a teachers' contract. Both activities run counter to the ideology of professionalism as invoked by central and local government to obtain good behaviour from teachers.

The militancy over salaries provides further evidence of the comparative solidarity of Scottish teachers. It covers a period from the early 1960s up to 1980, and the publication of the Clegg report, when the focus moved to conditions of service. The basis of the problem was dilution of the qualified teaching force - especially in the West of Scotland - in a period of extreme teacher shortage, linked to poor salaries. The shortage problem was not tackled, though after 1965 the problem of dilution was dealt with by the General Teaching Council - but at a time which, ironically, put immense burdens on teachers in chronically-understaffed schools. By 1973 the situation was serious, teachers in the most affected schools took action themselves, 'working to rule' and devising principles on staffing and maximum class size. The Executive agreed to the principle of a maximum of 35 in a class, and supported the campaign, which had its strongest manifestation in Glasgow, where over 6,000 teachers turned up at a meeting to discuss strike action.

The Houghton pay award took some of the impetus out of the campaign, and also deprived teachers of public support. The emphasis in campaigning shifted from salaries to working conditions, although organized strike activity over salaries occurred in both 1979 and 1980.

The question of agreed conditions of service,

class contact time, maximum pupil numbers etc. was
not unproblematic. It was less easy to maintain
membership unity on this campaign than on the
earlier salary campaigns. This was partly because
there were members from relatively prosperous
areas, with traditionally good educational
provision (e.g. the North East of Scotland) who
felt that the proposed national agreements meant a
levelling-down in their own conditions, even if
they represented an improvement for less fortunate
teachers in other areas, and who were therefore
hostile. The more militant membership, especially
in Glasgow, where much of the campaigning had
taken place and where conditions were often very
poor, were reluctant to give up the struggle for
what they saw as a compromise solution. However,
agreement was reached, and the EIS action
successfully achieved a scheme of Conditions of
Service in 1975.

This scheme has subsequently been revised,
and it covers a wide range of subjects relating to
teachers' work, including appointment procedures,
post-entry training, grading and salary scales,
hours of work and class contact time, class size,
annual leave, absence, allowances, disciplinary
and grievance procedures, consultation,
discrimination and so on. Where relevant, model
procedures and statements are set out. The most
important agreements are those relating to working
hours, class contact and class size.

It is perhaps worth quoting these in more
detail:

21   (i) Working hours
        (a) Normal working hours shall be 32.1/2
           hours per week, exclusive of lunch
           breaks and intervals.
        (b) Teachers will be required to attend
           school during the normal school day
           but there shall be flexible arrange-
           ments for the balance of time within
           normal working hours which is
           outside the school day. During this
           period essential-non-teaching duties
           (e.g. preparation, correction)
           should be carried out, either in
           school premises or elsewhere at the
           teacher's discretion . . .
    (ii) Class contact
        The amount of class contact time a
        teacher shall work is not to extend the

limits imposed by the following –
Primary teachers: A maximum of 25 hours class contact each week during the normal working hours
Secondary teachers: A minimum of 200 minutes of non-class contact each week during normal school hours.

22 Class Size

The maximum class size for time tabled classes shall be

		Number of Pupils Normal Maximum
Primary		33
Secondary	S1–S2	33
	S3	30
	S4	30
	S5–S6	30

9

The agreement proved of major significance as the recession worsened and the consequences of falling rolls become apparent. The cuts in government spending since 1976 have brought about a steady deterioration of the pupil–teacher ratio in England and Wales, but only in some of the best staffed areas in Scotland have pupil–teacher ratios worsened. Indeed staffing standards were improved in many parts of Scotland in order to meet the new contractual obligations, and it appears that these standards have been adhered to, despite the worsening financial position. Keir Bloomer claims that by 1979 the contract of service had guaranteed around 5000–6000 teaching posts "which would not have existed had the government and the education authorities enjoyed the same freedom of action as in England".[10]

The EIS, therefore, can claim past successes in two important areas, salaries and conditions of service. In terms of salary negotiations they have retained membership support, because of the fact that the salary settlements won by the union followed union policy of across-the-board improvement, rather than increased differentials between teachers. Since 1975 the EIS has become increasingly committed to using its slaaries policy as a means of promoting membership unity.

THE CONTRACT AND TEACHER 'PROFESSIONALISM'

The success of the conditions of service campaign is, however, not unqualified. There are obvious strategic advantages in a period of recession in a scheme which establishes precisely what a teacher may or may not be asked to do. Equally obviously, as cash becomes scarcer and the employers' freedom of manoeuvre even more restricted, there may be circumstances in which adherence to the contract may hinder the teachers' attempt to protect the education service. It is this dilemma which Keir Bloomer addresses when he argues that the agreements on class sizes and class contact time –

"represent, at the same time, the biggest recent improvement in working conditions and the biggest retreat from professional standards. The implications for the organization of schools and hence for the education they provide are profound. The total effect of the agreements may be seen as the enforced reordering of priorities by education authorities. Whereas, previously, protection of the working conditions of teachers occupied a very low priority in comparison with curriculum change, subject balance, curtailing costs etc., employing authorities were suddenly placed under an absolute obligation to guarantee certain minimum conditions and to provide the staff required to meet them . . . The unions now face a difficult decision: whether or not to respond to the considerable pressure from members to negotiate further improvements in the contract, thus imposing fresh restrictions on the schools and increased staffing requirements upon the authorities."[11]

Bloomer's conclusion is that the arguments against wholesale improvement of the contract are overwhelming – the major objection being the restrictions that would be placed upon the individual teacher by contractual requirements "and the effect upon the collective attitude of the profession brought about by frequent resort to such restrictive practices".[12]

This is an interesting quandary. At one level it can be readily illustrated by the fact that minority subjects have undoubtedly suffered as a result of operating the scheme of conditions of service. Given little room to manoeuvre, savings have had to be made through the loss of provision of 'extras' and through a reduction in the options available in the curriculum offering, especially in classics, minority modern languages and music. It may also be the case that the protection afforded to full-time teachers by the scheme has exposed their part-time colleagues to even harsher job losses than in England and Wales. This, too, cannot be looked upon by teachers as simple expediency: like the shrinking curriculum, the loss of experienced part-time teachers, who are overwhelmingly female, diminishes the breadth and quality of the teaching force, and reduces the level of the service.

This is the underlying tension which Bloomer recognises, the conflict between self-interest and self-sacrifice for the 'greater good' of the education service, and the fact that self-interest can, in the long run, produce detrimental effects for the service as a whole and the teachers in it. It is interesting that he should describe the dilemma in terms of a retreat from 'professional' standards. Earlier I suggested that there is a link between the 'partnership' status accorded to organized teachers in England and Wales and 'professional' behaviour, i.e. that professionalism may be interpreted as an ideological form of control of teachers by the state. I have written about its use in this way elsewhere,[13] and argued that the interest of professionalism as concept lies not in attempting to define it and determine whether this or that occupation has achieved professional status, but rather lies in taking account of the different meanings which professionalism may have for the different groups which make use of it. Most of the literature on teacher unionism adopts a relatively uncomplicated attitude to professionalism. It is linked to increased state provision; as the service grew, so did the status of those who taught in it. The teachers' development into professionals enables them to enter into dialogue with their 'partners' at central and local level, their professional expertise becomes the basis of their influence.[14]

My interest lies much more in the uses of professionalism as an ideology of control by the state over teachers, a use which is particularly pronounced in times of economic crisis, such as the late 1920s, and currently. The intention, however, is not to suggest that 'professionalism' is, purely and simply, a means of control. It is a complex concept, and one that does not easily lend itself to manipulation. It may have been intended as a powerful means of inhibiting teachers from 'union'-style activities - professionalism being presented as the antithesis of unionism - but it is a concept full of contradictions. Its use, however intended, raises expectations - particularly of autonomy in relation to supply, quality and training of teachers, not to mention payment - which cannot be fulfilled. Indeed the contradictions become even more apparent as the gap between professional rhetoric and harsh reality is widened by diminishing resources for the service.

And there are elements of professionalism which do not lend themselves easily to its use as a means of control, and which are not inherently antagonistic to unionism. Concern about entry and training has already been mentioned, to those may be added the idea of high standards of service and devotion to the task above and beyond financial reward. These aspects of professionalism are important to teachers and have enabled them to expand and develop their role, particularly within the confines of their own classrooms. It is this broader commitment which Bloomer perceives to be at risk when he identifies the scheme of conditions of service as "the biggest retreat from professional standards".

Here we see the contradictory elements of professionalism clearly displayed. The idea of commitment to, concern for, and involvement in, the education service contains sources of strength for teachers - at the same time those very ideas, when contrasted with the narrow definition of commitment emphasized by the contract encourage teachers to make concessions to their employers rather than see the service suffer. Or, if their instincts for self-preservation and their concept of themselves as employees has been strengthened by a contract which was won by hard-fought struggle, then at the very least they feel themselves torn between the need to adhere to what they have fought for, and their broader loyalties. This may be a particularly difficult situation when the direct employer - in this case, the Region - may be able to deny responsibility for events which are set in motion at SED or Treasury level. In this instance, at least, the often quoted tension between professionalism and unionism may exist.

But it is not the professionalism invoked by the employer, and linked to 'responsible' behaviour which sets up the tension. It is the professionalism which has links with craft unionism, which is concerned with quality and with standards of service. Bloomer is surely right to recognize that concentration on a limited form of unionism, which focuses on financial reward alone, would seriously weaken the teachers' unions. (He categorises the restricted form of unionism as industrial trade unionism, but it is not always the case that industrial unions take such a restricted view of their functions.)

The great strategic problem is to see how the commitment of teachers may be effectively put to use without its being manipulated by their employers. At least while the recession lasts, the possibility of the restricted use of 'professionalism' as a strategy for co-option of teachers is diminished. As I have already noted, that use in Scotland has been fairly limited, although it is sometimes suggested that the existence of the GTC demonstrates the 'professional' status of Scottish teachers.

The General Teaching Council for Scotland is often described as a major achievement for Scottish teachers, and the idea of a Teaching Council for England and Wales has been invoked as part of various campaigns to improve teachers' 'professional' status. Yet it is rather difficult to establish precisely what the GTC has achieved. By controlling the registration of all teachers in Scotland, who must be recognised as qualified teachers by the GTC before being allowed to teach, the GTC did effectively solve the problem of dilution mentioned above and does continue to exercise a degree of control over teacher supply. That influence also extends, to some extent, to teacher training. But it would be inaccurate to perceive the GTC as a major professional body, somewhat analogous to the BMA. It is extremely limited in what it can achieve by its shortage of full time staff. It is probably more correctly understood as a necessary part of a very well-defined system of operations - it fits into the general pattern of agreed regulation of the teaching force in Scotland - along with the Red Book on teacher supply, and the teachers' contract. Consultation with the GTC is part of a recognized process through which the SED must go when matters relating to teacher supply and training are considered. There is, for example, some evidence that the GTC provided a focal point for resistance to government policy on teacher training college closure in Scotland, and that it proved relatively effective because it could take a broad overview of the needs of the system.

The GTC then, is perhaps more significant as part of an agreed, formalised system of employer-employee relations than as a plank in the professional platform. This interpretation of the uses of the GTC may reflect a rather more realistic interpretation of 'professionalism' among Scottish teachers than their English colleagues. The concentration on practical issues is reflected in the fact that teachers in Scotland have shown little interest in attempting to influence educational policies. As Bloomer notes, the publication in 1977 of two major reports, which resulted in significant changes in the curriculum and examination system of secondary schools did not produce a demand for a general meeting in any single branch of the EIS. He contrasts this with the regular demand for meetings in connection with the annual salary settlement.[15] Possible explanations for this lack of activity have already been suggested - and they must all be placed in a context in which teachers were not encouraged to think of themselves as 'partners' in policy-making in the same way as their colleagues in England and Wales were brought to.

It is possibly also the case that the Scottish tradition of innovation from above allowed superficial changes: 'innovation without change' to be made while not disturbing the fundamentals of the system. Thus comprehensivation caused little trouble, but was restricted to patterns of organization and rarely led to changes in teaching methods, the introduction of teachers of guidance was a method of extending promotion opportunities rather than the injection of much needed personal education into Scottish schools, and it remains to be seen if either Munn or Dunning will succeed in breaking the grip of the traditional examination system with its emphasis on academic success. There is a certain complacency about Scottish education, an assumption of superiority which goes hand-in-hand with resistance to change which may also play its part in explaining lack of activism on educational issues among Scottish teachers. Yet another instance of the contradictions inherent in this subject is the possibility that it is belief in this superiority which strengthens teachers' commitment to an endangered service.

CONCLUSIONS

A number of contradictions in the position of EIS members and the operation of the teachers' contract have been identified. The major ones are those which are thought to occur as a result of conflict between professionalism and teacher unionism. However it may be that the concept of teacher professionalism in general has been interpreted in a limited way, and its application in Scotland in particular may have different meanings. The failure to incorporate Scottish teachers into the 'partnership' with government, their relative unity and their militancy may all combine to produce concentration on what are perceived to be 'union' rather than 'professional' matters: salaries, conditions of service, definition of duties, control of supply and training.

Yet the operation of the teachers' contract is not without its difficulties. These stem not from contradictions between 'professionalism' as defined in the literature and as used by LEAs and the DES to bring pressure to bear on English teachers, but from neglected aspects of professionalism such as commitment to the service which are played down by government in times of financial crisis because of the strength they give to resistance from teachers to the destruction of the service.

For Scottish teachers, then, a major difficulty lies in maintaining the position of relative strength which the contract has given them, while retaining commitment to standards of service. Perhaps the only possible way forward is for the EIS to attempt an alliance with parents and other organized workers, but the involvement of parents in Scottish education would be something of a departure from tradition. The widespread belief in the value of education and the dominance of the state sector in Scotland might make such an alliance both feasible and fruitful. This would mark a departure from the 'distancing' effect of traditionally-defined professionalism, with its emphasis on expertise, but would accord well with those aspects of professionalism given emphasis above, namely loyalty to the service and defence of the clients' interest.

NOTES

1. Many writers make use of this characterization: Weaver, Kogan and Briault among them. Briault in 'A distributed system of educational administration: an international viewpoint' in <u>International Review of Education</u>, Vol. 22, No. 4, 1976, developed the idea of the triangle of tension.

2. Weaver, T.: <u>The DES, Central Control of Education?</u> Unit 2 of E222, The Control of Education in Britain. Open University Press, 1979.

3. Presidential address of Dr. William Brunton, 1858, quoted in the <u>Centenary Handbook of the EIS</u> by A.J. Belford, Edinburgh, 1946.

4. For an assessment of the impact of the mythology of Scottish education on secondary education in Scotland since the war see Gray, McPherson and Raffe <u>Reconstructions of Secondary Education</u>, R.K.P., 1983.

5. This point is not valid for the whole of the period under discussion, but for the last 25 years a higher proportion of Scottish teachers has voted Labour than in England.

6. The sources of the material on which this section draws are EIS publications, including the Constitution, Standing Orders and Rules of the EIS, 46 Moray Place, Edinburgh, EH3 6BH.

7. Bloomer Keir, 'The teacher as a professional and trade unionist' in Hoyle, E. and McGarry, J. (1980) (Eds.) 'Professional Development of Teachers' in <u>The World Yearbook of Education 1980</u>, Kogan Page.
   This article, written by the then Deputy General Secretary of the EIS, was the source of my interest in the union. Not only is it one of the few sources of information about the EIS, it contains a very interesting discussion of the possible conflict between trade union style organization as reflected in the 'contract' and 'professionalism'. I have used many of Bloomer's ideas in that article as a basis for discussion here. In

passing it is also worth noting Bloomer's point about the union leadership being "to the left politically". This contrasts to some extent with the position elsewhere in the U.K., especially if one is talking about Union Executives. The leftwards inclination of the EIS leadership seems to be acceptable to the membership, partly, presumably, because of the Scottish political context and partly because, according to Bloomer, the Executive have incorporated former Rank and File leaders, thus preventing fragmentation of the union and presumably also controlling unacceptably 'left' tendencies.

8. Bell, Leslie Arthur 'An Analysis of the Branch Level Activities of the Coventry NAS/UWT with particular reference to the role of the Local Executive'. Unpublished Ph.D. thesis. Warwick, 1983.

9. Scottish Teachers Service Conditions Committee (1975, reprinted 1980), Scheme of Conditions of Service.

10. Bloomer (1980) op.cit.

11. Bloomer (1980) op.cit.

12. Bloomer (1980) op.cit.

13. See, for example, Ozga, J.T. and Lawn, M.A. Teachers, Professionalism and Class, Falmer, 1981.

14. Examples of this type of discussion of professionalism are numerous. See, for example, Roy, W. (1968) The Teachers Union (Schoolmaster Publications), or Tropp, A. (1957) The School Teachers (Heinemann) or Gosden, P.H.J.H. (1972) The Evolution of a Profession (Basil Blackwell).
Margaret Archer argues that teachers achieve influence over educational policy making by virtue of their educational and professional expertise (Archer, M.S. (1979) The Social Origins of Educational Systems, London, Sage).

15. Bloomer (1980) op.cit.

ACKNOWLEDGEMENTS

I would like to thank Keir Bloomer, former Depute General Secretary of the EIS, for his comments on this article. The opinions expressed in it are, of course, entirely my own, and not those of either Mr. Bloomer or the EIS.

Chapter Ten

TEACHER 'BURNOUT' AND INSTITUTIONAL STRESS

Sara Freedman

In 1983, a rash of Presidential and/or blue ribbon commissions-on-excellence reported their findings on the current state of the American educational system. One common stance of all the reports is, again, that the right people are not teaching, and as a consequence, the American educational system has seriously deteriorated. The chief of these reports, titled 'A Nation at Risk', issued by the National Commission on Excellence in Education, perceives a "rising tide of mediocrity" within education, a tide they believe to be so strong that it has brought America to the shores of economic ruin and decay.

> "Our once unchallenged pre-eminence in commerce, industry, science, and technological innovation is being overtaken by competitors throughout the world. This report is concerned with only one of the many causes and dimensions of the problem, but it is one that undergirds American prosperity, security and civility." (NCEE)

The seriousness of the problem is emphasized by the terminology used - apocalyptic and, not incidentally, militaristic.

> "If an unfriendly foreign power had attempted to impose on America the mediocre educational performance that exists today, we might well have viewed it as an act of war." (NCEE)

The impression conveyed is that anyone responsible for this decline has committed an act of treason and is part of a fifth column that is destroying America from within. "We have, in effect, been committing an act of unthinking, unilateral educational disarmament". The gender of those targeted for criticism in these reports is never mentioned, but it is naive to ignore the

255

unstated belief - women are undermining America's economic and military strength. The reports thus continue the attacks begun by the New Right on the achievements of individual women and the increased influence of the women's movement as a whole. As we shall see, the solution offered for the deterioration in education is to remodel teaching, and the goals of teachers, along the lines traditionally employed in male-dominated professions - perhaps in the hope that turning teaching into 'men's work' will stem the flow of this "rising tide of mediocrity" by attracting more suitable candidates to the field.

The reports chastise the American educational system, singling out parents and teachers for not producing a workforce of sufficient quality to keep the American system competitive. Rhetorical pronouncements declaring teacher incompetency, parental neglect, and a general drop in moral standards are actually designed to change the pattern of educational funding established in the 1960s. Since that time, compensatory programs have shifted some amount of money to poorer sections of the community, although it has often been argued that much of this money was spent on elaborate rote learning systems that answered the needs of employers rather than the demands of the communities who had pushed for needed reforms. The use of the word 'skill' in education illustrates this point. The emphasis on 'skill learning', embodied in the minimum competency testing and 'back to basics' movement, replaced the positive definition of the word 'skill' to reflect the type of work today's students can expect to find when they enter the job market. Its metamorphosis demonstrates the transformation of a community demand for quality education for previously neglected segments of students to a fixation on measuring those students according to easily quantifiable criteria devoid of political or cultural content. It appears the employers in large corporations such as those represented on the boards of these commissions have come to believe that they can no longer afford even the illusion of this type of equal opportunity embodied in 'skill learning'. According to these reports, sufficient amounts of money are not going into programs which would train the kinds of workers corporations need in order to maintain or create a competitive edge - highly skilled technocrats and managers. Yet even if these companies succeeded in channeling large amounts of money into educational systems which support creative, self-directed programs for the few and rote sessions for the many, they may not be able to stem the process of deskilling that their dual systems of job classifications - a few highly trained managers vs. a large pool of unskilled labour - inevitably create.

'Deskilling' is a term recently coined to explain a new type of work situation. From its traditional base in factories and filing pools, this process of deskilling or 'proletarianization' has been observed spreading to the professions, particularly ones that are female-saturated or are now more hospitable to women joining their ranks. In all of these professions we now see women and minorities ghettoized into the less lucrative, lower paying and routinized areas while white men continue to dominate the remunerative and powerful sectors.

In addition, new positions within these fields are being created. Even though all nurses, lawyers, engineers and social workers share the same title, a portion of them now manage the others. In female-saturated occupations some are recruited into those professions with the express purpose of having them fill those new positions. The two key proposals of the Commissions on Excellence - the creation of a 'master teacher' slot and the allocation of merit pay - reflect attempts to restructure teaching along similar lines in the belief that these incentives will recruit and retain better teachers.

It is important to note that the deskilling of the labour force isn't just happening to workers 'out there', or to the students in the classrooms. A part of the workforce also labours in schools, and the deskilling of that labour force - teachers - is occurring in ways that affect that particular group of workers as well as those they train.

"When I was a kid in the fifties I went to a strict, traditional school. The teachers were thirty and forty year veterans. They never varied from plans written many years ago. In September the same pictures were posted on the blackboard. The construction paper borders were replaced each year but the paper faded early in November and was a dull sheen by March. I loved those teachers. They conformed to many of the stereotypes of longtime women schoolmarms - stern, swift in justice, unimaginative, inflexible, sure of their methods. They praised the docile, hard-working, quick-to-grasp pupil and were alternately punishing or neglectful of the silent majority. The wicked were quickly subdued.

In fifth grade a spate of male teachers arrived, returning GIs straight out of college, who had a fertile field in the burgeoning school industry. They were different - young, creative, with lots of energy. They introduced SCIENCE!, giant papier-mache animals, and new seating patterns. We all wanted to be in their classrooms. Most of them soon moved to other positions in the quickly expanding system - principal, science co-ordinator, creative arts department. The children were left with the old women teachers - and with a disdain of old women teachers.

When I began teaching ten years ago, I had a clear image of the kind of teacher I wanted to be - Mr. Williams, the fifth grade teacher who had introduced the most daring educational experiments and who worked tirelessly, coming to school on Saturday. He was the closest person I actually knew to the figures portrayed by Jonathan Kozol, Herb Kohl, and John Holt in those books coming out of the sixties. And I managed. I worked tirelessly, tried all kinds of experiments, came in on Saturdays. It was exhilarating - for the first few years. But as the years wore on and on, I began to notice that the drive was being replaced by myriad frustrations. Many teachers who arrived with me on the crest of the sixties' waves, felt tethered in place. We became less experimental, angrier, more isolated. I was turning into my present perception of one of them - those female teachers of long ago who worked year after year in a closed space, each class merging into the next, stale ideas, frayed construction paper."[1]

'Burnout' is the term now popular to describe the phenomenon. The term has begun to appear regularly in the magazines directed to the teaching profession to explain widespread feelings among teachers of inadequacy, listlessness and decreased dedication to teaching. It is important to question the implications of using such a term to explain teacher frustration. 'Burnout' implies that at some point a finite amount of energy has been consumed. The number of articles and workshops that explore the issue of teacher burnout has greatly increased during the past few years. This is occurring at the same time in which many teachers face layoffs and a shrinking job market. The coining of the term 'burnout' at the same time that teachers are threatened with the loss of their jobs serves to direct the focus of each teacher's growing anger away from a critical analysis of schools as institutions to a preoccupation with her own failure.

No one changes from a dynamic teacher into a conservative pedagogue from mysterious personal reasons. Schools as institutions create contradictory feelings and demand contradictory actions from teachers. The rhetoric surrounding the institution of public education often proves to be in direct conflict with the function a teacher finds herself required to perform. The dissonance between the goals teachers presume they are striving for and the realities they encounter may be more or less pronounced depending on where they teach, but the contradictory requirements of schools have always existed. Attempts to improve schools offered today, as in the past, do not address the contradictions - the inherent barriers to the growth of teachers within the structure of schools. Rather the solutions buttress the 'blame the victim' approach. This approach defines the problem as an aggregate of disaffected or incapable teachers whose deficiencies are seen as personal rather than as a reflection of the failure of the educational system to grapple with and confront these contradictory demands. Examples of the main conflicts inherent in public education are:

Teachers work in an institution which supposedly prepares its clients for adulthood, but which views those entrusted with this task, the teachers themselves, as incapable of mature judgment

"When our principal is talking to a first, or second, or third grade teacher, . . . I find that she's repeating directions one, two, or three times, almost as you would to a first-, second-, or third-grader. When you get higher up, fourth, fifth, and sixth, the directions are not repeated as much, but they're more done in like an outline form as

you would give to kids who are a little bit
older." (AA, 1980)[2]

When the teachers' work has created a major
program their contribution appears publicly as
negligible and secondary. Their isolation from
each other and the need to funnel any request and
information up through the levels of the hierarchy
and back down again rather than directly to each
other has not allowed them to use their unique
knowledge of classroom life, which they alone
possess, as a basis for determining system-wide,
or even school-wide policies.

"After working for months on the fourth grade
reading curriculum, we brought it up to the
Assistant Superintendent. We had put a
blanket statement at the beginning stating
that we would assume that the teachers would
be responsible by consulting the textbooks
and other resource materials and their
expertise and so on and so forth . . . He
made it quite clear that he didn't think they
were capable of going over anything by
themselves, finding the materials, using them
appropriately . . . We're smart enough to do
all the busy work but not smart enough to
carry it out." (D, 1980)

Professional development courses for teachers
are frequently planned by others in the school
hierarchy and dictated to the teacher whose
concerns and opinions are disregarded. Faculty
meetings, which could provide a forum for issues
and ideas, a place where group discussion and
decision-making might be encouraged, are more
likely to be organized for the presentation of
previously made decisions to the assembled
teaching staff.

"Every Tuesday is a half day for faculty
meeting. The boss does all the talking.
They are just sit-and-listen types of things
. . . If he asks for suggestions on things,
it usually is put like this, 'Now this is
what I have planned. If there's anybody who
wishes to disagree or there's anybody who
doesn't care to go along with that . . .'
That might not be his exact words, but he
really doesn't care to open anything to
discussion. People sit there with a deadpan
look because they don't want to commit
themselves, you know, get themselves into any
kind of hot water, a little afraid sometimes,
depends on who the principal is." (E, 1979)

When the weekly faculty meeting is replaced or supplemented by a list of notices prepared and disseminated by the principal's office, the message is that teacher input is unnecessary, a discussion of issues is not called for - and the teacher's control of her work environment is further limited.

Anger and resentment build as the teacher realizes that the control she wields over her workplace and her working conditions is being sharply limited by restrictive administrative policies and practices.

"That's the thing that really kind of aggravates me about education: we as educators are not treated as adults. I feel that administrators still look upon us as being one of the children. So you teach elementary education, so you have an elementary education mind, and we can tell you just about anything and you will believe us. And at this point I would like to get into a situation where . . . I would be respected for my thinking as a person, as an individual, and I find that in this particular field, I'm not always treated that way, and I resent it and I'm angered by it too." (AA, 1980)

Fostering independence in children has always been an avowed goal of our educational system. Too frequently, however, the teacher is told to encourage independent thought and action in her pupils, while at the same time being cautioned never to leave her charges unattended. The same lack of trust implied here is mirrored in the school's careful monitoring and control over the teacher within her classroom.

"The intercom is something that many people have been paranoid about. There is a button on this that can be pushed to Privacy, which means the office can talk to you, but they can't hear you unless you press it onto Open . . . It has been rumored . . . I believe the rumor . . . that the principal can in fact override that and listen to anyone he chooses. And that's something that has upset people at different times. Yeah, I mean if you're a teacher who's having problems, that is definitely something that you're very aware of . . ." (C, 1980)

Education is an institution which holds that questioning and debating, risk and error develop one's thinking ability.   But learning situations are structured to lead to one right answer,   and both teachers and students are evaluated in ways that emphasize only quantifiable results.

"The principal was a marvelous person for handling the paper work, organizing the building, but when it came right down to the individual child, I think sometimes he missed the point a little. Once I remember he came into the classroom and said, 'Look at that, and that, and that'. He was pointing to the reading scores of three children. And these children were so, so unbelievably slow. I thought they were doing beautifully. They really sustained their interest to the end of the year and slow children don't do that. And I was enthusiastic. I was pushing a new program in reading for all it was worth. I can remember feeling awful, just awful when he said that. I felt I had been put down, a terrible put-down. I used to work like a son of a gun, always that push to do your best. And I felt awful. I don't think I dwelt on it forever, but I can remember getting feelings of like what a thankless job, you know. Really." (E, 1980)

A teacher who works day by day alongside a youngster knows which words a child will more likely stumble over, what words must be introduced in several different contexts, and which stories excite interest or increase the shuffling of feet and emergency trips to the bathroom.

"I can learn something by the papers that a kid turns in but I learn more by watching them do it, and that's particularly useful with kids . . . When kids really know something, I know it. They have a confidence about it. When they do it, they make the comment, 'Oh, boy, I love doing it', or 'this is easy' . . . I have to hear that or see that." (B, 1979)

Parents, school committee members, researchers, and future employers would like to have the same information the teacher has without spending six hours every day in the classroom reading stories and learning times tables. If the teacher's own description of the child's progress is dismissed as too biased and personal, the only way to communicate what a child knows to those outside the classroom is to abstract that experience by quantifying the results.

"A couple of years ago they developed a
reading checklist in this district. Each
year you are supposed to check off what the
child has accomplished during that year in
your classroom. They developed a math
checklist, and we have to give what is called
a test of essential skills in reading, and
that's supposed to measure their progress.
Then we enter all the stuff on the checklist.
And they have these little punch cards that
during the year you're supposed to punch out
each time they've learned something in math,
and then you fill out the little checklist at
the end of the year. I piloted one in
writing last year, and writing is too
subjective to evaluate in that way. All of
these things are absolute killers for
teachers, and personally, I don't think they
are valid." (Y, 1981)

This involves a distortion. The teacher, who
knows the children as idiosyncratic, highly
individual people, must administer tests that
yield quantifiable results easily transferable to
charts and tables. The teacher cannot simply stop
to share a child's joy over her accomplishments or
commiserate with her in her problems. The teacher
must first officially 'translate' the pupil's
progress as defined by testmakers and publishers.
Only then can it be officially recorded that the
pupil has learned a fact or is able to reach an
opinion. The role of comforter and educator
yields to that of recorder and judge.

"We were all so very conscious of teaching
subject matter that we're not teaching the
children; we were just teaching the subject.
I had made the determination, 'I'm not going
to teach like that'. I almost don't care if
a kid doesn't know how to add if he knows how
to be nice to another human being and if he
respects himself. I think that's very
important." (W, 1980)

The same teacher in a later interview:

"I think the happiest day of my life was when
I got back the reading tests and found out
that the exact percentage of kids in the
other two first grades were all reading on
the same level. They had twenty-five per
cent of the kids who were below grade level
and so did I." (W, 1981)

Once she has entered the child's progress
into her book or on the blackboard, both the

teacher and her pupils are easily understood and evaluated. The desire to nurture and support students, a major reason for many to enter teaching, is transformed into the drive to keep each student on a predetermined grade level.

"My principal gets upset because he doesn't see enough low science and social studies marks that should correlate well with reading . . . He complains about this in general . . . if they don't read well, how could they be doing well in science and social studies. He's also the same person who told us that . . . if they're in the eighth or ninth stanine that means they're an A or B student and their report card marks should reflect this." (C, 1980)

The teacher, under attack for failing to help children reach arbitrary grade level goals, accedes to the greater wisdom of the commercial test makers and the research academics. Once started on the road to quantification, the method becomes addictive, even for attributes other than achievement.

"I went to a very exciting convention about learning style. They have been doing a lot of research on it and finally validated a reliable test so that you can give it to kids so that you can determine learning style ... It's a multiple choice test of a hundred questions, just very simple questions ... It's like the Stanford Diagnostic that tells you exactly what you need to know about a kid and all. Even if you did it yourself you wouldn't really figure it out — what the computer can do, put all the little things together." (F, 1979)

Principals and school board members then use the same types of evaluation created by the researcher to evaluate the teachers. The new 'objective' type of teacher evaluations that have recently been introduced into the schools are examples of such quantitative methods. They take great pains to code and enumerate the type, number and direction of the interactions of the teacher with her pupils within the classroom. She is not evaluated outside the classroom because presumably these contributions to the school as a whole, enhancing the sense of community of the school, are not properly considered her responsibility or more strongly, not really 'her business'.

When she helps a teacher reorganize her

classroom, when she 'takes in' a difficult child so that teacher and child can have a rest from each other, she is simply being nice. She is not being 'professional' and no professional benefits will accrue.

What is left for the evaluator to write down are the concrete manifestations of the interactions of the teacher with her pupils that can be observed by the examiner himself. Only those moments become part of the meticulously documented, seemingly exhaustive evaluation of the teacher. It seems as though the examiner is riveted to the teacher, but it is actually the teacher who, in a more important way, is focused on the principal. What the principal does not see or is not done for his eyes becomes irrelevant, even counterproductive.

"My principal says, you know, he could look in the room and in one second he knows everything that's going on. Well, yeah, he might get an idea of what's going on, but that doesn't mean it's the right idea, and you know, sometimes it's not . . . One day . . . I came back to my room after dittoing off papers, and there I am sorting out my papers out on the table, and all of a sudden I realize there's a presence in my room - all my kids are all at art or music or something. And I look up, and there's the principal sitting in my room, with an evaluation sheet . . . writing down - he's looking at the questions on the board, he's looking at the bulletin boards I've got up, he's looking at everything around and he wrote me up a detailed evaluation based on what he saw in my classroom when my kids weren't there and I wasn't there." (C, 1980)

The more quantitative measures and national exams are used to evaluate the teacher, the more she will feel the need to use such quantitative methods to judge her students and other teachers. She is now the in-class representative of the national norms and countrywide bell curves. Once she has entered the child's progress into her books or on the blackboard, both she and her pupils are assured to be easily understood and evaluated.

The schools have the responsibility of developing the whole child. But the structure of the institution constricts the types of behaviour acceptable in teachers and pupils.

Teachers, especially those in less affluent districts, often feel that they and their colleagues are encouraged to show only a few facets of their personalities within the confines of school.

> "I don't think that there are people who are really close. I can just not picture one teacher going to another one in tears. I really can't. There's no one to run to. Not just for me. People really just don't get that close. And I think part of it is working in an impersonal system. You do what the boss tells you. You don't have choices. You file at 10:10, whether you like it or not . . . Everything is impersonally handled - time, bells." (A, 1979)

The message quickly gets across that order and quiet are the primary goals, leaving teachers to stifle, in themselves and their students, any activities that might be disruptive.

Teachers of working class children are not surrounded by the many signs of their pupils' affluence - and probable future success - that bolster the teachers' and the students' sense of worth. It is difficult for such a teacher to justify 'developing the whole child' when the local paper publishes yearly standardized test scores. The teacher's ability to identify with her job and with her students is threatened.

> "When I changed from kindergarten to first grade teaching, it was a whole new scene. I just seemed to take on a first grade personality. I think you just become a different type of person because you're more instructor and you don't have time to develop their personalities. The whole point in kindergarten was to develop this child so he's happy and likes school. If he's uncomfortable about something in his life, you try to make him loved. You get to first grade, forget it. I haven't got time for you. You've got to learn to read. You've got to finish that book before the second grade teacher sees you . . . Somebody raises their hand, in the kindergarten you would listen. You're hoping to develop their language, and you listen . . . You get to first grade, it was 'Put your hand down. That's all the stories for now. Pay attention. Sit up.' And they go to talk to you, 'I don't want to hear your story. We're

lining up. You have to go out. The clock doesn't wait for anybody. Be quiet. Be quiet. We have to leave the room.' A whole new emphasis." (E, 1980)

The definition of 'skills for life' varies according to the social class of the school and the teacher. A teacher in a working class school:

"In my school it's a luxury to think about those things - inter-personal relationships, how to encourage spontaneity - we have to teach the basic skills for life. Basic skills, that's the most important thing I teach them. Reading and math because those are the tools to succeed in life, you know, to help you in life." (H, 1980)

A teacher in a middle class school:

"One parent said, 'What's important is the tools that you are giving kids to be excited about finding out things and feeling okay about being wrong, too. You're just giving them lots of tools for the future and how you look at things and find things out.' I felt very good about that." (B, 1979)

Sometimes areas which a teacher might consider very important are dropped or ignored because they are not part of the mandated curriculum which takes up more and more of the day's schedule.

"I've learned a lot about how scapegoating needs to be stopped at the first possible opportunity. My first instinct is to say, 'Stop the world, we're going to talk about this'. But in this school I can't suspend the schedule. So there's not any time for soul-searching, heart to heart. I could stick a little in that twenty-five minute math block. I could stick a little in that one-half hour when you get to passing papers. So I'm really stifled in handling things my way by that. Yet I'm not placing a whole lot of faith in traditional discipline. So I'm in a real conflict - I'm doing what I feel is wrong." (A, 1980)

Ironically, those teachers who want to provide 'enrichment activities' - creative writing, improvisational dramatics - must increase the pace and pressure of the classroom in order to cover the real work already established by the basal reader. The extras can be added only by a furious winding-up of prescribed work.

267

Education is charged with the social task of providing equal opportunity for the school-age population of a pluralistic, multi-level society. But
the structure of schools emphasizes comparative
worth and increases competition not only among the
pupils but also among parents, teachers, and administrators.

> "We never had any administrative
> encouragement to work together. There was
> never any time, there was never any made,
> there were very few group decisions. It's a
> very individual thing, if you found someone
> you wanted to share materials with, you did
> it on your own. No, nobody has ever
> encouraged that route . . . It only comes
> from the individual teachers in our building.
> None of it is encouraged by the principal."
> (D, 1979)

The goal of the best education for each child
is thwarted when feelings of envy and competition
divide a school staff.

> "The teacher in the room next to me seemed to
> be very friendly. I'd been in and out of her
> classroom, sort of looked around and made
> some nice comments about it. I asked her
> once if she would mind sharing a ditto sheet
> or something . . . She said, 'No! You come
> in here and look around the room.' She was
> really, I mean I couldn't believe it . . . I
> don't know why she felt threatened. What was
> I going to do with this paper? Do one
> better? Put it up on the wall? I don't
> know. But it was a terrible, terrible
> feeling." (B, 1980)

Rather than working on problems together,
teachers - and pupils - are labelled, categorized,
and divided. Ironically, the desire to ensure
equal opportunity to what have been termed
disadvantaged children has led in practical terms
to an increasing reliance on abstract
quantifications that document inadequacy and focus
the attention on what the child does not know.

> "If there's a kid in the classroom that a
> teacher is having a problem with, and it
> looks like there might be something the
> matter, they go through the core evaluation
> process, and they discover that he does, he
> has an auditory figure ground problem, so
> automatically he's going to get picked up by
> the person in charge of auditory figure
> ground problems. So now we've created a

label for a kid and a person to deal with
that label. There's a pattern and the
pattern is they're minority kids, they are
ESL (English as a second language) kids, they
are the kids who walk to the beat of a
different drummer." (W, 1980)

For teachers caught up in the demands of
school there is no time to think about the
divisions among the staff and how these divisions
often undermine the school's atmosphere and
educational effectiveness. Resentment and
competition can split teachers along many lines -
older vs. younger, traditional vs. innovative,
classroom teacher vs. specialist, those whose jobs
are 'safe' vs. those threatened by lay-offs, those
teachers requested by parents vs. those who are
not, those who are given aides vs. those who
aren't.

"We have to have kids till the last day of
school. Why doesn't everybody have to have
kids? Now people who are specialists in
tutoring kids have to do a lot of testing and
writing of reports. We have to write reports
four times a year. We have report cards. I
have to write my core. I have three of those
to write. I realized I was really pissed."
(B, 1979)

The competition among children in the
classroom and among teachers in the school
building is often echoed in the antagonistic
feelings fostered among schools in the district.

"The superintendent made it very clear that
the quote-unquote more aggressive schools
would get funding and materials for the
programs they wanted . . . He said, 'The
more aggressive buildings will get the money.
If there's something you want to do in your
building and you can give us a good reason
for it, then we may be able to make it
available to you.' Some schools took
advantage of that, like the ___ School. They
have a lot of parents who know how to write
proposals and they always get their way.
(W, 1981)

Public education is charged with upholding democracy by developing an electorate capable of critical thinking and the intelligent balancing of
alternatives; but teachers are required to pursue
this goal by increasingly mechanical, technical
means.

"The principal started another program in

kindergarten that he wanted to adopt, working with small groups, using electronic equipment like head sets and things, very carefully planned individualized instruction with the children. He was structuring, planning fifteen minute segments. He wanted to try something new. We would have a half-hour of concentrated teaching in small groups . . . So you worked on listening to sounds or you worked on your workbooks in small groups and then after fifteen minutes it was [clap hands] change groups. And no matter what you had to stop at that point. There was one little girl who had had kidney surgery in my room who wasn't learning and had a lot of problems and I felt I couldn't sit and do the work like that. And I remember one day when I said, 'You know, she just had kidney surgery', he said, 'I'm tired of hearing about her kidney surgery. I'm tired of hearing emotional things blamed for reading problems.'" (H, 1981)

In poorer and working class schools, where standardized test scores provide the major indicator of how much a pupil has learned, the teaching of discrete mechanical skills takes on primary importance. Expertise is seen to lie in the books, not in the teacher. These tools are seen as the crucial determining factor in the education or miseducation of the child. If the teacher adheres strictly to the text, the child should learn.

"We can't use any supplementary materials until we've finished all the textbook work . . . I can show you the memo. [The memo read: 'Teachers are reminded that only materials found in the adopted textbooks can be duplicated. Supplementary materials are not to be stenciled and duplicated. It is the feeling of the administration that materials in the textbooks are adequate and must be completed before other materials are to be introduced in the curriculum.'] Even the kids who are repeating go back through the same materials . . . Last week I was teaching a reading lesson and the story was about Galileo. Now I have a wonderful ditto about Galileo and telescopes. But it's from the science unit, so I couldn't use it. The administrator's aide controls the ditto machine and files all the dittos that are run off. If we have any supplementary dittos, they have to be cleared first."[3]

Computers and other advanced technical equipment, supposedly designed to make the classroom a more productive place, reflect an assumption built into the newly acquired equipment of what is considered 'productive'. By establishing a centralized control developed from abstractions of 'real' students, helping a child become 'productive' means asking the child to compete with a pre-set standard rather than developing the unique skills and qualities of each pupil. For the teacher, these types of equipment limit the teacher's control over the pace and manner in which the skills are presented far more narrowly than possible by using only the basal reader.

"I'm not a machine-oriented person, for one thing. Not a bit. Not at all. And I just cannot see feeding stuff into a machine and have it talk back to me. I know what's going on in my room. With a small class, I'm getting to know them better and better, and I'm much more sensitive to them, it being a small class. And I've done it with bigger classes, too. I don't need a machine to tell me this child doesn't know this or doesn't understand that." (E, 1979)

Teachers also recognize that this equipment is not introduced to enhance their capabilities, nor those of their pupils.

Richard Bueschel of Time Share Corporation which prepares materials for Houghton Mifflin said,

"The approach in the 60s was to replace the teacher. Technically it was correct . . the computer can replace the teacher. But it missed the practicalities, missed the point that education is student interaction with the teacher . . . Besides, teachers weren't going to go for it."

J. Kenrich Noble, Jr., publishing analyst for Paine, Webber, Michell, Hutchins notes:

"Though student enrolments have dropped 5.5 per cent since 1969, largely among elementary and high schools, there are segments, particularly in the earlier grades, that are flattening or rising. Several years from now declining numbers of teachers may cross rising student numbers, making any instructional tools that make the teacher more efficient high priorities."

Knowledge is, therefore, seen as residing in the machine, not the person.

"I think these diagnostic tests are another one of these things where somebody came up with the idea. Somebody who has a little empire to run sold somebody in the school department. Descriptively it sounds wonderful. You test each child and you know exactly what they need. It's a prescriptive thing. You look at their profile and you say, 'Oh good, this child needs to study this and this and this.' It sounds wonderful. Now that's based on two assumptions. One is that we don't know ourselves how the children are doing. Secondly, the other assumption is that the kinds of things that are being tested there are more important than the kinds of things such as general comprehension and following directions and understanding that the whole thing has to hang together. The whole paragraph or sentence has to hang together to mean something. The tests simply don't test for that kind of general reading ability." (Y, 1981)

Retaining teachers then becomes a question of choosing the person who will most strictly adhere to that mechanical solution, rather than the one who will weigh and discuss, choose and implement.

"I'm realizing that the other third grade teacher who is my colleague, with whom I exchange children for reading, has what is presumably the middle group. I have presumably the top and bottom group. I find out that her top group is almost where my top group is, and we've been on our book since the beginning of the year, and she didn't start it until just two months ago. It makes me feel that maybe I'm holding these kids back, but consensus is that these books are pretty hard. They've got some rather intriguing stories, ones that are not just run of the mill ordinary kinds of stories, with a lot of metaphorical language and different kinds of fiction and fantasy. We do a lot with that sort of thing. I just feel really that I don't know if I'm doing the right thing in spending all that time on each story and having the children do a lot of things with each story. She's obviously bombing through the book. A story a day, I

guess. it makes me nervous that somebody is
going to say I'm not a very good teacher. I
really feel as though my kids are getting a
great deal out of their reading. But it's
one of those things that doesn't look good on
paper." (Y, 1980)

The roots of these conflicts have never been
addressed within the context of analyzing
classroom issues. Rather, critics have focused
teachers' attention on the failure of the
individual - the teacher, the student, and the
student's parent - and his or her inability to
adjust to the established system. Understanding
how life inside the classroom is crucially
affected by the structure of the school system as
a whole is considered counterproductive to a
teacher's career.

"Many teachers are hired to do their thing in
the classroom, but that's as far as they're
supposed to go. They're not really part of
policy or curriculum in very meaningful ways.
I think that's what a lot of the isolation is
about. I certainly have the feeling - I know
I'm not alone in this - there's a lot of
futility in that and frustration." (B, 1979)

If every teacher would only be perfect -
responding fairly, efficiently, and effectively
with infinite wisdom and tact to every child and
exigency - we would have the perfect system.
Teachers know that they are incapable of such
persistent perfection. They often react in ways
that increase their sense of isolation and
reinforce their powerlessness in the institution.
When confronted with stereotyped choices that deny
or obscure the conflicting demands placed on
teachers, teachers frequently lash out in angry
denial while internalizing the negative message.
They are told, and have come to believe, they have
'burned out'.

"I had found that toward the middle of last
year I was beginning to feel - dead. And I
was beginning to feel frustrated and I was
beginning to feel sort of like this was a
drudgery. And I had never felt like that
before - I mean, classroom teaching was my
thing. I really loved it. Then this year
coming into the situation and getting such a
difficult class, I started off the year with
a tremendous sense of frustration. I
thought, 'My God, what am I going to do with
these kids?' I kept thinking, 'I'm not

really, really happy with what's happening in
this class and I wonder how much of it is my
own fault'." (W, 1981)

The present-day discovery of teacher
dissatisfaction as a recently recognized
phenomenon obscures the fact that the basic
contradictory demands on teachers have been
present since the doors of the brick grammar
school first closed behind a staff of schoolmarms,
a male principal, and a rush of youngsters.

The modern concept of 'burnout' is the
natural result of the new ideology of
professionalism which encourages teachers to see
themselves as more powerful than they actually are
and, therefore, more responsible alone to correct
complex societal and institutional dilemmas. What
has been labelled 'burnout' is, in fact, anger and
frustration. Today, the more publicized 'burned-
out' teacher has come to represent the 'true
identity' of all dedicated teachers. The concept
encompasses even those who haven't burned out. If
burnout is the natural end to a dedicated teacher,
those who have managed to survive are seen as
callous and self-serving.

The two labels of 'burnout' and 'deadwood'
further divide the teaching workforce. Younger
teachers or those still with other career options
are told they have worked too hard and have
therefore 'burned out'. Older teachers are told
they aren't working hard enough and have become
'deadwood'. The fact that both are demoralized
points to similar concerns, but the labels obscure
the commonalities.

'Burnout', however, does not come from
overtaxing one's intellectual and mental
capacities. Burnout comes from not being able to
use those abilities to handle difficult emotional
and managerial problems. These problems are often
the result of administrators' analysis of a
situation far removed from their personal and
immediate responsibility. The establishment of
the master teacher position which would remove
teachers from classrooms to oversee other teachers
would add another level of managers who are
separated from the rank and file.

"In short, the paradox that to become
increasingly professional in teaching means
increasingly subjugating personal values and
interests to system maintenance functions
tends not to be confronted except in
isolation. With rare exception, professional

274

organizations that have followed the American labor union model for organization and action continue to ignore quality of life issues."[4] The reward offered to master teachers - removal from the classroom and a chance to participate in curriculum development, supervision, and decision making or institutional concerns - confirms the true confinement of being inside the classroom and the dearth of possibilities for classroom teachers to influence the more content and structurally oriented areas.

In contrast, those who exhibit managerial, i.e. distant, 'objective' relationships with colleagues and students, would have the edge in being chosen master teacher, much as they now have the edge on being chosen principal.

"You have to make yourself very well known to get any recognition in this system. I've decided that. You have to belong to the teachers' union and the negotiating team and negotiate with these people. Then I think they get a feeling for your strengths and weaknesses and get to know you . . . I was just thinking the other day, 'Who are the busy little bees that do all the dirty work, put together minimum competency standards and tests, do all the background work for curriculum decisions? Women. Who's on the negotiating team? Men.' And I think if you don't do those things there is no other way they get to know you because they certainly don't go in classrooms. No one would ever recognize you for that. And that's what I've done all my life and I don't think they know me from a hole in the wall. Or if they did, it doesn't really count."

These reports also deplore the level of intelligence of teachers, particularly those presently entering the field. They do not investigate the absence within teaching of opportunities for exhibiting this characteristic. This critique of teachers is not new, despite the nostalgic assertion of the majority of these reports that teachers just aren't what they used to be. It may be that intelligent women were lured into teaching as these reports contend, but it wasn't their intelligence and the promise of being able to use it that was seen as an effective hook. To the teachers themselves, their now much vaunted intelligence was never mentioned. What was emphasized was their 'natural' ability for working with children, a trait that earned teaching the label 'women's true profession'. The emphasis on the nurturing qualities of good teaching - empathy, patience - made irrelevant any discussion of the intellectual abilities of teachers.

Intelligence is only the latest in a string of attributes reported to be lacking - each attribute having been seen at the time of its exposure as part of the essential make-up of a good teacher. Rather than investigating how the system often deadens teachers, these reports concentrate on the individual, who alone in her classroom creates the soft pockets of civilization. Focusing criticism on the individual person, who - for different reasons at different moments in history - 'just shouldn't teach' or is not of master teacher quality, perpetuates the idea that it is the individual alone who must make a difference, or that by being the right kind of person a teacher will be exempt from the failures others have experienced. There is no recognition within these reports of the structural barriers to enhancing educational potential for either student or teacher and no incentive to look at how the institutional frame-work of schools frequently creates stagnation while punishing attempts to challenge and improve bad school practices.

Precisely when intellectual challenge and opportunities for nurturing are being curtailed even more than in the past, the panacea of merit pay is introduced as a way of defusing or obscuring the true roots of that alienation. The overriding concern of the authors of these reports - reversing a declining rate of profits - explains their solution to the problem of teacher alienation - merit pay for the few, luckily also a neat justification for maintaining the rest of the teaching staff at present or lower levels of salaries. Their recommendation of merit pay is gambling that teachers will accept the replacement of a cash reward for the goal of helping individual children and society as a whole. Merit pay quite baldly tells teachers they should recognize that that goal is old-fashioned, a pipe dream, a mirage used to lure them into teaching.

Merit pay/master teacher will appease the few by co-opting their anger and frustration. It will standardize the work of every teacher anxious to follow the method of the present master teacher and eager to discern what teaching style would best fit in with the principal's present conception of a good teacher. Thus, merit pay can easily increase mediocrity, as teachers hold on to a sure thing or seek to emulate other 'sure things' practised by favoured teachers.

The end result will be that those who seek a creative outlet, whether or not they receive merit pay, will leave teaching. They will be greatly lamented by concerned parents who may well turn their anger on the remaining teachers. The dual career mother/professional woman moving into banking, law, or computer programming may not understand why an intelligent woman is willing to spend her day with children. The rising corporate woman, thrilled with her new career but mindful of her children's needs, explains to herself that she needs a fulfilling job in an important area. She would like to be convinced that being with children and finding such a job are incompatible.

Paradoxically, for the working class woman the teacher represents the powerful professional woman who the media has suggested is secure in a demanding position. Both sets of mothers will not understand that their desire to secure the excellent teacher for their child - with their varying conceptions of what that means - often ends in the departure of some of those same teachers and the demoralization of the others who will teach their remaining children. As the teacher packs her homemade games, her aquarium and rock collection, and carts them off, the teacher herself now wonders about her own future and her ability to adjust to the world outside and its reflection in the interior world of the classroom. She may also wonder about the further adjustments to be made by the pupils and teachers who remain in schools.

NOTES

1.   Freedman, S. (1979) Personal Journal.
2.   Letters are used to indicate specific teachers interviewed by the Boston Women's Teachers' Group. Single letters indicate teachers interviewed bi-weekly over a year's teaching schedule. Double letters indicate teachers interviewed bi-monthly over a school year calendar.

3. McCutcheon, G. (September, 1980) 'How Do Elementary School Teachers Plan?' in The Elementary School Journal, 8, p.27.
4. Bullough, Jr., R. (1982) 'Paradox and Professionalism', in The Educational Forum, Winter, p.208.

Chapter Eleven

THE NATIONAL UNION OF TEACHERS (ENGLAND AND WALES)

Ken Jones

To read the educational output of the
National Union of Teachers is to experience the
power of the past over the present. Looking back,
the union emphasises its overriding aim of
securing expansion of opportunity; it stresses
the reasonableness of its cause and the supporters
the cause has attracted, across the political
spectrum. Governments may sometimes have
obstructed expansion, short-sighted councils may
have sought immediate economies at the expensive
of long-term interests, but the lesson of history
is that allies will be found to press the struggle
on. The future of the nation's children is the
future of the nation itself, and enough will
realise this axiom to make the union's efforts
eventually worthwhile. This outlook is plainly
that of a body which claims, not simply trade
union status, but co-responsibility for the
education service. It colours the rhetoric and
strategy of the union's present campaigns, which
enumerate once-consensual themes:

> "All children should have equal opportunity
> to develop their abilities and talents to the
> full.
> Access to a public education service of the
> highest quality is a fundamental right for
> all children . . .
> The united support of all who care for the
> nation's future is vital if these principles
> are to be upheld and our children offered the
> opportunities they deserve."[1]

These propositions are offered as re-statements of
well-known truths, which scarcely need argument.
The full range of present educational crisis -
which comprises more than cuts and crass anti-
egalitarianism - is not discussed.

That 'equal opportunity' as it has previously been defined has foundered on inequalities of class, sex, race and power; that 'quality' has become a term of an immensely problematic sort; that 'united support' cannot easily be invoked when the community of 'those who care' is divided about the value and purpose of education - these problems, which are all aspects of a breakdown of consensus, are not registered. Yet these difficulties are at the heart of the union's current situation which arise from the combination of economic recession with a very marked shift in the relationship of major social forces to state education. The union's traditional pathways of advance are blocked. The assumption that educational expansion is synonymous with economic benefit is not widely shared. Governments no longer think that the teaching force can be relied upon to adjust itself to official perceptions of educational need; on the contrary, it is argued that new routes of policy-making have to be constructed, that by-pass the union's channels of influence. The teaching force must not only contract. Just as important, it must be subject to increased control both of its educational work and its conditions of service.

The NUT thus faces a Conservative government committed not only to financial restraint, but to radical revision of the 1944 educational settlement. This settlement, and its renewal in the 1960s, provided the conditions for the extension of the union's influence, as well as the matrix in which the attitudes of its leaders and many members were formed. The union has been accustomed to rising membership, educational expansion and increasing curricular influence. The accelerating revision of the settlement has shaken the NUT. Its membership falling, its influence lessened, the conditions of service of its members worsening, the union is attempting to develop a new strategy that in its basics revives and consolidates its traditional outlook, and yet also faces problems that require responses more associated with trade union than professional forms of struggle. This article examines the tensions that arise in this difficult process.

No single great governmental battle plan has forced the union onto the defensive. But the cumulative effect of a number of distinct processes has been to face the union with problems on every front.

SALARIES

The average salary of a teacher has fallen – by comparison with average earnings in the workforce as a whole – by about 30% since 1975[2]. The early 70s were a time of teacher shortage and successful pay campaigns. By contrast, 1984 finds management in a strong position. Teacher numbers are falling – by 10% between 1979 and 1983. Teacher unemployment is rising to an official level of about 15,000[3], 3-4% of the teaching force.

In addition to their low pay increases, many teachers find that their automatic progression by yearly increments has come to a halt: they have reached the top of their particular pay scale, and no further movement is possible without promotion. Promotion is difficult because, with a fall in student numbers, schools are less able to make appointments above the lowest scale of the 5 scale salary structure.

The teaching unions have turned their attention to renegotiating the salary structure. The employers (representatives of local authorities with whom teachers negotiate on the Burnham national salary committee) have used the occasion to link issues of pay to those of the management and control of the teaching force. Their proposals for restructuring would make salary progression dependent upon assessment of the teacher. There would be a three year 'entry grade' for new teachers, with the elimination at the end of this period of teachers who were declared professionally incompetent, or who failed to display something called 'long term career potential'. There would be an annual assessment of teachers on the 'Main Professional Grade' with accelerated progression through the pay scales for teachers certified as good, and the withholding of increments from those who did not satisfy. A condition of being paid at all would be a willingness to accept as contractual activities which are now voluntary: lunch-time supervision, staff meetings, 'in service training', parents' evenings. These proposals will, of course, be modified in negotiation. Even so it is clear that the employers envisage a teaching force more flexible in its interpretation of 'professional duties' and subject to assessment as a condition of advance. And, since criteria for assessment

The National Union of Teachers (England and Wales)

will be influenced by new educational policy goals, employers will also be able to develop a surer means of translating curriculum policy into school practice.

JOB SECURITY

The years since 1979/80 have been marked by a reduction in educational provision which has in many cases increased workloads and lowered morale. 'Morale' in this context should be understood in a strong sense. It is not simply a question of increased stress arising from a decline in resources. It entails, also, a sense of the breakdown of an educational project: that of attempting to develop a pedagogy based on principles of equal opportunity. The attitudes created by the expectation of unemployment, the perception of a lowered public status, the pressures from inside and outside the school to emphasise differentiation of curricula, and the new vocationalism all combine to create a general crisis of teaching purpose.

The particulars of job security should be set against this background.

Compulsory redundancy is very rare - though hundreds have been prevailed upon to accept premature retirement with compensation, and thousands have left teaching voluntarily, under similar agreements. But redundancy is not the only threat to job security. The number of teachers employed on fixed-term (temporary) contracts is slowly increasing; an NUT survey put the proportion in 1983 at 4.6% of the teaching force. About half have been placed on such contracts in order that their employers can more easily eliminate jobs in time of cutback.

Compulsory redeployment is also on the increase. The White Paper of March 1983 on Teaching Quality recommends its use, not just as a means of dealing with a teacher 'surplus' at a particular school, but as a permanently available tool of managerial policy.

This policy, though directly affecting only a small number, can only weaken the sense that all teachers have of belonging to a particular staff at a particular school. It 'de-collectivises' the teacher's conception of his/her status, and thus helps to increase the influence of centralised authority both within the school, and within a local authority area.

EDUCATIONAL INFLUENCE

In the union's best years, government influence on the curriculum was indirect. Teachers, though subject to advice, resisted stipulation. The main advisory body on the curriculum was not a government department but the autonomous Schools Council, on which the union was strongly represented. The Council is now dissolved and has been replaced by committees on the curriculum and examinations appointed by the Secretary of State. At the same time there is an abundance of state and independent initiatives, all of which have the effect of reclaiming from teachers much of the curricular ground they occupied in their heyday. The proposed common examination at 16+ will lessen the influence teachers have exercised through the CSE exam boards. Encouraged by the DES, the two main (private) vocational examining bodies are to promote a new 'practical' curriculum leading to a system of pre-vocational and technical awards[4]. Likewise, the government's 'Technical and Vocational Initiative', funded not by the DES but through the Manpower Services Commission, represents a direct national influence upon a curriculum traditionally open to school-based decision. Other government initiatives, outside the control, even, of the DES are setting a context for the school curriculum that installs at the heart of the educational system a goal different from that of equal opportunity, in that by stressing the relationship between education and occupational destiny it emphasises that the school must provide appropriately vocational forms of education for students destined for relative failure in the labour market. The Youth Training Scheme has an educational basis which is rudimentary in the extreme[5]. Yet its educational criteria are influencing school curricular developments, and the union can do little to modify them.

As the union's national influence on the curriculum diminishes, its members experience in their schools the emergence of different criteria and new demands. Stimulated by DES circulars, local authorities are requiring of their schools an account of their curricular objectives. As the schools redefine their work, the initiative passes from the subject departments to the administrative centre; and the recommendations of heads and deputies, curriculum co-ordinators and working parties are increasingly inflected by the new vocationalism.

ACCOUNTABILITY

The corollary of teacher control of the curriculum has always been an objection to 'outside interference', whether governmental, industrial - or parental. In practice this has entailed not only a justifiable suspicion of government's centralising tendencies but also a resistance to dialogue with popular organisations about educational objectives. At a time of consensus, the weakness of this latter position was not crucial: teacher activity could at least parallel the public mood even if there was little explicit interaction. However, when with the publication of the Black Papers in the late sixties, the right wing began to depart from the consensus, teachers had to face something more than the usual lobbying and infighting against particular government policies. They now had also to cope with a populist critique of the comprehensive principle which, utilising the slogan of accountability, appealed over the heads of the usual protagonists of debate to win some support among parents and public opinion. The NUT has found it difficult to respond to a challenge of this kind. Too much associated with the character of post-war reform to respond critically to the shortcomings of 'equal opportunity', it has never investigated the sources of discontent with the school system and is thus vulnerable to criticisms which play upon concern about the discipline and knowledge presently transmitted by the school in order to advocate a return to a form of schooling in which order and a sense of purpose would allegedly be secured by the unambiguous matching of types of education to types of future occupation.

Mainstream Conservative policy borrowed from the Black Papers the slogan of accountability and deployed it as a tactic in educational debate. The accuracy of the charges that linked a supposed decline in 'standards' to the secretive and unresponsive nature of the system was questionable; but this was less important than their political effect. Conservative policy was able to exploit a gap - caused partly by failures of communication and partly by real differences in

educational conception - between the activity of
teachers and the expectations of parental opinion.
A diluted form of 'parental choice' is now
embodied in the 1980 Education Act, which gives
parents the right to indicate a preference for a
particular secondary school. It is a device which
assures some schools of substantial demand and
certain survival, while alongside them unpopular
schools face falling rolls and the possibility of
closure. Given that parental choice is exercised
in a manner influenced by the new themes of
educational policy, schools are under pressure to
provide an education in line with the redefined
priorities. It thus serves as another pressure
towards conformity and as a further, if distant,
instrument of control over the teaching force.

This survey should be enough to indicate that
the problems the NUT faces are not simply the
classic ones of trade unionism in a period of
recession. Though they encompass the defence of
jobs and conditions, they also go beyond it.
Teacher autonomy in determining the curriculum,
relative freedom from management control, and
organisational influence upon national policy-
making have been among the union's major
objectives, and have formed the practical content
of its claim to professionalism. Each aspect of
this policy is now under threat. Much of the
anger that fuelled the union's 1984 salary action
- which involved refusal to take on 'voluntary'
activities, or to cover for absent teachers, as
well as widespread strike action - arose as a
response to this combination of factors, and not
from the pay issue alone.

Before examining the responses of union
policy to these issues, it is necessary to look at
the varied composition and attitudes of the union
and of the teaching force. These must be
appreciated before any account of the development
of union policy can become comprehensible. It is
useful to begin with a description of some of the
major points of division among teachers.

SALARY AND MANAGERIAL FUNCTION

Salary differentials are large enough to
sustain differences in outlook between groups of
teachers, especially when combined with the
interests arising from the managerial functions
carried out by a surprisingly large percentage of
the workforce[6]. In September 1981, there were

nearly 60,000 head teachers and deputies in
employment: 13% of all teachers. Of the rest
9.5% were on Scale 4 or Senior Teacher scale[7].
Though it is impossible in any exact way to read
off from teachers' position in the school
hierarchy their attitude towards trade union
issues, there is a rough but evident correlation
between status and 'political' practice. The
tendency for heads to leave the NUT or NAS/UWT
over the last decade, in order to join less
militant head teacher organisations is one
indicator of this.

PRIMARY AND SECONDARY TEACHERS

Secondary teachers are on average better
paid, have greater opportunity for promotion, and
more time in school to prepare lessons. Working
in larger units, they are better able to resist or
escape close supervision of their work. Protected
by their numbers, more remote from parental
pressure, and less vulnerable to the argument that
militancy causes children to suffer, they are -
though in many senses better off than their
primary colleagues - more likely to take
'industrial' action. Yet, in the NUT, primary
teachers are the majority: the implications of a
situation in which the part of the union with the
lesser implantation within its own sector plays
the more militant role needs further consideration.

GENDER

Sexual discrimination permeates teaching.
Women are 59% of the teaching force. They occupy
the lower salary scales, hold 96% of part-time
contracts (which are usually temporary), and 81%
of full-time temporary contracts[8]. They are less
likely to be graduates and more likely to be 'non-
specialised' teachers or to work in the less
prestigious areas of the curriculum.
The effects of discrimination are as
pervasive in the major teaching unions as they are
in the schools. The NUT (which has a much better
record on 'equal opportunities' than its rivals)
has only 8 women on an elected executive of 42 -
yet nearly 60% of its membership is female, and in
every region of the union there are more women
than men members. Over two thirds of women
primary teachers are in the union, but less than

half of male primary teachers. In secondary schools, too, women members outnumber men: nearly one in two women secondary teachers are in the union; less than one in three men. Yet these proportions are not reflected in the composition of school and area leaderships.

UNION MEMBERSHIP AND POLITICAL ALIGNMENT

Only about half the teachers in England and Wales belong to the NUT - about 220,000. Of the rest, the National Association of Schoolmasters/Union of Women Teachers claims 120,000 and Assistant Masters and Mistresses Association 80,000[9]. Both organise mainly in secondary schools. The Professional Association of Teachers (23,000) and the head teacher associations claim the rest.

Only the NUT and NAS/UWT are affiliated to the TUC. PAT never strikes; AMMA hardly ever. The NAS/UWT built its reputation as a militant union of male teachers - 'the men's movement', it called itself[10]. It gained many members in the 1960s, as a result of its salary campaigns. It maintains a militant rhetoric on questions of pay and conditions, and has a highly competitive attitude towards recruitment. It is much more distant than the NUT from the reforming tradition in education. It is less concerned with the establishment of alliances with extra-educational bodies, and less likely to co-operate at local level with non-educational unions. It is inclined, in its educational pronouncements, to authoritarianism, as befits a union which for many years championed the cause of 'men teachers for boys'. Although it established itself as a union in the course of campaigns against equal pay (which would, it said, reduce the male teacher's salary, and prevent him earning a 'family wage') it has in recent years been forced to moderate this stand, first by the Sex Discrimination Act, and recently by the need to maintain membership levels - a concern which is leading to attempts at recruitment in primary schools.

It will be plain from this account that union membership and political orientation to some extent overlap. It would be improbable that a Labour voter would join PAT, and unlikely that any organised socialist tendency of teachers would arise outside the NUT. No union, though, can claim that its membership is firmly aligned on the

287

left. An opinion poll[11] taken before the 1983 general election indicated that 44% of teachers, the majority in primary schools, would vote Conservative. The rest were fairly evenly divided between SDP/Liberal and Labour Party. These differences are probably not reproduced in exactly the same form in the NUT, where Conservatives are less assured of support. Nonetheless, the general picture of political heterogeneity does also hold true for the union.

But differences in overall political allegiance are not directly translated into particular alignments in NUT debate. They are, instead, refracted through conceptions that the nature of the union requires a special form of politics. Executive members who have long been in the Labour Party will argue against activity that might be considered as over-sympathetic to Labour. Thus, also, campaigns - such as that to defend existing abortion rights - which achieve reflex (if not always vigorous) support in the trade union movement as a whole are shunned by NUT leaders. The basis of this dissociation between private belief and public action is discussed later. One of its results has been that it falls to those groups - particularly the Socialist Teachers' Alliance - which were originally connected with organisations to the left of the Labour Party, to defend positions which in other, non-teaching, unions would be common ground.

It is important that, of this catalogue of divisions, none is seen as politically immutable. The teaching force has always been divided - particularly along lines of sexual discrimination and status. The degree of sharpness of the political splits that arise from such differences has depended upon the effectiveness of the strategy advanced by the major organisations: the rise in NAS membership in the 1960s after a salaries debacle attributed to the NUT is one case in point[12]. The secession of the now defunct NUWT from the NUT on the issue of equal pay is another[13].

. . . . .

Having considered some of the main features of the NUT's ideology, of the policy changes it has to face, and of its constituency, it is now possible to look more closely at the effectiveness of its strategy, as a means of maintaining the strength and influence of the union in the context of a sharp and sometimes frantic fight to defend educational provision.

The NUT has always presented itself as the transcender of differences; with justice, it points to its non-sectional nature. Unlike AMMA it has no history of representing the interests of grammar school teachers in an exclusive way; unlike the NAS/UWT it has no record of explicit support for the almost literally patriarchal demands of male teachers. Its aim has been: to unify a profession. The two terms of this brief phrase have to be read together. The unity that it seeks is of a specifically professional kind. The union has for many years supported the setting up of a General Teaching Council, which would have the power to control both entry to the profession, and discipline within it. If such a body were to be established, it would increase the consultative weight of teachers and raise their status.

It is doubtful whether this aspiration is realistic. If teaching is a profession, it is largely a self-recognised one. Neither in pay nor security, institutional authority nor curricular influence do teachers share the position of doctors or lawyers. The trend is rather the other way. Yet although the hope of professional self-government is ill-founded, it has real effects. The NUT, having set out its aspirations for the future, cannot in the present behave in a manner which departs too sharply from them. Professionalism, while not incompatible with episodes of 'industrial action', certainly inhibits the systematic development of a trade union orientation.

A too-consistent pattern of militancy, political alignment and educational controversy seems from the perspective of professional unity to jeopardise the union's highest ambitions, since the conferral of self-government upon an unruly teaching force would be impossible.

In this way professionalist traditions lock into and reinforce the union's reliance upon the achieving of educational progress, not through combativity or political partisanship, but through alliance with the broadest possible forces on a narrow front of issues.

The phrase 'unity of the profession' can be glossed in another way too: that it is only as a profession that unity can be achieved. This is the rational basis of professionalism at the present time. For even when the hope of a self-

governing profession is shown to be false, it can
still be argued that among such a heterogenous
teaching body, political alignment is ruinously
divisive, and that it is only a teaching force
which demonstrates a deep concern, quite beyond
politics, for the fate of education, which can
secure public support and its own cohesion.
This argument overlooks the deepening
ideological divisions among teachers. Nevertheless it is employed within the NUT to justify the
union's abstention on an important range of
issues. It is the basis of a double, self-denying
exclusion. It discountenances, first of all, the
formation of a school-based politics of the
curriculum. It is not for NUT members to develop
collective policies on what should be taught in
their school; that is the responsibility of the
heads, in consultation with their staffs. This is
a responsibility which can be devolved to individual teachers, but which cannot be mediated via
the school union group. This conception rests in
turn upon a belief that the nurture of children is
a task which is politically and ideologically
unproblematic and must therefore be kept free from
political controversy and 'interference'.

Yet state educational policy, though doing
lip-service to education's non-political status,
has in reality taken a series of political
initiatives that have shifted the ground of
educational common-sense rightwards, and are
changing the ideological character of an important
part of the school curriculum - 14-19. The
union's belief in the neutrality of the
educational process does not assist it in coping
with these developments.

The second forbidden zone is that of extra-
educational politics. The union's constitution
codifies the relationship it should have with
political parties and the trade union movement: a
distant one, that is made still more remote by the
way that the present executive interprets the
union's 'aims and objects'. For an issue to be
supported, it must have an explicit educational
content; for an organisation to be worked with it
must have educational objectives.

The problem with this approach is that it is
not at all symmetrical with government policy.
For the government, education occupies just a few
degrees of a wider arc of vision. Thus measures
to privatise aspects of education (meals,
cleaning, some YTS courses) are not unique to the

sector, but part of a broader policy. Likewise, the fall in education spending is not independent of the rise in spending on defence. When the union decides that only a single aspect, selected from the general movement, is relevant to its concerns, then it renders impossible co-operation with other unions across the broad front. Here arises the union's dilemma. The nature of the problems that it faces impel it towards consideration of issues that arise outside the educational sector. But traditional politics and the pressing fears that a politicised union, in attempting to alter a century-old configuration of teacher attitudes, will lose members and influence, pull it back towards conservatism. In the arguments of the majority of the union's executive this difficulty is the reason for a high rate of abstention on 'political' issues, exemplified in the union's votes at the TUC, and in its attitudes to central issues of trade union politics.

But while professionalist ideas are still powerful in the NUT, they are increasingly modified by the pressing necessities of trade union action.

It is not as if the changes described at the beginning of the article have occurred outside the teachers' organisations, and are only now provoking a debate on the strategies needed to deal with them. In an uneven, spasmodic and overlapping way, changes in teachers' status, educational spending and curricular policy have been in motion since the mid seventies. Combined with changes in the composition of the teaching force, they have already had an effect on the relationship of teachers' organisations to each other, and on their internal life.

As early as the end of the sixties, in the late afternoon of consensus, long, premonitory shadows were being cast. The pay strikes of 1969/70 brought about the growth of 'trade union' methods of struggle and organisation, and, in reaction, the development of 'non-political' and non-militant organisation. This was the period when the NAS and NUT affiliated to the TUC, as well as that of the founding of the PAT.

Throughout the seventies these shadows took on more substance. Legislation of the Labour Government of 1974-79 strengthened the process of trade unionisation by encouraging the development of training courses for local union officers. At school level, the function of the NUT 'correspondent' was evolving into that of 'representative'. At the same time, the generation of activists who had come into the union at the end of World War II reached retiring age. These men were gradually replaced, in the local union structures, by members of the generation which arrived in teaching in annual batches of 40,000 in the early seventies. The processes of trade unionisation and generational change were speeded up as the union came into collision with the cuts. A more hectic pace of activity and the demands of a higher level of mobilisation have led in many areas to a recomposition in union leadership.

Developments in union organisation have been accompanied by a drift of union policy to the left. This movement centres on local action against cuts. In addition, where the TUC is united behind an action, the union, seeing in unanimity a legitimisation of action, hs sometimes offered support: on the TUC 'Day of Action' against government policy in 1980, and, in support of the health workers, in 1982. These are the modest frontiers of expansion into areas which, because they encompass broader-than-educational objectives, are new territory for the union. They find their cautious parallels in union policy in the endorsement by Union Conference of the need for 'an alternative economic policy' to that of the government. (The indefinite article establishes a distance between the union's policy and that of the TUC and Labour Party.)

Neither educational action, nor that of the wider sort, should be seen simply as developments of <u>policy</u>. The process of organising action alters (even temporarily) the composition, structures and outlook of the union's local associations. Always, there are a few members who resign; others become involved in the union for the first time; in circles which extend beyond the usual activists, NUT policies are debated and questioned. In this process, the previous certainties of union life are put in doubt - without, necessarily, approval being given to a coherent new strategy.

These were all features of the highest recent point of teacher union militancy - the NUT's seven-week strike in the London Borough of Barking and Dagenham in 1982. The strike is worth examining for what it reveals of the potential of teacher militancy, of the relationship between the NUT and non-teaching unions, and of the way that parents responded to teacher trade unionism. Implied in the strike were fragments of a strategy that, developed in a coherent way, could with some optimism address the present educational crisis.

The Labour council of Barking and Dagenham announced in September 1981 that it intended to cut 160 teaching jobs - about 10% of the total number - starting the following April. About 30 of these jobs would be lost through compulsory redundancy. This package provoked a strike - the union's longest since the 1920s - which was in many ways squarely in the NUT tradition: ultimate control, and conduct of negotiations, rested at Hamilton House; strikers were fully sustained by the union; the issue which triggered it related to the defence of existing levels of jobs and provision. But the way it was organised has a significance of its own, in what it showed of the way that, in order to oppose severe attacks on their jobs and on education, teachers adopt new tactics and new relationships with parents and with other trade unions.

Apart from the more rapid tempo of union life - mass meetings at least weekly, strike committees every other day - the action was remarkable for its combination of union militancy with popular support: the two were not at all incompatible. A measure of the extent of 'trade unionisation' in the NUT was the readiness of teachers to carry out the controversial public activity of picketing. Official picket lines appeared outside primary and secondary schools - intended, though, to turn away supplies rather than teachers in other unions. Unionised oil-tanker drivers refused to cross the pickets; the council therefore employed scab drivers. Teachers lay down in front of their lorries, tracked them to their depots and spread word of the council's tactics in the local Labour movement. Next, a council driver was suspended for respecting the picket lines. The resulting strike of the council's drivers was almost fully sustained by donations from NUT members.

Just as important, the local union was able, first to mobilise and then to work alongside newly-created organisations of parents. Widespread leafleting and the assiduous collection of names at lobbies led to a volatile inaugural meeting of a 'Parents' Action Committee' which in turn set up groups in about half the schools. These parents organised meetings in the schools, occupations of the Town Hall, and demonstrations in Barking and in Central London. Although many parents did not support the strike, efforts to organise a 'go back to work' campaign failed, since the 'Parents' Action Committees' clearly had the initiative.

The union was able to build such support because it linked the issue of jobs to that of educational provision. A fight against redundancies alone would have had nothing like the same impact. In the context of cuts of this size, in an area which was predominantly working class, the slogan of equal opportunity became the basis of a militant, if limited, campaign and inspired an attitude among parents which was strong enough to sustain the burden of making arrangements for child-care during a long strike.

In the policy of the union nationally, however, the relationship between militancy and parental support is not explored. Propaganda aimed at parents is written for those who are thought to inhabit the middle ground of politics - 'young executives in tree-lined suburbs' as one union leader put it - who must be won away from Thatcherism to a belief that 'investment in education is the basis for national prosperity'. Unsurprisingly, the committees, demonstrations and occupations of the Barking strike are not a reference point. Nor is its insistence on equal opportunity as a working class right. Instead, the union executive appeals to another tradition, that descends from Disraeli to Edward Heath, and that sees educational expansion as entirely compatible with conservative social philosophies. An early parliamentary justification for universal schooling is quoted with approval:

"Upon the speedy provision of elementary education depends our industrial prosperity . . . Upon this speedy provision depends also . . . the good safe working of our constitutional system."[14]

So the occasional necessities of strike action are bound within an overall framework that endorses the most conventional values of education policy.

The strike was fairly successful - nearly two-thirds of the threatened jobs were retained, and there were no redundancies. But like every action, it had its cost and aftermath. 'TEACHERS

TRIUMPHANT' wrote the local paper, hyperbolically, and as if the strike was a sporting contest in which the winners would be secure in their victory for all time. In reality, the strike represented an enormous collective investment of energy, of a kind which could not easily be repeated. The action over, members returned to their schools. Some frustrated that the action had not achieved all it seemed to promise, others to schools where censorious heads and non-strikers (the other teaching unions at no point joined in) exerted the pressures of conformity. Nevertheless, the strike not only brought lasting benefits, in terms of the number of jobs protected, but also demonstrated the way in which militant trade union action can develop in ways which alter the usual relationship of the NUT to other sections of society.

It is not only the union's response to 'economic' questions which has changed. The women's movement has also had an effect on union policy. In danger of being outflanked from the left, and responsive to changes in the ideological climate, the executive has taken up issues related to 'equal opportunities', and in 1976 produced a memorandum on the issue. This document concentrated on aspects of sexism in the curriculum, women's conditions of service, and questions of promotion. Since then, there has been a gradual movement towards consideration of the role of women in the union.

The 1984 Conference of the union voted to set up national union structures which would have the effect of encouraging the organisation of women: an 'equal opportunities' department; an advisory committee on 'equal opportunities'; the possibility of an annual conference on 'equal opportunities'. Small steps, but important in that they establish a framework for future activity. A lot has still to be done. At the moment, the union has six national officers, all men; six senior officials, one of them a woman; twelve regional officials, all men. Local associations are, in the main, led by men. The union is beginning to become aware that these proportions comprise a problem, but its most usual way of explaining the difficulty is to refer to the (learned) passivity and non-assertiveness of women: the problem lies in the consciousness of women, rather than the activity of men. This diagnosis, itself symptomatic, explains the

untroubled persistence of a range of behaviour,
from the generic use of the masculine pronoun to
the platforms weighted down with male speakers and
the prioritisation of the major areas of the
union's activity. It is a factor which helps
explain the union's relative neglect of primary as
against secondary education, as well as the
absence from its main campaigns of discussion of
the way in which the issues involved - from
salaries to nursery education - particularly
affect women.

It is important to see changes in the NUT as
only one side of the response of teacher
organisations to the changes in educational
politics. If the activity of 1969/70 prefigured
some welcome changes in NUT policy, it also
foreshadowed some less heartening developments. It
was in the aftermath of the pay strikes of those
years that the PAT was founded - an organisation
whose policies are less important than its
embodiment of a single principle: that teachers,
being professionals, should not take any form of
industrial action, let alone strike. Thus the PAT
abstracted, from the strategy of professional
unity and educational reform developed by the NUT,
just one element, and then exaggerated it.
Though the present Conservative Government
has been eager to recognise PAT, its influence is
not great. But its existence as, in effect, the
newest teachers' union provokes important
questions: why is it that the unification of the
education system which has occurred with the
ending of the 11+, and the many problems that
teachers have faced over the last decade have not
created either a general unification of teachers'
organisations, or else established more firmly the
hegemony of the NUT, as the union most willing to
take defensive action? Why is it, rather, that
the trends of consciousness most acutely
dramatised in the founding of the PAT actually
seem to have increased their strength in the
teaching force, so that it is necessary to speak
not simply of a 'drift to the left', but of a more
complex process of polarisation?
To ask these questions is to draw attention
to a number of developments: the fact that AMMA,
far from collapsing with the decline of the
grammar schools, seems to have established a
stable position; that the NAS/UWT, which has done
far less than the NUT to oppose cuts in education,

The National Union of Teachers (England and Wales)

claims not to have lost members during the recent
fall in teacher numbers; and that the NUT is
struggling to prevent, not just a decline in its
numbers, but also a fall in its share of the
teaching force.
These 'membership' issues are an index of the
attitudes of teachers to the problems of
recession and sharp educational change. Whereas,
undoubtedly, the number of those willing to
campaign against education cuts has grown, so has
a reluctance, on the part of others, to involve
themselves in activity of a sort which is
strenuous, controversial and contrary to the
policy of the government they may well have voted
for. The attitudes of parents, heads and
colleagues combine with the belief that the
'children come first' to produce quiescence. In
addition, the overall political crisis of the
Labour Party and trade union movement provides no
attractive or plausible alternative to the
difficulties of the present, and makes it less
likely that teachers will see anything purposeful
in union activity. It is not that, in this
situation, the NUT's competitors have any
effective strategy to put forward - but their
continued numerical strength is the indicator of a
considerable political problem.
Are, then, the kinds of radical policy
implied in the previous sections really a feasible
basis on which to maintain the NUT's strength?
Will they not simply sharpen the divisions within
teaching and ensure the collapse of the union's
remaining positions? Against these self-made and
anticipatory accusations of ultra-leftism, the
first point to make is that, while the union's
traditional strategy is capable of some defensive
victories, it is, overall, demonstrably losing
ground. It is the failure of the old approach -
rather than the wholesale adoption of something
new - which gives rise to the union's crisis of
strategy, and the membership problems associated
with it. (Though the fact that the conflict
between the two approaches is unresolved and
ubiquitous adds to the union's problems a
dimension which is absent from the policy
development of other, less ambitious teacher
organisations.)
To offer a detailed 'solution' to the complex
of political and ideological problems that face
the union would be both grandiose and implausible.
Nor do I want to suggest that there is only one

possible solution to the union's crisis, and that
the adoption of a left-wing programme will
simultaneously raise the level of militancy, win
over wavering members and establish widespread
popular support. On the contrary; even if the
dangers outlined earlier in this article were all
to be realised, the union would still have a role,
albeit diminished, in educational politics, as
well as a large membership.

So rather than asserting in inevitablist
fashion that <u>either</u> the union must move to the
left <u>or</u> collapse, I would argue from the
perspective that teachers have the potential to
play a useful part - trade union and, more
important, educational - in the development of a
popular left-wing current in Britain. At the same
time, for the union to adopt such a position would
allow it to make a more effective critique of
state educational policy, to construct alliances
to replace those that, developed in an earlier
period, are now ineffectual, and to produce a less
sectoralist answer to the conservative populism
which has influenced parental opinion. This, in
turn, would strengthen its position among teaching
unions.

A pre-condition of a successful change in
overall strategy is a militant 'trade union'
response to issues of jobs, conditions and pay.
But this hardly represents in itself an adequate
alternative to the rightward drift of educational
policy. That alternative would have to
incorporate, not just defensive responses, but a
fully-rounded educational politics.

The first area where, from this perspective,
change is needed is that relating to policy on the
<u>content</u> of education. Much of the effectiveness
of populist assertions that 'education isn't
working' has stemmed from two propositions:
first, that education has become irrelevant to he
'world of work'; second, that the standards of
the state school - largely as a result of the
shortcomings of teachers - are too low.

No progress is possible unless these
propositions are questioned.

Vocationalism presents the functioning of the
economy as something quite beyond social
determination, and consequently offers no
understanding of the world of work for which it
claims to prepare students. It is an approach
that has been challenged surprisingly little. Yet
it is possible to discover, even in the

unspectacular history of British 'civic' education, alternatives to it, which present economic decisions as subject to popular control. This, for instance, is from the teachers' manual of the largest pre-MSC effort at mass education on economic questions, the Army Education Council's wartime British Way and Purpose:

"Few people are likely to confuse masses without work, half-derelict mining communities, the slums of Glasgow, the under-sized bodies of under-nourished children, or the shocking scars on the loveliness of the English countryside with any heavenly thing . . . The war has been among other things an excellent teacher of economics. It has shown conclusively that unemployment is not inevitable . . . Given a clear expression of the democratic will of the people . . . there is no reason why we should not make the fullest use of all our resources to create a much finer civilisation than anything we have ever known."[15]

Such eloquent arguments can be utilised against the politically-willed depoliticisation that is embodied in the educational content of the YTS. At present, the union has little to say about the content of the Youth Training Schemes, or their school-based derivatives. It concentrates on questions of administration, selection, resources. In questioning the educational content of the schemes, the union would be beginning the work of formulating different objectives for state education, and of influencing public debate on those objectives.

Likewise on the issue of standards. The present Secretary of State has been able to win a strategic advantage by seizing as his own the issue of 'intellectual standards'. This is the high ground of educational debate, which any opposition aspiring to popular success must take.

In reality, the claim to intellectual seriousness is not soundly based. It is not just that the segregation implicit in vocationalism excludes the majority of students from the high levels of education to which Sir Keith Joseph, the Secretary of State for Education, claims aspire. It is also that the curriculum he defends in the name of high intellectual standards is archaic and seriously incomplete. It should be quite possible for the NUT to come forward as an advocate of a curriculum which aims to deliver a knowledge of

the world well in advance of what the Secretary of
State can offer: instead of vocationalism,   a
general and critical education around the world of
work, including its planning and decision-making
aspects;   a greater commitment to the study of
science in a social context;   the incorporation of
ecological, north-south and feminist themes into
many areas of the curriculum;   the development of
media and communications studies.   Because such a
synthesis could justifiably claim to create a much
higher level of understanding among a larger
number of students than present policy will allow,
it   would   have   the   advantage   of   combining
intellectual force with its radical momentum, and
could achieve a real popular resonance.
     There are two further areas in which change
is required.   That aspect of professionalism which
is   suspicious   of   parental   and   student   demand
lessens the chances of winning broad support for
change.   It is through encountering and debating
criticism from the 'consumers' of education that
the union will be best able to take an authorita-
tive position in a movement for reform.
     Secondly, an alliance on educational issues
should be complemented by an alliance with the
labour movement on broader questions of social and
economic policy than the NUT at present allows.
It is difficult to see how otherwise a strong
section of teacher opinion can be won to support
of a movement of the left.   Continued abstention
on major issues insulates the NUT, not only from
controversy,   but   also   from   exploration   of
alternative economic and social policies to those
ofthe government,   and   thus   impoverishes   all
aspects of its work, educational, as well as trade
union.
     It is possible, then, for the union to
establish itself as a force capable of leading a
response to those new issues of educational debate
which are at present a virtual monopoly of the
right.   Winning hegemony on issues of curriculum
content,   vocational   education,   and   the
relationship between education and economic and
social policy would allow a membership campaign
based   on   the   union's   ability   to   present   a
popularly-accepted case for educational change:
the union would be offering its members more than
a grimly attritional defence of equal opportunity
and diminishing provision.   (Though this defence
would remain essential.)   It would not end the
division of teacher opinion - but it would greatly

strengthen its progressive wing. At the same
time, a greater alertness to feminist issues, and
a manifest willingness to ensure that the local
and national leaderships of the union - as well as
its base - are predominantly female, would do a
lot to increase the involvement of primary and
women members, as well as opening up new areas of
educational policy.

The support for campaigns on cuts and pay
shows that there are considerable reserves of
militancy within the union. The difficult thing is
to extend these attitudes into areas which the
union has not previously entered. The development
of educational battles in Britain depends to a
considerable extent on whether this enterprise is
accomplished.

NOTES

1. Our Children, Our Future   NUT Pamphlet.
    London 1983.
2. Memorandum on Salaries.   Presented by NUT
    Executive to 1984 Conference.
3. Statistics presented by DES to Pay Data
    Working Party of the Burnham Committee, 1983.
    The NUT considers this figure to be an under-
    estimate.
4. Times Educational Supplement   6.1.1984.
5. See A. Green 'Education and Training: Under
    New Masters' in Donald and Wolpe (Eds.) Is
    There Anyone Here From Education? (London,
    1983).
6. Management Panel of the Burnham Committee -
    Submission to Arbitral Body on Teachers' Pay
    1982.
7. Ibid.
8. NUT Survey of Fixed Term Contracts, 1983.
9. Times Educational Supplement   24.9.1982.
10. Action 1919 - 69:   A Record of the Growth of
    the NAS   NAS Pamphlet 1969.
11. Times Educational Supplement   27.5.1983.
12. M. Kogan, in Educational Policy-making: A
    Study of Interest Groups and Parliament (Lon-
    don 1975) gives the following figures for NAS
    membership increase: 1960-22651; 1973-60230.
13. A.N. Pierotti The Story of the National Union
    of Women Teachers, Kew 1963.
14. Quoted in NUT Executive Memorandum to 1983
    Conference: Education for National Survival.
15. The British Way and Purpose   Directorate of
    Army Education.   1944.

LIST OF CONTRIBUTORS

Leon Boucher	Chester College, Britain
Mary Darmanin	University of Malta, Malta
Roger Duclaud-Williams	University of Warwick, Britain
Sara Freedman	Boston Women's Teacher's Collective, U.S.A.
Ken Jones	National Union of Teachers, Britain
Martin Lawn	Westhill College, Britain
Susan Mann	Monash University, Australia
Jenny Ozga	Open University, Britain
Haruo Ota	University of Illinois, U.S.A.
Andrew Spaull	Monash University, Australia
Stephen Stoer	Higher Institute of Sciences of Enterprise and Work, Portugal
Wayne Urban	Georgia State University, U.S.A.
Rob White	University of Saskatchewan, Canada

302